HELPING YOUR CHILD SLEEP THROUGH THE NIGHT

Joanne Cuthbertson
and Susie Schevill

BROADWAY BOOKS

NEW YORK

This book is dedicated with love to Nicky, Jenny, Jimmy, Alex, and Vanessa, our champions at sleeping through the night.

A previous edition of this book was originally published in 1985 by Doubleday, a division of Random House, Inc. It is here reprinted by arrangement with Doubleday.

Broadway Books titles may be purchased for business or promotional use or for special sales. For information, please write to: Special Markets Department, Random House, Inc., 1540 Broadway, New York, NY 10036.

PRINTED IN THE UNITED STATES OF AMERICA

BROADWAY BOOKS and its logo, a B bisected on the diagonal, are trademarks of Broadway Books, a division of Random House, Inc.

Visit our website at www.broadwaybooks.com

First Broadway Books trade paperback edition published 2002.

The Library of Congress Cataloging-in-Publication Data has cataloged the previous edition as:
Cuthbertson, Joanne
Helping your child sleep through the night.
   Bibliography: p. 229.
   Includes index.
   1. Child rearing. 2. Children—Sleep. I. Schevill, Susie. II. Title.
HQ769.C975 1985   649'.6   84-18807

ISBN 0-385-19250-9

32 31 30 29 28 27 26 25

CONTENTS

FOREWORD

It is unusual and fortuitous, in being asked to review a new book, that one of the reviewers, an alleged expert in the area of infant sleep disorders, is also the parent of a nine-month-old son with disturbed sleep. Max, the youngest of three boys and son of two "high powered" professionals enjoyed falling asleep in his mother's arms while nursing or being rocked. In fact, it was difficult for anyone but Mom to get him to sleep. He seemed to enjoy particularly the middle-of-the-night feeding and his "private" time at that hour. Everyone but Max, however, was becoming increasingly fatigued and short-tempered. The parent who was the sleep expert provided advice; but the other, a pediatrician, wasn't convinced. (A good example of why professionals shouldn't "treat" their own). Then in the mail came the manuscript *Helping Your Child Sleep Through the Night* by Joanne Cuthbertson and Susie Schevill. The two professional parents read it together, and, lo and behold, Max now continues to nurse contentedly (during the daytime), but falls asleep by himself and sleeps through the night more often than not. What better introduction for this book than the reviewer's enthusiasm generated by a personal success story. Was the treatment simple? Not quite. Are Max's sleep problems over? Probably not. But, the book was clearly instrumental in helping us in this venture, so already there is one grateful set of parents, and we predict that there will be more.

One benefit of the book will hopefully be that parents who have a child with a sleep disturbance will not feel so alone. Once, a few years ago, when some of our material appeared in an article on childhood sleep problems in *Parents* magazine, we were amazed by the number of letters and phone calls we received from desperate parents across the country who felt that their child's sleep problem was unique. Few problems of infancy and early childhood are as exasperating for parents or as challenging for clinicians as sleep disturbances. They emerge at various stages in the course of development and for a variety of reasons. Most infants have some disruption of sleep at one time or another during their early development.

What constitutes a bona fide sleep problem, in contrast to a minor disturbance, a bad habit, or an atypical family practice? Some sleep problems may be associated with brain mechanisms controlling sleep, whereas others may be related to environmental perturbations. It is also possible that sleep problems arise from an interaction of constitutional and environmental factors. Certain genetic or familial propensities may mark an infant as "vulnerable" and lead to sleep problems under certain environmental circumstances or "stresses."

Our knowledge of sleep problems remains scanty; they do not lend themselves to easy explanations or solutions. More large-scale research studies are required, as many of the findings now in the scientific literature are derived from small samples of infants and from families of homogeneous composition and socioeconomic class. Nevertheless, sleep researchers from laboratories around the world have begun to piece together an understanding of normal sleep in the first months of life and some of the factors that influence early sleep pattern development.

In this book, Joanne Cuthbertson and Susie Schevill provide a good overview of current knowledge about both normal sleep and the most common sleep disturbances in infants and young children: what are the sleep "states," how much sleep is adequate, how do such things as environmental disruptions (e.g., trips, moving, illness) and sleeping arrangements influence sleep patterns, what is the difference between nightmares and night terrors, etc. The book provides parents with a basic understanding of sleep and guidelines for when they should seek professional help.

In the early months of life, the infant gradually develops the ability to sleep for longer periods at night. The sleep pattern that develops during this time, the authors suggest, becomes a foundation for later sleep habits. In this regard, they provide a set of important suggestions for establishing "good sleep hygiene" from the early weeks of life—a safe, quiet sleeping environment at night; a soft toy, pacifier, or "special blanket" to aid the infant in comforting himself/herself during brief awakenings; a consistent bedtime routine; and, especially important, allowing a young infant the experience of falling asleep on his/her own, without always being rocked or nursed to sleep.

Combining their own experiences as parents with current knowledge about sleep, the authors describe how sleep problems can develop and recommend specific methods for managing a child's disrupted sleep. Several of their points deserve emphasis. When parents consider their child's sleep a problem, before attempting one of the book's treatment strategies, they should consult their pediatrician to ensure that the child is in good health and that there is no medical reason for the sleep difficulty. If some parents find that a particular technique does not seem to work, though they have followed the clearly written instructions carefully, it may be helpful to consult a specialist in childhood sleep disturbances, or a sleep disorders clinic, to evaluate the possibility of a less common sleep disorder; or, for aid and support in formulating and maintaining an individualized treatment plan that may be more effective. Above all, parents should proceed with any method slowly, especially with older infants and toddlers. Sleep problems that develop over several weeks or months are rarely resolved in a few days. When there are multiple problems (for example, a child who resists going to bed, wakes frequently, and demands bottles during the night), parents should focus on one problem at a time. By proceeding slowly and tackling one problem at a time, the child will more readily accommodate to the changes being made.

Two general principles which seem to underlie the suggestions for treatment in the book ought to be made more explicit. First, parents should be in control of their infant's sleep and feeding, and not vice versa. Regularity and structure are indeed important in managing a child's sleep habits. However, we hope that the authors would agree that parents should not be excessively concerned with either scheduling and control or permissiveness, but rather strive for sensitive understanding of their individual baby's needs at a particular point in his/her development in the context of the family's personal values and beliefs.

A second belief of the authors relates to fostering independence in the infant and competence in the parents. Who could take issue with such ideals? Yet, an acceptance of the goals, without consideration of how they are achieved negates the importance of both cultural traditions and class differences in child rearing. In several cultures, infants share the parental bed for the first year or two. We do not know whether this compromises their independence or whether such practices lead to sleep problems. We suspect that such infants do not have sleep problems and that they grow up to be independent adults. However, the issue is not where the infant sleeps, but whether the sleeping arrangement is congruent with the family's values. An infant is most likely to develop physical independence and psychological autonomy and parents are most likely to develop feelings of competence, in an environment of comfort, familiarity, and support, where relationships develop through sensitive and flexible communication.

But the authors' approach and instructions certainly will not satisfy all parents.

The study of infant and early childhood sleep disorders is a relatively new endeavor, and many of the factors which may be important in shaping sleep patterns still remain speculative. For the most part, the techniques described by the authors are consistent with our own treatment approaches to sleep-disturbed infants and children. The step-by-step directions and the question/answer section at the end of each chapter provide helpful guidelines for parents in adapting the methods to their own situation. However, as the authors concede, some of their suggestions have not been tested by systematic research study. Yet, the methods are nonetheless intriguing and certainly merit evaluation by further research. In conclusion, we can recommend heartily this lively and well-written book, and we can wish well those families that embark upon its precepts.

THOMAS F. ANDERS, M.D.
Brown University

MARCIA KEENER, PH.D.
Stanford University

ACKNOWLEDGMENTS

We would like to take this opportunity to thank all the people who have helped us prepare this book. We are especially indebted to Dr. Marcia Keener of the Stanford University Infant Sleep Laboratory, who so generously provided us with information and guided us through our research; Drs. Elmer Grossman, Howard Gruber, Jane Lande, John Harris, Nancy Salter, and Judith Klein, who thoroughly and patiently reviewed and contributed to our manuscript; and to the many parents, in particular Anne Van Dyke, Susie Peterson, Sandy Bails, Linda Walker, Carol Cosman, Lyn Lorber, Terry Gillen, Gail Berland, Martha Blanchette, Elizabeth Kibbey, Susan Berman, and Susan Fisher, who generously shared their experiences and wisdom with us.

We would like to extend special thanks to Marilyn Fabe, who encouraged us to write this book; to Katinka Matson, who believed in our idea; and to our editor, Marie-Denise Kratsios, who has made our publication process a pleasure.

And most of all, we would like to thank our husbands, Jim Cuthbertson and Robert Sinai, for their enthusiastic, loving support and countless hours of help in planning, organizing, and reviewing our manuscript.

HOW TO USE THIS BOOK

This book is made up of a general introduction and five age-specific chapters. We encourage all of you to read the introduction, which outlines our general principles, and then to turn to the chapter that corresponds to your child's age. We have designed the book so that each chapter stands on its own. In this way, if you are the parent of a young toddler, for example, you do not have to work your way through material that is more appropriate for a newborn. You should simply read Chapter Three: From Ten to Eighteen Months. As your child gets older, you can read subsequent chapters.

Chapters One through Five contain methods and guidelines that are addressed to specific types of childhood sleep disruption. Where appropriate, we have devised detailed step-by-step methods in each age group. Other sleep problems do not require a night-by-night program but can be solved by following more general guidelines.

For ease of discussion, we have divided sleep disruptions according to habits, development, and specific situations. Keep in mind, though, that any organization, including ours, is somewhat artificial. As we all know, life isn't always so easily categorized, so you may have to combine points from a few of the discussions to help your child. Your specific family situation or your child's temperament might also suggest a minor change in one of the methods. This is fine; just keep in mind the basic goals of positive interaction with your child and ultimate nighttime independence. The questions and answers, located at the end of each chapter, are all drawn from real life, and thereby show you how you might apply our principles and strategies to a specific situation.

Note: Throughout this book, we alternate by chapters using male and female pronouns to refer to children. We do this to avoid awkward he/she constructions and at the same time to help balance out the historical usage of only male pronouns. Except for the parasomnias, which are discussed in Chapter Five, there are no gender-related differences in the way boys and girls sleep, so your approach should be the same whether you have a son or a daughter.

INTRODUCTION

It is difficult to appreciate the value of sleep until you try to get by without it. As new parents, being deprived of sleep just when you're trying to adjust to having an infant in your life can seem like an extraordinarily cruel twist of fate. If you have an older child who has been keeping you up at night for months, you are likely harboring feelings of resentment as well as suffering from the long-term effects of sleep deprivation. Or you may have a child who has been sleeping through the night for a long time but suddenly develops a nighttime waking pattern. In any of these cases, this book is for you.

Good sleeping habits are essential for both your child's personal development and your own well-being. Sleep can mean the difference between an enjoyable, rewarding life and stressful months or even years for everyone in your family. If you and your family are well rested, you will be able to face your daily lives with joy and enthusiasm. The cumulative effect of weeks of sleepless nights, however, can interfere with your normal behavior and good judgment and rob you of this joy.

When your baby is young, it is primarily you, the parents, and other family members who suffer from her nighttime awakenings. In most cases, your baby is able to make up her sleep needs during daytime naps, but the rest of you have to suffer through your days being tired. Eventually, though, poor sleeping habits will also catch up with your child. If she is excessively tired during the day, her social interactions, intellectual curiosity, and even physical development can suffer. If she continues to depend on you throughout the night when she is no longer a baby, her sense of self-esteem and independence may be impaired. It is much better to help her establish good sleeping habits early, so that she will continue to thrive throughout her childhood.

To that end, this book is devoted to showing you how to establish and maintain good sleeping habits for your children. We provide you with strategies, geared to different age groups, for implementing the principles outlined in this introduction. Our methods are tailored to work for normal, healthy children between the ages of five weeks and five years. We do not deal with the special problems that can arise in brain-damaged, emotionally disturbed, or chronically ill children. Nor do we cover rare sleep disorders such as narcolepsy and sleep apnea. These situations are beyond the scope of this book and must be dealt with on an individual basis with a pediatrician, child psychiatrist, neurologist, or sleep specialist.

WHAT DO WE MEAN BY "SLEEPING THROUGH THE NIGHT"?

The phrase "sleeping through the night" is somewhat misleading in that most people periodically awaken throughout the night. In most cases, though, we fall back to sleep so quickly that we don't remember our brief surfacings.

Children are no different. Numerous studies have shown that the child who sleeps all night long without waking up is uncommon. For example, Dr. Thomas F. Anders has found that almost half of the parents of two-month-olds and three quarters of the parents of nine-month-olds reported that their children "slept through the night." When the children's sleep was recorded on time-lapse videotape, however, it was found that only one sixth of the two-month-olds and one third of the nine-month-olds really did sleep the whole night. Similarly, in Dr. Isabel Paret's study of nine-month-olds, all of the children woke up at least once during the night. In many cases, the children were able to get back to sleep on their own, so their parents never knew that they had awakened.

Our goal, then, is not to have our children sleep for an uninterrupted eight, ten, or twelve hours. Rather, we want to help them be independent during the night and not require our assistance to fall back to sleep when they do wake. This is what we mean by "sleeping through the night."

A LOOK AT STATISTICS

If you are thinking that your child's bedtime resistance or inability to sleep through the night is unusual, don't. Studies have shown that childhood sleep disruptions are much more common than most people realize.

Statistics gathered by Drs. A. U. Beltramini and M. E. Hertzig from the New York Longitudinal Study of Temperament and Development reveal that nearly 90 percent of the normal, healthy preschool children studied required more than thirty minutes to fall asleep at one age or another. This proportion increased as the children grew older, from one fourth at one year to two thirds at five years. Also as the children grew older, they became less willing to entertain themselves before falling off to sleep. After being tucked into bed for the night, 14 percent of one-year-olds called their parents back again for another good-night kiss, a drink of water, or some other form of attention. The percentage of children using these delay tactics continued to grow steadily, from just over 25 percent at two years to a full 50 percent at five years.

Statistics concerning middle of the night waking are equally impressive. Drs. Beltramini and Hertzig found that during the first five years of life, 95 percent of the children went through a period of middle-of-the-night crying or calling for their parents at least once a week. A full 70 percent of the children went through a stage of awakening one or more times *every* night during their first five years. Broken down by ages, approximately 30 percent of the children at ages one, two, three, and four demanded parental intervention at least once every night. It wasn't until the children were five years old that this statistic dropped to 20 percent.

In a frequently cited study of early childhood sleeping habits, T. Moore and L. Ucko found that 70 percent of infants regularly slept from midnight until 5 A.M. by three months of age. This statistic increased to 83 percent by six months, and 90 percent by one year. This is not a very long stretch of nighttime sleep, however. And to put this into perspective, further corroborating the data from the New York Longitudinal Study, Dr. Anders estimates that approximately 40 to 50 percent of those infants who do at one point sleep through the night develop night-waking problems in their second year of life.

WHAT CAN WE DO?

There seem to be three primary factors that affect a young child's sleeping patterns: development (neurologic as well as emotional and social), temperament, and environment. Several researchers have also looked for possible gender-related differences, but none has been found. Because there is nothing anyone can do (or would want to do) to alter the course of a child's development or change the characteristics of her basic personality, the strategies we have adopted in this book focus on the child's environment. In a review of the relationship between temperament and night waking, Dr. William Carey of the University of Pennsylvania Medical School concludes, "There probably is still no better method of trying to overcome night waking than a program of habit training. . . ." In addition, a number of behavioral studies have shown that the way parents deal with their children and organize their lives can have a profound effect on their child's ability to sleep through the night.

Yet even though your child's individual development and temperament cannot be changed, they cannot be ignored. A strategy that works with one child may not work for another. You cannot assume, for example, that one of your children will respond in the same way that your other child has. At any particular point in your child's life, it always makes sense to try to work with, rather than against, her individual personality and the natural course of her development. Without this framework, a behavioral analysis is meaningless.

Throughout our book then, the emphasis remains the same: the importance of helping your child develop solid sleeping habits early on. Childhood is so full of changes and new situations that we can pretty safely say that all children will, at one time or another, experience at least a few nights of disturbed sleep. We contend, however, that those children who are used to sleeping through the night will be much less vulnerable to sleep disruption from the developmental issues (for example, separation anxiety, bursts of motor achievement) and situations (for example, illness, birth of a sibling, moving to a new home) that inevitably arise in any child's life. Even young children respond so well to routines and form habits so easily that getting on the track from the beginning isn't difficult. The biggest problems arise when you are faced with changing an undesirable habit that has been established over the years. A child with good sleeping habits and a positive attitude about sleep will sail through the rough spots with relative ease.

On occasion, doctors prescribe sedative drugs for even very young children with sleep problems. This decision to use drugs such as chloral hydrate, barbiturates, or diphenhydramine can only be made on an individual basis and after careful evaluation. It is our feeling, however, that in the vast majority of cases, not only are drugs unnecessary but they may even be harmful. We urge you, then, first to try the methods described in this book. If, as a last resort, and on the advice of your doctor, you finally do use medication, don't abandon our techniques. You should still work on reshaping your child's sleep behavior because in the long run, once the drug is withdrawn, it is her habits that will remain.

THE SCIENCE OF SLEEP

Amounts of Sleep

One of the most obvious changes during the first five years of a child's life is the amount of time she spends sleeping each day. On the average, sleep needs decrease by about one third during this time, from sixteen to eleven hours. Although the specific amounts vary greatly from individual to individual, the tendency to need a relatively large or small amount of sleep seems to remain constant over time. That is, a person who sleeps more than the average amount as a young child will probably continue to need a lot of sleep. Or, the infant who seems to get by happily with much less than the average amount of sleep will most likely continue that pattern. So that you may compare your child's sleep needs to what are generally considered to be the averages, we include the following list. Remember, though, that there is nothing especially desirable about these figures. Your child's behavior is the best indicator of how much sleep she needs.

AVERAGE AMOUNTS OF SLEEP PER DAY

Newborn	16 hours
3–5 months	14 hours
6–23 months	13 hours
2–3 years	12 hours
3–5 years	11 hours

(Data from Roffwarg et al., "Ontogenetic Development of the Human Sleep-Dream Cycle," *Science*, 1966, Vol. 152, p. 608.)

Biological Rhythms

The bodies of all people, including young children, are monitored by cyclical forces. In the last several decades, scientists have shown that body temperature, blood pressure, respiration, digestion, the secretion of hormones, and other biological processes, including sleep, all vary according to the timing of a person's internal clock. The healthy human body normally maintains an incredibly delicate balance of its interwoven cycles, whether they be hourly, daily, or monthly. Scientists are only recently beginning to link certain medical and psychological problems with a disruption of these rhythms.

It turns out, then, that age-old advice advocating a regular schedule, with regular meal and sleep times, may have more merit than some of us were previously willing to concede. As an extreme case, it has been well documented that night-shift workers suffer from chronic fatigue, psychological troubles, and increased susceptibility to disease. Their bodies simply can't keep up with the irregularities of their schedules. Similar problems make up what is commonly referred to as jet lag: the traveler's internal clock has a hard time adjusting to the new setting of the external clock.

Sleep-Wake Organization

One of a person's most powerful biological rhythms is the "sleep-wake cycle." Although subject to individual and day-to-day variations, the average newborn tends to sleep for about two to four hours, wake up for one to two hours, fall asleep again, and so on throughout the day. During the first several weeks of life, these combined periods of sleep and wake, or sleep-wake cycles, occur randomly throughout the day and night. Dr. Arthur Parmelee, one of the pioneers of childhood sleep research, has found that a one-week-old sleeps about 7 3/4 hours in the day and 8 1/4 hours in the night. None too soon for the parents, a pattern begins to emerge at about four weeks of age, with daytime sleep decreasing and nighttime sleep increasing. Dr. Parmelee found that, in his sample, a sixteen-week-old baby was likely to sleep about 4 1/2 hours in the day and almost 10 hours at night. This emergence of day-night differentiation is one of the most significant milestones in the young infant's road toward a more mature sleep pattern.

These figures take on even more significance when you consider that the young baby also lengthens her longest time asleep during her first four months of life. Dr. Parmelee has found that, on the average, this stretch doubles between birth and four months of age: from 4 to 8 hours. Dr. Anders' observations are similar: between two weeks and five months of age, this time increases from slightly less than 4 hours to more than 7 hours. In both cases, this represents a significant change in the way the baby's sleep hours are distributed throughout the 24-hour day.

After concentrating her hours asleep in the night and lengthening the amount of time she sleeps at one time, a young baby begins to stretch out the length of time she stays awake. In their study of sleep pattern development, Dr. Carol Nagy Jacklin and associates found that between the ages of six and thirty-three months, the children studied doubled their longest period of wakefulness from 4 to 8 hours. And then, usually around their third birthday, and most often before their fifth, children give up their daytime naps altogether, so that all of their time asleep (about 11 hours) is in the night.

The Physiology of Sleep

Until thirty years ago, everyone, scientists included, assumed that sleep was a passive and stable condition. It wasn't until the early fifties, when Dr. Nathaniel Kleitman and his associates at the University of Chicago first monitored the eye movements of their sleeping subjects, that the concept of two separate sleep states was conceived and modern sleep research was born. Since that time, advances have been rapid. The two basic sleep states, REM (rapid eye movement) sleep, commonly associated with dreaming, and NREM (non–rapid eye movement) sleep, a much deeper state of sleep, have been well described in adults.

There are many differences, though, between the way adults sleep and the way children sleep. But before we get to those differences, let's first briefly describe adult sleep, beginning with a synopsis of a typical night's sleep. That way we will have some perspective for understanding how sleep matures.

The first sleep of an adult's night is, under normal conditions, NREM. Characterized by slow, regular brain activity, slow, regular breathing, relaxed muscles, and infrequent body movements, this state is also called "quiet sleep." Quiet in all but one sense of the word, that is, because it is during NREM sleep that people snore. To make things more complicated (or interesting, depending on the way you look at it), NREM sleep is further subdivided into four stages of progressively deeper (less arousable) sleep, each clearly differentiated by its distinct brain wave patterns. As the night goes on, the sleeping person proceeds through each of these stages, starting with Stage 1, until the deepest stage of NREM sleep, Stage 4, is achieved. He or she then begins to ascend into progressively lighter sleep, to Stage 3, Stage 2, and back again to Stage 1 NREM sleep.

This NREM sleep is then followed by the first REM, or "active" sleep of the night. REM sleep is characterized by rapid eye movements, irregular breathing and heart rate, and more intense brain waves than in NREM sleep. The body does not move, but the fingers and face muscles may twitch. When awakened from REM sleep, most people report vivid dreams.

The time from the first onset of sleep (NREM) through the first REM period is called the first "sleep cycle." Although individual cycles may differ quite a bit, the average adult sleep cycle takes about ninety to one hundred minutes. NREM and REM sleep continue to alternate throughout the night, so that an average night of about eight hours of sleep is likely to include about five complete cycles.

The categorization of sleep states is not as clear-cut in infants and children as it is in adults. Because young children's brain waves are relatively immature and not as well differentiated as adults', the terms "active" and "quiet" sleep are generally used to describe their sleep, rather than REM and NREM. It isn't until about two years of age that the four stages of NREM sleep are fully differentiated, although the process begins at about six weeks. Dr. Anders has also described a third category of poorly organized sleep, termed "indeterminate sleep," which occupies 10 to 15 percent of the newborn's sleep time. There is controversy about the actual significance of this type of sleep, but it appears to predominate in premature and some abnormal term infants and disappear completely in the older child.

Among the most significant differences between the sleep of young children and adults is the amount of time spent in active versus quiet sleep. As compared to adults, who spend about 20 percent of their time asleep in REM sleep, newborns generally spend 50 percent, and premature babies 70 percent, of their sleep time in active sleep. Researchers seem to agree with Dr. Roffwarg and his associates, who were the first to speculate that this predominance of active sleep in the very young child serves a definite purpose: providing the maturing brain with adequate stimulation to develop. Perhaps this is nature's way of making up for the newborn's relatively unstimulating life, largely so because she spends so much time asleep! Active sleep drops to about 40 percent of total sleep time by three months of age, and continues to decrease to about 30 percent by age two, 25 percent by age three, and to the adult proportion of 20 percent by age five.

Along with the young child's decreasing amounts of active sleep and increasing amounts of quiet sleep comes a reorganization of when these sleep states occur. At birth, the newborn goes directly to active sleep. It isn't until after six months that the more mature pattern of quiet sleep onset begins. Gradually, throughout the first year, quiet sleep becomes more prominent in the beginning of the night, and active sleep more prominent toward the end of the night. Throughout these changes, though, the young child's sleep cycle (one period of active sleep and one period of quiet sleep) remains considerably shorter than the adult's: about forty-five to fifty minutes as opposed to ninety to one hundred minutes. In other words, the young child passes through her various sleep states much more quickly than the adult, which perhaps in some way influences her arousability.

By now you may well be saying to yourself, "All of this is very interesting, but how does it relate to my child's problems in sleeping through the night?" Unfortunately, there are no easy answers. The link between physiology and behavior is no clearer in sleep than it is when a person is awake. Nevertheless, sleep researchers have provided us with the framework for better understanding and dealing with many of the most common as well as the most esoteric problems of sleep. We now know, for example, that some of the most common childhood sleep disturbances, night terrors, sleepwalking, and sleeptalking, are associated with arousal from the deepest stages of NREM sleep. Our nighttime hours have been, to a large extent, demystified and brought into the realm of scientific observation. Although many questions remain unanswered, the groundwork has been laid, and the promise for the future is unlimited.

FAMILY DIFFERENCES

In the same way that each person is an individual, bringing to this world his or her own specific personality and talents, so is a family. It is no more appropriate to expect families to be the same and to have the same needs than it is to expect this of individual people. Varying situations, lifestyles, and schedules may all affect how an individual family feels about its child's sleep.

For this reason, what one family perceives as a sleep problem might not be a problem for another family. You and your spouse, for example, might not mind if your child calls for you once a night but become distressed if this turns into several interruptions a night. Another set of parents might tolerate one nighttime awakening a week quite well but not cope well if their child wakes up and expects attention two or three times a week. And then a third family might consider any nighttime awakenings a problem. It is all just a matter of degree and personal opinion.

Given the individual nature of such opinions, however, each family has to decide what is best for it. In practical terms, each set of parents has to reach that point when the sleep disruption represents more of a problem than the effort needed to alleviate it. Unfortunately, young children's sleep disturbances often don't resolve themselves, and in many cases they get worse. If you haven't established good sleeping habits early on in your child's life, changing a well-established habit can be difficult. No one can say when you will make your decision to reshape undesirable sleep patterns, but we encourage you to start working on it sooner, rather than later.

WHEN A FAMILY SLEEPS TOGETHER

In recent years, more and more American families have reacted against separate sleeping arrangements and joined together in "the family bed." This concept, advocated in a recent book by Tine Thevenin, is really not new; it has been practiced for hundreds of years in a variety of cultures. Citing the desire to breast-feed, promote family bonding, enhance the child's sense of security, and alleviate sleeping problems, many families are giving bed-sharing a try.

There is no doubt that this issue of family bed-sharing is highly personal, and one that each family will have to grapple with on its own. A lot of the reason that this issue has become so emotionally charged is that the practice of a family sleeping together has been taboo in our culture for so many years. But this in itself isn't an adequate reason not to try something. You have to look deeper and, in making your decision, think carefully not only about what you are doing in the present but what implications your decision will have for the future.

Hardly anyone would disagree with the wonderful feeling a mother and father can have when they are cuddled up in bed with their peacefully sleeping infant. Somewhere along the line, though, if this practice continues, you will be creating definite expectations for your baby. A baby or toddler who is used to sleeping in bed with her parents will not take well to suddenly being placed in her own crib. On the other hand, the baby who has been used to sleeping in her own crib since a very young age can form positive associations with her bed and sleep there happily. Before you let her become dependent on your bed, then, you should decide where your baby will sleep in the long run and spare her this distress.

Let's move on, then, to examine the way family bed-sharing can

affect your child as she matures. We feel that the respected pediatrician
Dr. T. Berry Brazelton has addressed the issues in a most sensitive way:

> In our society, at least, to be able to sleep alone in childhood is
> a part of respecting oneself as an independent person.
> Whether or not that is right in absolute terms can certainly be
> questioned, but it is difficult at this time for a child or a parent
> to reject the general consensus without the danger of lowered
> self-esteem and a feeling of being inadequate to establish au-
> tonomy. . . . I am convinced that although independence
> may not be an easy goal for parents to accept, it is an exciting
> and rewarding goal for the child. Being able to manage alone
> at night helps a child develop a positive self-image and gives
> him a real feeling of strength during the day. [Redbook maga-
> zine, October 1978, pp. 92, 216]

It is our conclusion, then, that co-family sleeping arrangements are
not in the best interest of the child. This is especially true if there is a
sleep problem. We feel this way not because of cultural disapproval but
because of the developmental implications in the context of our culture.
We agree with Dr. Brazelton that if you don't allow your child to develop
independent sleeping habits, you may also be interfering with the growth
of her daytime independence and perhaps her sense of self-esteem. Children are often more perceptive than we give them credit for. If you are
feeling that your toddler is incapable of making it through the night on
her own, her behavior will most likely mirror your uncertainty. Or if it is
you who are missing the contact with her through the night, and not the
other way around, she will also pick up on your motivation. It is most
important, then, that you do some real soul-searching and sort out these
issues. Growing up and moving toward independence is never easy, but as
a parent you owe it to your child to help her achieve this goal in any way
you can.

This is not to say, however, that you shouldn't occasionally have your
child in bed with you, either for a weekend morning treat or when she is
ill or frightened. There are times when a family cuddle will do everyone a
world of good. We are also not basing our decision on some of the most
common objections to families sharing a bed: that the baby will smother
in the bed, that one of the parents might roll over onto the baby, that the
baby will interfere with the parents' sex life, that the baby will spit up on

the bed, that there isn't enough room in the parents' bed, and so on. Babies do not get smothered in bed by their parents, and we consider the other factors to be matters of personal preference.

To summarize, then, let's get back to the basic goals of cofamily sleeping: while we agree 100 percent that breast-feeding and family closeness are desirable, these can easily be achieved without sharing a bed. And while we definitely agree with the goals of building your child's security and helping her to feel comfortable enough to sleep through the night, we think that a cofamily sleeping arrangement will, in the long run, hinder rather than encourage this achievement. A child who depends on her parent's presence to sleep through the night cannot be as secure as the child who has learned to feel comfortable with herself.

BED IS A SPECIAL PLACE

One of the most important things you can do to help your child sleep through the night is to build her positive feelings about her bed and bedroom. The time you spend making her sleeping quarters safe, comfortable, and inviting will be well worth your effort.

Bedroom

As we have stated in the previous section, young children (after the first few months of life) are best off learning to sleep without their parents. If you don't have a separate bedroom for your child, arrange a little sleeping nook in a hallway or corner of another room. You can block it off with screens, bookcases, or other pieces of furniture.

It is also fine to have your young child share a room with an older brother or sister, especially if they are only a few years apart in age. Parents' fears of their crying baby or talkative toddler disturbing the sleep of an older sibling almost never materialize. Instead, young children often get so much reassurance from seeing a sister or brother sleeping that they are able to relax themselves and sleep through the night.

Although some children don't seem particular about the way their bedroom is decorated, many others do. Interesting pictures, cheerful wallpaper, special toys and books, and brightly patterned bed sheets can all help a child feel good about her bedroom.

Light

Some young children are sensitive to the amount of light in their rooms and wake up with the sun. If you are having this problem, roller shades on the windows may help. As your child approaches her first birthday and begins to experience normal developmental fears, a hall light or dim night-light can make her feel more secure during the night.

Temperature

A room temperature between 65 and 68 degrees is ideal for sleeping. If the room is too cold or too hot, your child might wake up from discomfort alone.

From Bassinette to Crib to Bed

Newborns are notorious for being able to sleep anywhere and through anything and many parents take advantage of their willingness to sleep in a number of different locations. You can alternate putting your infant to sleep in a crib, bassinette, or carriage. During the first weeks of your baby's life, you might want to set up a bassinette or cradle (even a large drawer will do) in your bedroom. In addition to giving you quick nighttime access to your baby, she will love the secure feeling of a smaller sleeping space.

At around eight to ten weeks of age, watch for signs that your baby is outgrowing her bassinette. Once this happens, it is time to move her into a full-sized crib. Besides being too crowded, she'll become more particular about her sleep environment in the coming months. And because she will spend so much time in her crib over the next several years, be sure to check it carefully for safety features. Federal standards for cribs are now quite stringent, so if you are buying a newly manufactured crib you can be sure that it is safe. Otherwise, if you are looking at a secondhand crib, make sure that it is sturdy and in overall good shape. The slats should be no more than 2 3/8 inches apart; every year babies die from getting trapped between slats that are too widely spaced. To protect your baby from falling, the raised top rail of the crib should be at least twenty-six inches from the top of the mattress. Also make sure that the mattress fits snugly into the crib. Even a small gap can be dangerous for a young baby's bed. When she is an infant, crib bumpers can cushion her against the hard sides of the crib and provide extra assurance that she won't get caught between the edges of the crib and the mattress. Bumpers are now available in a variety of brightly colored and patterned fabrics, so they can also make a visually interesting addition to her bed. For maximum safety, make sure that the bumpers are securely attached to the crib slats with at least six straps. It is time to remove the bumpers once your baby is pulling herself to a stand. Physically precocious nine-month-olds have been known to use them as a step-up to hurl themselves out of the crib.

There is no set time when you should move your child from a crib into a big bed, but many children make this move between their second and third birthdays. For suggestions on making this transition a positive experience, see our discussion in Chapter Four.

Crib and Bed Toys

Because many infants and young children spend a fair amount of time in their bed awake and unattended, all crib and bed toys must be safe. Federal regulations are quite stringent and specific in outlining safety requirements for children's toys, so you can be pretty sure that any new toy manufactured by a major American toy company is safe, provided that you abide by the age guidelines. If you are using older or imported toys, or making your own toys, keep in mind that they must be able to withstand rough handling and chewing. Every year hundreds of babies suffocate by choking on small objects, so make sure not only that the toy itself is large enough but also that it doesn't have buttons, wheels, or other small parts that can come loose (according to federal regulations, any toy that is smaller than 1 1/4 inches in diameter or 2 1/4 inches in depth is unsafe for a child under the age of three). *Never* leave any type of battery-operated toy in the crib. Batteries can come loose and leak caustic acid if chewed. Also make sure that a toy does not have any sharp or rough edges. Particularly in bed, you don't want your baby rolling over onto a sharp or hard object. Finally, any paint used on baby toys should be nontoxic.

Once you have selected toys for your baby's crib, be sure to check them periodically. A toy that looked fine a week ago may now be showing unsafe signs of wear. A cracked toy may have a sharp edge, or the stuffing from a torn doll may be hazardous if swallowed.

Safety considerations aside, you will want to select crib toys that are both interesting and aesthetically pleasing to your child. Young babies enjoy looking at bright mobiles, experimenting with brightly colored teethers, rattles, and other objects of different shapes and textures. Toys such as a crib gym or activity center will help her develop her eye-hand and fine motor coordination and amuse her at the same time. Children of all ages like having stuffed animals, dolls, and books in bed with them. By the time your child is two or three, she may also enjoy bringing her special action figures, cars, or trucks to bed with her.

Sleepwear

Dress your child for comfort. Drawstring nightgowns and snap-up stretch suits are long-standing favorites for infants. Because older babies and children tend to move around during the night and often kick off their blankets, a one-piece footed blanket sleeper can keep them warm. During the winter months, you might want to put thermal underwear underneath the blanket sleeper. In the summer, especially if you live in a climate that doesn't cool down at night, a diaper and short-sleeved undershirt may be the most comfortable. Once your child is three or four, she will probably enjoy helping you select her nightwear.

Many parents find that their babies urinate profusely at night, and sometimes wake up sopping wet. If this sounds familiar, you can use two diapers at night, with securely fitting plastic pants. Disposable diapers come in a special nighttime thickness and can also be doubled up; if you put a small slit in the plastic coating of the inside diaper, the urine can then seep out into the outer diaper, providing double protection.

CONFIDENT PARENTING

Establishing good sleeping habits for your young child may well require all the confidence you can muster. From a very early age, many children resist sleep, and if you are the parent of an infant, this may be the first time you find yourself in the position of having to enforce limits on her behavior. As your child grows and becomes more opinionated and determined, your confidence as a parent becomes increasingly crucial. On the one hand, you respect your child for her individuality and want to encourage her independence. But on the other hand, you realize that she needs your guidance in many areas, such as getting a good night's sleep. Learning to meet and balance both of these goals is what makes parenting such a dynamic and interesting process.

Therefore, it is most important that you learn to feel confident in your role as a parent. While most new parents occasionally feel bewildered and inadequate in the face of new challenges, recognize that these feelings will give way to confidence as you master each milestone with your baby and young child. Your love for your child, combined with some common sense, is worth more than you can know. Also don't mistake confident parenting for perfect parenting, because that doesn't exist. We all make mistakes. But having a sense of humor and learning from your mistakes will allow you to meet the challenges of parenthood in an increasingly relaxed and easy fashion. Try as you might, life doesn't always work the way you planned. If you smile or joke to a friend about what you or your child has done, you are much more likely to ride through the rough times and concentrate instead on the good.

In fact, one of the most effective ways that parents can build confidence is to talk to each other. This sounds so obvious and is so simple that you might wonder why we are even bringing it up. The truth, though, is that many families tend to keep their questions and concerns to themselves. Reading a book like this one or talking to your pediatrician or an advice nurse can help, but it won't substitute for sharing your experiences with friends who are in a similar situation.

Many parents are fortunate in that they live in a community with lots of young families and have daily contact with other parents. Other families are more isolated, though, and they may have to make more of an effort to find people to talk to. To fill this need, family support groups are springing up all across the country. Other, smaller, infant and baby groups give parents a chance to get together, with their babies, to compare notes and discuss their concerns.

Whichever tack you prefer, we encourage you to give it a try. By sharing tips with other mothers and fathers, you will quickly learn that your experiences are not unique. It's true, your child isn't the only one who makes her parents stand on their heads before she falls off to sleep. A sense of community and camaraderie about the general ups and downs of parenthood often helps a lot. In our society, many of us no longer have strong role models in an extended family; the support of other parents can fill this gap.

Experience also helps you build confidence. As your child grows, you grow as a parent. Because of this dynamic process, you continually get to build on the parenting skills you have already acquired. Birth to five years covers so many developmental milestones that you will undoubtedly be tested and rewarded many times over. And no doubt about it, some of the stages will be difficult. But if you keep in mind that oppositional behavior is part of normal development, you will have a much healthier outlook. Try not to be overly impressed, for example, when your two-and-a-half-year-old falls kicking and screaming onto the floor of the supermarket because you won't buy her a pack of gum. And although it is definitely harder to maintain your cool in the middle of the night, try to react with similar authority when your toddler climbs out of her crib for the fifth time. And sometimes parents can renew their confidence with a simple reminder that babies and young children act as if they had radar. If you are confident about enforcing your child's routine, she will respond more easily than if you act with uncertainty.

A final way for you to develop the art of confident parenting is to set realistic goals for your child. Setting goals can both focus your efforts and help you monitor your progress. And once you are determined to meet your goal, you will find it psychologically much easier to weather the process. Like so many sound and wonderful goals in life, the process of establishing good sleeping habits may be hard work, but the results are well worth the effort.

SECURITY OBJECTS COMFORT
CHILDREN AT SLEEP TIMES

Kids have been carrying around security objects (also known as transitional or love objects) for a long time, and with good reason. Growing up and moving toward independence isn't always easy, and a security object can help ease the way. In this book, because we are concerned primarily with sleep, we focus on the comfort a special blanket or cuddly toy can offer your child when she is falling off to sleep or when she wakes up in the middle of the night (if she feels secure with her blanket or teddy bear, she won't need you).

This attachment at sleep times usually carries over to the day; many children like to have their love object close by when they face a new and stressful situation or are experiencing separation anxiety. Most experts agree that there is no harm in letting a young child have a security object during the day as long as this attachment doesn't evolve into an overdependence and prevent her from engaging in normal activities. We therefore advise you to restrict the security object to your child's bedroom or other specified places and only let her use it at sleep and comfort times. If you find it too difficult to monitor your child's daytime attachment to her love object, at least try to limit it to your home. In this way you eliminate the risk of losing the security object at the park, supermarket, or friend's house and you also minimize its wear and tear. But most important, your child will develop a natural ability to get along outside her home without the perpetually clingy, self-comforting behavior associated with around-the-clock use of a love object.

We tend to take for granted that all small children have this magnetic attachment to a special object because it is so helpful. In reality, though, there are plenty of babies and children who don't. Some young children never form close attachments to love objects because they receive the same comfort from their thumbs or pacifiers, or just don't need anything. This is fine. If your baby or child is like this, you can be sure that her ability to comfort herself is an indication that she can learn to rely on herself to fall off to sleep.

If you are the parent of a young baby, you can start to encourage an attachment to a love object (we recommend a blanket or thin quilt) by comforting her with it at sleep times. Toddlers and two-year-olds will become attached in this way, too. You can hold her special blanket or teddy bear next to her as you rock and sing to her at bedtime, and then make sure that it is tucked into bed with her. Over the weeks and months of repeating this, she can learn to associate this object with you, and in that way derive indirect comfort from it, comfort that before only you were able to provide. Then, if she awakens during the night, the feeling of her blanket or animal next to her (or sucking her thumb or pacifier) will help comfort her back to sleep.

BABIES AND YOUNG CHILDREN THRIVE ON ROUTINE

As we have discussed in the section on biological rhythms, most people benefit from a regular schedule. Variations in individual sleep needs are quite large, but everyone is better off by having approximately the same amount of sleep, at approximately the same time, each day. This doesn't mean that you can't put your child to bed a little later on the weekends or occasionally let her stay up late or miss a nap on a special occasion. Just don't expect her to fare well with enormous daily fluctuations.

As a young child matures, she takes great pleasure in anticipating the regular sequence of events in her day, culminating in bedtime. She can't tell time, but she still has an internal clock and is likely to feel better if it is in synchrony with her daily activities. A routine also provides a child with a buffer of security against other changes in her life. It can help protect her from the upsetting effects of a move to a new home, the birth of a baby brother or sister, or even her parents' divorce.

Parents, too, benefit from a regular schedule. In today's busy world, with many two-career families, parents often don't have the time to improvise. Routines take care of this, as everyone understands what is expected of whom, and when. When bedtime is part of a child's normal expectations, she no longer resists—provided, of course, that the nightly experience is pleasant and you are firm about your expectations.

We do appreciate, though, that there are plenty of wonderful parents who have unstructured life-styles. Most, however, aren't allowed total flexibility. It is difficult to find families who don't live by the clock and who don't even occasionally have to put their children to bed for their convenience. Children who are accustomed to falling asleep on the living room floor whenever they are tired do not respond well to having a once-in-a-while bedtime enforced when the parents are having friends to dinner. Also, if a child goes to daycare, a sitter, play group, or nursery school, the obvious advantage of a bedtime is that she will be up in time to get a fresh start on her morning activities. Sooner or later, parents have to face the fact that going to bed at 11 P.M. is incompatible with a regular school schedule.

Some parents shudder at the words "routine" and "schedule" because they evoke feelings of an old-fashioned rigid upbringing. This isn't our point of view, nor is it our intention to be rigid. Paradoxically, though, we have found that the more regular and predictable routine a young child has, the *more* flexible you can be as a parent, without calamitous effects when you occasionally make an exception.

THE IMPORTANCE OF A BEDTIME RITUAL

A regular bedtime ritual is one of the most natural and obvious ways of preparing a child for bed. Like adults, children often need a relaxing, winding-down time after a hectic day in order to fall asleep. A bedtime ritual can help your child bridge the gap between her active, busy day and a quieter, soothing state from which she can release herself to sleep. For this reason, her bedtime ritual should be calming and enjoyable; a bath, putting on snuggly pajamas, a book or a story, a song or two, or even a cassette or record all fit the bill.

All of this, of course, should be adapted to the age of your child. An infant doesn't need much of a bedtime ritual. And although an older preschooler generally benefits from a predictable, relaxing end to her busy day, she usually doesn't demand as elaborate or rigid a nightly ritual as she did when she was two years old.

A second, but we think no less important, function of the bedtime ritual is giving the two of you some happy, one-to-one time together. Once you learn to handle bedtime well, this can be one of the most relaxing and intimate times for you and your child to share every day. This is especially true if you work away from home and have little time with your children during the day. It is also true if you have several children at home with you or if you have many other commitments in your life.

Bedtime also provides busy fathers with a unique opportunity to maintain close contact with their child. For many children, this is the one time of day they can count on seeing their father. Many parents also find that alternating putting their child to bed works well because it gives both of them the opportunity to have special time with their child, because they alternate having time to tend to other children or other tasks, and because the child gets used to more than just one person at bedtime and during the night should the need arise.

If properly handled, bedtime rituals can both enrich the fantasy life and allay the fears of a young child. This task becomes more interesting and challenging as she becomes better at expressing her thoughts. Bedtime books and stories not only switch her mind to a more passive state, but they can also defuse fears, organize facts in her mind, and feed her effervescent imagination (see our suggested reading list for children at the end of the book). Starting young children on a regular bedtime book or story provides the foundation for a later love of language and literature. We can't emphasize enough the future rewards of this aspect of a bedtime ritual.

Just because we are such advocates of the bedtime ritual, however, don't be discouraged if your experiences don't live up to our happy, idyllic description. Of course, every parent occasionally experiences difficulty getting a child to bed! Either the child resists bedtime, the parent is too tired to cope with all the work entailed in putting a child to bed and finds herself following the path of least resistance, or a parent goes through a wonderful bedtime ritual only to be disappointed and aggravated moments later with constant, testing cries or forays out of bed.

Many children (especially around the age of two) try to draw out their bedtime ritual, so you may find yourself spending an unreasonable amount of time saying good night to every stuffed animal and doll in the room, or going through so many rigid steps that you begin to feel a bit of a fool. A special piece of advice, then: If your two-year-old has a fairly short, easy bedtime ritual, keep it that way, at least for the time being. If you start adding new characters to a made-up story, for instance, she may well insist that these additions be fixed into her nightly routine. One of your biggest challenges may be learning how to put time constraints on your bedtime attention without communicating impatience. If your child feels that she is being rushed, she is almost sure to balk and all your good intentions can go out the window.

WHEN TO GET PROFESSIONAL HELP

Extreme behavior problems and rare or persistent sleep problems are beyond the scope of this book. Sometimes, profound sleep disturbance can be a symptom of an underlying emotional problem. Other times, an otherwise normal child may exhibit signs of a recognized, although rare, sleep disorder. In either case, we recommend professional help.

When it comes to emotional or severe behavior problems, chances are that you know, deep inside, whether you and your child need the help of a counselor or therapist. It isn't something that comes up suddenly; rather it has built up slowly, over the years, to the extent that you now have a very difficult situation on your hands. The situation need not be disastrous; it is simply one that you, for one reason or another, can't deal with on your own.

Fortunately, children are usually more transparent than adults. They haven't learned to hide behind a false exterior, so their behavior is a pretty good indication of what is going on inside. In other words, you will know, by the way your child acts, if she is troubled.

Not all short-term troubled behavior warrants professional help. If, however, you find that your child has continual problems relating to other people, if she is extremely withdrawn or hostile, or if her behavior spins out of control a lot of the time, it is probably worth investigating. And particularly if these problems seem to center around your child's relationship with you, your spouse, or another family member, family counseling is advised. On the whole, your relationship with your child should be positive; if you find that the two of you are not enjoying the time you spend with each other, this is a danger signal.

Almost more than any other behavior, sleep is an indicator of problems, both in a child and in a family. If your preschooler is too fearful to fall asleep in the evening and wakes up frequently with severe nightmares, these may well be symptoms of serious emotional stress. On the other hand, if your child does not seem unusually fearful, but you are having no success in getting her to sleep through the night despite all your efforts, you probably need some outside help in learning to set limits on her behavior.

If any of this sounds familiar and you are now wondering where you and your child can go to get professional help, your first step should be to talk to your family doctor or pediatrician. Your doctor may well be able to provide you with the guidance you need, or perhaps he or she will suggest another professional. (If finances are a problem, most communities have facilities with sliding-scale fees.)

Or, if your child's problems seem focused around sleep abnormalities, your pediatrician may refer you to a sleep clinic. Sleep disorder clinics are emerging as part of many major university hospital centers. Doctors at these clinics are equipped to study individual sleep patterns and can diagnose and offer programs for a variety of problems, including the most rare and disabling disorders such as narcolepsy, sleep apnea, and hypersomnia. Recently, there have been enormous strides in understanding some of the most perplexing sleep disturbances. Even if a cure is unavailable, a sleep clinic will be able to provide you with appropriate counseling.

A FINAL WORD

We hope that this introduction has given you a new perspective on early-childhood sleeping problems and encouraged you to move on to the next several chapters of practical applications. Our general principles outlined in this introduction and our methods are based on our reading and stem from our personal experience with our own children, the professional experience of our husbands, who are both in private pediatric practice, and the experiences of our friends and acquaintances. In a field as young as childhood sleep research, methods such as ours have not yet been tested by large controlled studies. We feel that our recommendations are consistent with what work has been done, however, and we encourage psychologists and sleep researchers to incorporate our methods into future studies.

As you work your way through our methods, don't expect instant

results, especially with a toddler or preschooler. Keep in mind the importance of a long-term goal triumphing over short-term frustrations and
fatigue. Feel confident that you are developing happy and secure bedtime
and sleeping habits that will benefit your child for the rest of her life.

Chapter One

FROM BIRTH TO FOUR MONTHS

Welcome, New Baby
Getting on the Right Track
How to Help Your Baby Sleep Through the Night
    Illness
    The Nursing Mother's Diet
    Colic
    Your Three-to-Four-Month-Old

Questions/Answers

No one ever told me the power of love! I was looking forward to having this baby, but I didn't anticipate that my feelings would be this intense. It sounds crazy to say this, but my feelings of protection for him are so strong that I would kill for him. I wonder if other fathers experience such strong feelings at the birth of a first child. All the parents I know tell me that this bonding will serve me in good stead for all the sleepless nights we're about to endure!

—Father of newborn

WELCOME, NEW BABY

The first several months of a child's life are a period of adjustment for any family. It is a time when parents and older brothers or sisters get to know the baby and adjust to having a new family member. It is an equally eventful time for the newborn, who is faced with new stimuli and challenges every day. Intensifying all of this newness are the emotional aspects of having a new baby in the family. Frequently, all the joys and stresses are felt most intensely during these first months. No matter how prepared parents are, the unexpected often occurs and plans can go awry. Life is full, but not always easy. Fatigue can take its toll.

The first four months of life is not a period of major physical milestones, but more of laying the neurologic groundwork for achievements to come. During these first months, a baby begins to get control over his body and continues to get stronger, first supporting his head and upper back when he is held, and then learning to roll over, usually first from front to back, and then from back to front.

Many parents feel that the fourth month of their baby's life represents a real turning point. He begins to interact purposefully with other people and his environment. His crying decreases dramatically, especially if he has suffered from colic. By three months of age, most babies develop a social smile, and many try to mimic sounds they hear. Near and far vision continue to improve, and by four months of age, babies can see as well as adults. At around three months of age, babies develop an interest in their own hands, watching them intently as they move, grasp, and explore objects. This is the first step toward the eye-hand coordination that will continue to develop in the months to come.

The newborn's needs during these first months are simple. Beyond the basics, food and sleep, he mostly needs lots of love and calm, consistent attention. Most experts agree that there is no such thing as a sleep disorder during the first several months of life; babies know how much sleep they need. Provided a baby is not mistreated, he will sleep as much as he needs. It is up to you, as a parent, to gradually make these sleep times fit in with the rest of the family's schedule.

Happily, this seems to be the norm. Most babies begin to show day-night differentiation within a couple of months. Whereas a newborn sleeps randomly around the clock, most two-month-olds show a preference for sleeping in the night. And around this time, parents begin to get an idea of how much morning and afternoon sleep their baby needs, even though it probably isn't organized into predictable nap times. At two months of age, a baby may take from two to five naps a day, depending on the parents' schedule and the baby's temperament. By four months of age, most babies take only two or three naps a day, usually at about the same time every day. A four-month-old may continue to sleep just about as long as he always has, but his longest stretch asleep may well double to about eight hours.

Another part of the picture is that the newborn's sleeping patterns revolve around his stomach: he is likely to wake up hungry and fall off to sleep when he has had enough to eat. Gradually, this connection between eating and sleeping begins to fade, so that a four-month-old is more likely to fall asleep when he is tired, rather than when he is full, and wake up because he has had enough sleep. And at the same time, his pattern of small but frequent feedings is replaced by one of larger, but fewer, feedings. A newborn who wants to eat ten times during the day, for example, may be contented with only five larger feedings by the time he is three months old.

The connection between the physiologic changes in an infant's sleep and the reorganization of his days, if indeed there is any, is not at all clear-cut. As we pointed out in the introduction, however, the proportion of active sleep rapidly decreases during these early months, while quiet sleep increases. The changes in the way a baby sleeps may—although this is purely speculative—have some effect on his increasing ability to sleep longer and more soundly.

All in all, these changes combine to make life much easier for you as a parent. While it isn't always clear what is causing what, you do have a definite say in how your child's sleeping patterns shape up. To get an idea of what you can do, read on!

GETTING ON THE RIGHT TRACK

For many parents, their baby's sleep patterns improve just in the knick of time, coinciding with their own growing need for uninterrupted nighttime sleep. Although it usually doesn't take parents long to realize that fatigue is making life harder for them, it often isn't until four to six weeks after the baby is born that the cumulative effect of sleepless nights becomes profound. At this point, many mothers express varying degrees of depression and confusion. Most likely, exhaustion contributes not only to the first-week postpartum blues but also to the more profound depression that can continue. Under the best of circumstances, sleep deprivation can interfere with a mother's ability to carry on a normal life.

With the tremendous increase in father-infant bonding and the father caretaking role, fathers also experience this exhaustion. Even when babies are exclusively breast-fed, many fathers are up at night, walking, changing, and comforting their infants. So, we not only have the traditional ranks of new mothers staggering around in fatigue, but we also have many new fathers suffering from sleep deprivation.

Working mothers have additional pressures on them. Many mothers are no longer able to single-handedly carry the burden of sleepless nights because they, as well as the fathers, are due at work the next day. More than ever before, babies must learn to sleep through the night at an early age.

Although there may be no particular harm in training a younger or smaller baby to sleep through the night, we prefer to wait until a baby weighs at least nine pounds, is five to seven weeks old, and does not fall into any high-risk category or have any health problem. In the meantime, though, there are several preparatory steps you can take:

1. As new parents, we all have the tendency to continuously hold, rock, or nurse our babies to sleep. This is okay in the first few weeks of life. This is not okay as a continuing pattern, though, as you will be teaching your

baby to depend on you to fall asleep. In fact, this is one of the most common causes of sleep problems in young children: they are unable to fall asleep on their own either at bedtime or when they surface in the middle of the night. Since building a close relationship is so important during these early weeks, you should hold your baby as much as possible during his wakeful rather than sleepy times.

Therefore, get used to putting your newborn to sleep without fanfare. Wrap him snugly in a receiving blanket after feeding and changing him. Put him down in his cradle and leave the room. If you find yourself unable to stop thinking about him, go admire him from the doorway, but don't pick him up or otherwise interfere with his falling asleep on his own. You can distract yourself by telephoning a friend, listening to the stereo, or involving yourself in some other activity. Similarly, don't let your baby get used to sleeping in your bed. As a newborn, he won't mind sleeping alone, but if he gets used to your company, you may well find yourself with a habit that is difficult to break.

During the first weeks of life, a baby is safest sleeping on either his side or his stomach. Then, if he spits up some milk, there is little danger of his choking. Lying on his stomach, he also has the opportunity to use his neck and shoulder muscles to lift his head. When your newborn is lying on his side, you can prop him up by placing a rolled-up diaper behind him. Once he learns to roll over, he will most likely choose his own sleeping position. Then, you can try putting him down on his stomach or his side, but don't worry if he prefers sleeping on his back. In fact, customs vary from country to country. In England, for example, parents put their newborns to bed on their backs.

2. Babies don't require silence to sleep soundly. By nature, young babies will sleep through normal household noise, so don't eliminate these noises or your baby will learn to depend on an artificially quiet environment to sleep. This does not mean that you should have the stereo blaring, but don't worry about the telephone ringing, older children playing, or the dog barking. A baby can easily become accustomed to these noises.

3. Babies can be taught the difference between night and day. Because the average newborn sleeps about sixteen hours per day, this only leaves about eight hours that he will be awake. Therefore, try to concentrate these wakeful times in the daytime hours. It only makes sense that your baby will be livelier at night if he has been sleeping all day. Although you

may not see the effects right away, you will be beginning a process that will slowly evolve.

Your first step is to wake your baby every few hours during the day for feedings. Play with him before or after these feedings, depending on his inclination. If a friend or relative comes to meet him, don't hesitate to wake him up. You can also keep your house stimulating during the daytime hours by playing music and giving him brightly colored toys.

On the flip side, don't entertain your baby at night. When you go into his room, don't turn on the light. A light in the hall or a night-light can give you enough light to see what you are doing. Change his diaper only if he is very wet. After you have fed him, try to get him back to sleep as quickly as possible. It is important that you not stimulate him during the night, even if he seems anxious to play with you.

4. Starting as early as the third day of your baby's life, define one *focal feeding* time. This should be in the late evening, probably sometime between 10 P.M. and midnight. Then make sure that you feed your baby every night at this time. Do not be afraid to wake and feed him if he fails to wake on his own. Because babies are so unpredictable in their wakings and feedings during the first weeks of life, there might be times when you have just put your baby down as late as 9 P.M. Still wake him at 11 P.M. It is from this late evening focal time that we will "stretch" the early morning hours until we have achieved an eight-hour uninterrupted sleep for you and your baby.

Make sure that this late evening feeding is substantial. We are especially concerned that the breast-fed baby have a complete feeding at this time. Because breast-fed babies have to suck harder to get the milk flowing, they can become tired and fall off to sleep before becoming completely satiated. If your baby has this problem, try to keep him awake by unwrapping him or gently jostling him. Or you can try wiping his forehead with a moist washcloth. If he falls asleep after the first breast, try waking him up by changing him before you offer the other breast.

The purpose of this focal feeding is twofold. First, it ensures that your baby is full enough in the late evening to have a good start on sleeping during the night. Second, it puts *you* in control of his emerging schedule.

5. If you adopt the above routine of waking and feeding your baby at 11 P.M., he will most likely fall into a pattern of waking again around 1 or 2 A.M., and then again around 4 or 5 A.M., for additional feedings. Continue

these demand feedings during the early weeks and don't be surprised if there are time variations. Be sure, however, that you wait to pick your baby up until he is really complaining. In this way, you can begin to train yourself not to respond to a nondistressful whimper or a little cradle fidgeting. Soon you will learn to distinguish between real distress and simple infant wakefulness.

It is important to *never* wake your baby for any nighttime feeding *after* the late evening focal feeding time (at about 11 P.M.). If you are a nursing mother and your breasts are unbearably full, express your milk and put it in the freezer. If you are fortunate enough to have your baby waking only once between 11 P.M. and 7 A.M. before he is five weeks old, you are somewhat ahead of the rest of us. Give yourself a pat on the back.

6. Even if you are exclusively breast-feeding your baby, get him used to taking an occasional bottle. If you don't want him to have formula, you can express your milk and keep the bottles in the freezer. This will not only allow you to miss an occasional daytime feeding but also allow someone else to attend to your baby in the middle of night, as in our method. In order to get your breast-fed baby used to taking an occasional bottle, you should give him his first bottle somewhere between two and six weeks of age. Some parents find that their baby will refuse the bottle if they wait too long; other parents don't have this experience. In any case, if you don't have immediate success, try again in a few days. Some breast-feeding mothers find that their baby is much more likely to accept a bottle from someone else. So if you are having trouble giving your baby a bottle yourself, ask your husband or a friend to give it a try. In order to maintain your success, continue to give him at least two bottles a week.

7. You may have heard that a bottle-fed baby sleeps through the night sooner than a breast-fed baby. This is not true. You may have also heard people talk about cereal helping an infant to sleep through the night. Again, we disagree. Studies have shown that feeding cereal does not prolong the length of sleep. Therefore, cereal is unnecessary for the infant who is thriving on breast milk or formula.

HOW TO HELP YOUR BABY
SLEEP THROUGH THE NIGHT

You have finally arrived at the turning point. From now on, your immediate goal is getting your baby to sleep right through the night. Be sure that your baby weighs nine or ten pounds, has been gaining weight well, and is at least five to six weeks old. Research has shown that between four and eight weeks of age, babies frequently stretch out their longest sleep from four to eight hours. It makes sense, then, to take advantage of this natural tendency. But if he has a cold or any illness, wait until he is fully recovered.

If you are a nursing mother, the first five weeks or so of around-the-clock frequent nursing will have given you ample time to establish a good milk supply. Now, when you wean your baby from nighttime feedings, you in no way jeopardize your ability to breast-feed exclusively. If you are bottle-feeding, the same age and weight guidelines apply. By waiting until your baby weighs nine to ten pounds, you can be sure that he is able to go at least eight hours without a feeding.

Some of you may not feel ready to use our method yet. This is fine, as the method will work equally well when your baby is two, three, or four months old. In the meantime, though, be sure to follow our preliminary suggestions. Then, when you feel ready, you can proceed through the steps of our method. Or at that point you may find that you don't need to do anything else. Sometimes the focal feeding is the only step that is needed to get a baby to sleep through until morning. Also see our section on the three-to-four-month-old at the end of this chapter.

Preparation

Remove your baby from your room at night. Put him in his own room, or if this is not available put him in the hallway at night. It is time to reclaim your privacy as well as to introduce your baby to his own regular surroundings. Sometimes this is all that is needed for a five-to-six-week-old infant to sleep through until 5 or 6 A.M.

By now you should feel confident picking your baby up for his nightly focal feeding. Remember that you must be in control of this feeding, so you must wake him before he has a chance to wake you. This will allow the rest of our method to fall into place.

Our method is most effective with the help of a nighttime assistant, someone other than the biological mother. Make sure that whoever you choose understands what you are doing and clearly sympathizes with you. The baby's father is the most likely person for this job.

If you are a nursing mother, you absolutely must enlist the help of someone else for these three or four nights. This is because your baby can identify you and your breasts as his milk supply by smell and warmth; thus, as soon as you pick up your baby, he will start to root. Being physiologically primed to feed him (full breasts!), you can easily cave in and say, "The shortest route back to bed for me is feeding him." Therefore, don't attempt it alone!

If your baby is bottle-fed, there is no reason why you can't try the method yourself, except that you are probably so tired that you deserve a few nights off! In any case, it is important to have a clear understanding with your helper as to exactly what is expected of whom. It's too easy to make expedient decisions in the middle of the night.

Plan on devoting four nights to the method. We suggest that you choose Thursday, Friday, Saturday, and Sunday or Friday, Saturday, Sunday, and Monday. Weaning your baby from nighttime feedings on the weekend allows a working father or helper to recoup some sleep during the day. This is necessary, of course, only if he needs to tend to the baby for a good part of the night.

If your baby has severe colic, you may have to put off trying our method until he has recovered, usually at about three months of age. Or, if your baby gets a cold or any other illness during these four nights of training, abandon the method until he is fully recovered. He may well need your love and comfort in the middle of the night. You can start over again as soon as he is better.

NIGHT 1

Step 1: Have on hand a bottle of plain water or glucose water. Sweetening is not necessary, but it might encourage your baby to drink a little of the water. (You can use a bottle of glucose water from the hospital or you can sweeten the water yourself by adding 1 teaspoon of sugar or corn syrup to 4 ounces of tap water. Do not, however, use honey, as honey can cause botulism in infants. This is because the bacteria can grow in the baby's immature intestines and produce poisonous toxins.)

Step 2: Between 10 P.M. and midnight, wake your baby for his late evening focal feeding as you have been doing for the last several weeks. Get him back to sleep as promptly as possible.

Step 3: When your baby wakes up at 1:30 to 3 A.M., father or assistant, it's your turn to get up. First change him. Then wrap him up and try to settle him back into his bed. You can sing to him, turn on a musical mobile, offer him a pacifier, and rock the cradle or crib. This may or may not help him fall back to sleep. Do not pick him up at this point.

Step 4:

IF YOUR BABY FALLS BACK TO SLEEP

If you are fortunate enough that your baby fell back to sleep, hightail it back to your own bed. Don't give it a second thought! However, you'll probably be rudely awakened again in what seems like a very short time. He will probably wake up in as soon as twenty minutes, or if you're lucky, one and a half to two hours later.

When he does wake up, your purpose is buying further stretching time. Change him again. Wrap him up and go for a walk through your house. Put some music on, or the television—whatever. Just don't go back into the bedroom where the baby's mother is sleeping.

IF YOUR BABY DOESN'T FALL BACK TO SLEEP

If your baby has not fallen back to sleep after ten to twenty minutes of cajoling him as suggested above, pick him up, comfort him, and take him for a walk through the house or apartment. He was probably good and mad by the time you picked him up, so the change of being in your arms should be very comforting. You can install yourself in a big armchair and turn on the late late movie to help you stay awake and pass the time. Do not go back into your room, where the baby's mother is sleeping. Hold your baby close against your chest but don't put him in the feeding position.

Hopefully, you have succeeded in stalling your baby up to an hour with what we call *stretching.* Also, within the context of helping your baby sleep through the night, you are not being unduly harsh or unfeeling, although at the moment, in the middle of the night, you may feel torn. Be prepared for these feelings. Remember: You are, and have been, giving your baby all the love in the world.

In both instances in Step 4, you have achieved the goal of stretching your baby. The amount of time that has elapsed since your 11 P.M. feeding will vary considerably. Chances are that you can still be successful with a baby who is difficult to defer; it will just take extra patience, time, and consistency. For suggestions on how to deal with a colicky infant, see our section at the end of this chapter.

Step 5: Since you have stretched your baby as long as you possibly can (anywhere from an additional ten to forty-five minutes), you are now ready to offer the water that you prepared in Step 1. You might want to warm it or try sweetening it at the last minute if you are not having any success with plain water. At this point, some babies will chug down an ounce and others will spit out the nipple upon realizing that it's not milk. You may wonder in your middle-of-the-night stupor why you cannot just give a bottle of milk instead of a bottle of water. The process of having the father give a bottle, regardless of contents, does indeed allow the baby's mother to sleep, but a bottle of milk does not teach the baby that he doesn't need that nighttime feeding. Water is not food, and a baby will quickly abandon nighttime awakenings if water and love are the only reward. (This is not the case in older children!) Thus, this whole procedure discourages the baby from waking up for nourishment in the middle of the night. Remember: Giving a bottle of milk fills the need for the moment but does not meet the long-term goal of weaning your baby of nighttime feedings.

Step 6: Change your baby's diaper if necessary, and try as hard as you can to settle him down. Some of you will succeed, and some of you won't (as in Step 4). In either case, with the next serious complaining from your baby, the time has finally arrived to *feed* him. If your baby is bottle-fed, there is no point in waking the mother. But for all you fathers of breast-fed babies, unless you have a prior agreement to feed your baby breast milk from the freezer, your job is finally over for the night (phew!). *Congratulations* on the success of your first night—even if it is only 3 A.M. But the time really is not as important as having started the process of stretching your baby. Also, you are beginning to *not* reward nighttime waking with food, and in the process are extinguishing the stimulus-response pattern of "wake up: expect to eat."

To put this whole issue in perspective, remember that your baby can have as many demand feedings as he wants during the day, but *not* at night. We don't advocate letting your baby cry excessively. We simply want you to learn the difference between being appropriately and overly responsive during the night.

NIGHT 2

Before you start your second night, we would like you to review carefully both what we recommended for Night 1 and what you actually experienced. Some of you will relate a comedy act of everything that went wrong. That is fine, and it is especially encouraging that you are maintaining your sense of humor. Others of you will have frayed nerves, saying, "I can't bear hearing my baby cry," and feel a strong urge to give up on our method. Most of you will fall into the category of having achieved moderate success, expressing varying degrees of optimism and anticipation. Since most of you were able to stall your baby for some period of time, you should feel confident that you are on the right track. All you need is another few nights of extra resolve. If you are one of those many parents who argued in the middle of the night about what the other parent might be doing wrong, we suggest that you sit down during the day (not when you are trying over again at night) and review your experience and strategy. This daytime session allows parents to voice their grievances removed from the heat of 3 A.M. exhaustion. Usually, the problem is traceable to some specific event such as the baby's mother getting out of bed and interfering with the father while he was trying to care for the baby. Remember not to be hard on yourselves and don't amplify the importance of the events of last night.

So, now you are ready to start the step-by-step method for Night 2.

Step 1:   Prepare a bottle of water before you go to bed. Sweeten it or not, according to your preference. If your baby rejected plain water last night, you might try sweetening it tonight.

Step 2:   Pick your baby up for his 10 P.M. to midnight focal feeding as you have been doing for the last several weeks, but this evening make it a little later than usual (or if he wakes up himself, go ahead and feed him then). If you normally feed him at 11 P.M., this evening wait until eleven-thirty or eleven forty-five. Remember, your goal

FROM BIRTH TO FOUR MONTHS

is to stretch your baby through the night. Last night you were able to see how long he went without waking for a feeding. Was it three, four, or five hours? Tonight you want to see if he will sleep on his own a little longer by giving him the 11 P.M. feeding a little later than usual.

Step 3: Okay, father or helper, are you ready? When your baby wakes up in the middle of the night, go to him only when he is really fussing loudly. Then pick him up and comfort him. When he has settled down a bit, take your time and change him. Talk or sing to him as you wrap him up and try to settle him back into bed. All the aids you can use, such as a musical teddy bear, mobile, or pacifier, are fine. His thumb is fine, too, if he can keep it in his mouth.

Step 4: You are now at the point when your baby has either fallen back to sleep or is getting increasingly agitated.

IF YOUR BABY
FALLS BACK TO SLEEP

If your baby has fallen back to sleep two nights in a row, this is a good indication that he will be sleeping through the night soon. If this is your baby's first night of falling right back to sleep, congratulations! When he does finally wake up, continue the process of stretching him as you did on Night 1.

IF YOUR BABY DOES NOT
FALL BACK TO SLEEP

Pick your baby up again, and proceed with all the different strategies you tried last night. Remember, your immediate goal is to stretch the time between feedings. Your long-term goal of having your baby sleep through the night will be achieved when he gets the message that it is not worth waking up for water and love alone. Continue deferring him for forty-five minutes to an hour.

Step 5: It is now time to offer the water that you prepared in Step 1. This may be all you need to get him back to sleep for another two hours or so. Good luck.

Step 6: You have once again arrived at the point where you should finally feed your baby when he starts the next persistent round of complaining. You should have succeeded in deferring him at least an hour from the time he first woke up. If you have only been able to stall him for a short period of time two nights in a row, you are probably feeling somewhat discouraged about your ability to use this technique. Don't give up! You might be pleasantly surprised on Night 3.

NIGHT 3

You are now in a position to review two nights' experience. By this time we hope that you are entirely committed to having your baby sleep through the night. Because babies can vary so much, from the most easygoing to the active or colicky baby who never seems to settle down, don't expect your experience to be the same as your friend's. Most babies fall somewhere in between these two extremes.

If you are too discouraged to continue, go ahead and take some time off. You can always try again next week. In the meantime, continue the late evening focal feedings. For the majority of you who are left, good luck training your baby to sleep through the night on the eve of Night 3.

Step 1: As on the first two nights, prepare a bottle of water before going to bed.

Step 2: Pick your baby up for his late evening feeding, but again make it a little later than usual. You will actually be feeding him closer to midnight than at his regular time of 11 P.M. (Once your baby is sleeping through the night, he won't notice the difference if you pick him up at 10 P.M. or at midnight, so this late evening feeding can be at your convenience.)

Steps 3–6: Repeat steps 3 to 6 as in Night 2. By the third night your baby may initially waken at three-thirty or he may sleep until five-thirty. Hopefully, you're seeing progress, but if not, don't be discouraged.

NIGHT 4

Most of you must complete our method by reinforcing your accomplishments of the last three nights. If your baby has now already slept through until 5 or 6 A.M. (which many do by Night 3 and many more by Night 4), we suggest that you try staying in your bed, allowing him to fuss for ten to twenty minutes. By Night 4, many babies have made the adjustment to not eating and will go back to sleep without any intervention from you. If, on the other hand, your baby is still waking earlier, at around three or three-thirty, continue the stretching process on Night 4 (or for a few more nights, if needed). It shouldn't take him much longer to respond to your efforts and sleep through until the early morning.

If you have the occasional baby who is either very active or colicky and who won't go back to sleep, reread our preliminary suggestions. Try the method again in a few weeks after you feel comfortable with it. Active babies especially need to sense your confidence and will benefit from your loving but firm approach. If your baby has severe colic, check with your pediatrician to find ways to minimize his discomfort. You can try our method again in a week or two. If you still don't succeed, wait until your baby has fully recovered from his colic, usually at about three months of age.

Those of you whose baby has slept through the night until 5 or 6 A.M. deserve congratulations. Even though there is a significant difference from the parental sleep point of view between 5 and 7 A.M., you are finished with the real middle-of-the-night feedings.

The Final Touches

In order to complete your success, there are two things you still need to do. First, you need to work on your baby's early morning feeding. If after several weeks he is still waking expecting to eat at 5 A.M., we encourage you to be very slow to respond to him at this hour. If he doesn't settle down on his own after fifteen to twenty minutes, you can try the nighttime stretching technique. If that doesn't work, you can try putting him down to sleep an hour later in the evening. If he normally sleeps from seven to five, for example, you could probably switch him to eight to six. It's not a good idea to get into the habit of bringing your baby to bed with you at 5 A.M. and falling back to sleep while you nurse him. This pattern will be hard to break later on.

Second, continue to pick your baby up for a late evening feeding (between 10 P.M. and midnight) until he is at least three months old. This is because a baby under three months of age is not usually big enough to sleep for twelve uninterrupted hours. So if he isn't fed in the late evening, he'll likely start to wake up again at 3 or 4 A.M. We continued to pick up some of our babies for this feeding until they were three months old, and others until they were five months old. Suit yourself. This does not mean that your baby is or should be awake until 10 or 11 P.M. every night. When you are finally ready to wean your baby from his 11 P.M. feeding, you will be surprised how easy it is. Because *you* have been in control, picking him up at *your* convenience before your bedtime, you will find that the first night that you do not pick him up, he will not wake up on his own. That 11 P.M. feeding, then, is finally over, and it really is that easy. Your baby should now be sleeping for eleven to twelve hours a night, with minor deviations according to individual sleep needs.

Illness

Unfortunately, young babies often get colds and other minor illnesses that can temporarily interfere with their sleep. This is especially true of the baby who has older brothers or sisters or who is frequently around other children. If your baby has been sleeping through the night and now becomes ill, by all means take care of him whenever he needs you, regardless of the hour! Once you are sure that he is better, it shouldn't take more than one or two nights to reestablish his good sleeping habits.

The Nursing Mother's Diet

Occasionally, a nursing mother's diet may affect her infant's comfort and behavior. A number of substances, including caffeine and medications, can get into the milk supply, and some susceptible children may feel the effect and react adversely. It is probably a long shot, but if your child is having unexplained discomfort or trouble sleeping through the night, you might evaluate your diet and check with your doctor about possible changes you could make. Coffee, tea, and (to a much lesser extent) chocolate all contain caffeine, so these might be the culprit. If any of your family members are allergic to certain substances, you might be on the lookout for your baby developing an allergy. Keep this in perspective, though; it is really your attitudes about sleep that are the most important, and the best diet in the world won't by itself help your child sleep through the night.

Colic

One of the hardest challenges for new parents is helping a crying, colicky infant settle down. Although only 10 to 15 percent of infants develop colic, a much larger percentage of infants demonstrate some type of milder fussy behavior that develops into a regular daily pattern. Usually, this milder colicky behavior doesn't interfere with the baby's sleep in a significant way. On the other hand, true colic can include crying jags that last for hours. Most pediatricians diagnose colic if, in the absence of any physical problem, a baby cries inconsolably for several hours at a time every day.

There are many theories about the origins of colic, including one that implicates cow's milk in the mother's diet. In the final analysis, though, no one knows for sure why certain babies get colic, what exactly is bothering the baby, or how to treat colic. We do know that colic almost always resolves itself by the third to the fourth month of life, and that it causes no long-lasting problems. Parents of colicky babies should also feel reassured by the knowledge that colic develops in otherwise *normal* babies who have healthy family situations.

Soothing and settling down a colicky baby is the greatest challenge of this condition. Most parents find that close body contact, combined with gentle rhythmic movement, helps comfort their baby intermittently. A front baby pack, a cradle, a carriage, or an infant swing can bring temporary relief. Sometimes, a ride in the car can do wonders. In order to weather these difficult first months, parents of a colicky baby should be in frequent touch with their pediatrician or pediatric nurse practitioner for advice and reassurance. Parent support groups can also help during these trying times, as the most practical help often comes from other parents of colicky babies. And perhaps most importantly, parents should use stouthearted baby-sitters whenever possible to get some much needed relief! Sometimes, just a few hours' break will do a world of good. No matter how desperate parents of a colicky baby feel (and they *do* feel desperate), they must remember that their baby will grow out of his colic.

Nighttime colic probably demands the greatest patience and loving care. As a parent of a colicky baby, you can try rocking or massaging your baby over your lap. You can also reduce some of the strain and fatigue of caring for your colicky baby by alternating nights "on call" with your spouse or another adult. Because of your baby's need for nighttime attention and contact, he is an unlikely candidate for being trained to sleep through the night until his colic is resolved. When this happens, at about three months of age, you can then begin our method (see the following section on the three-to-four-month-old). At this age, gradually stop reinforcing behavior patterns that will interfere with good sleeping habits. A "cold turkey" approach is probably too abrupt, but over the next few weeks you must stop using your old soothing techniques such as walking, rocking, or nursing him to sleep or middle-of-the-night feedings and attention before you can expect him to sleep through the night.

Your Three-to-Four-Month-Old

Although we have explained our method starting from the first days of an infant's life (with the focal feeding), our method works equally well for a three- or four-month-old baby. In fact, if your baby is three to four months old and you are still up at night with him (as is often the case with a baby who has colic), you are probably extra keen to wean him of nighttime feedings. All you need to do is backtrack a little and use the same method.

Since the pivotal starting point of our method is having an approximately 11 P.M. focal feeding time, start picking your baby up for this feeding even if you have never done so before. *You* must be in control of this feeding by waking your baby before he has the chance to wake you. After establishing this feeding as a routine (give yourself a week to ten days and be consistent during this time), you can then proceed with the "stretching" steps of our method. Some of you may not even need to use the stretching steps; the focal feeding routine may be all that your baby needs to sleep through until morning.

If you haven't already introduced a love object for your baby, it is time to do so now. As you comfort him before his nap or at bedtime, hold him with the blanket or stuffed animal so that when you put him down with it, the object becomes an extension of you. Older babies, who are becoming progressively more sophisticated, can respond to this kind of reassurance. By promoting this security object, you are encouraging your baby's independence. Because a four-month-old baby is more established in his habits than a newborn is, you may need a little extra time and patience to change his nighttime waking patterns.

On the positive side, though, a four-month-old is still young enough to respond easily to your efforts. Your baby, more than ever, does not need a nighttime feeding. Your parenting skills should now be developed to the point that you can proceed with confidence in the knowledge that you are doing what is best for your baby.

QUESTIONS/ANSWERS

1. My three-week-old baby daughter has started sleeping through the night (from 11:30 P.M. to 6 A.M.) on her own. Is she too young to go that long without a feeding?

You are very lucky indeed. Provided that your baby was a good size and healthy at birth, continues to gain weight, and is otherwise thriving, she does not need that middle-of-the-night feeding. She can go six and a half to seven hours without harm. If you are breast-feeding her, you must also make sure that your milk supply is ample. If it is, your baby can meet her caloric needs by nursing more during the day. Since your baby has already made the adjustment to sleeping through the night, we want to encourage you *not* to revert back to middle-of-the-night feedings.

2. I can't get my three-week-old infant to settle down before 9 or 10 P.M. I am afraid of waking her just an hour after she has fallen asleep, especially since it was such an ordeal to get her to go to sleep in the first place. Are you sure that we are doing the right thing by waking her for the late evening focal feeding?

It is common for new parents to be reluctant to wake a sleeping baby, regardless of the hour. This reluctance is easy to understand, especially if this is your first baby and you haven't seen how well this system works. Let us reassure you, then. The focal feeding is important because it (1) gives your baby the best chance of being full enough to sleep at night and (2) puts *you* in control of her emerging schedule. Your baby will quickly become accustomed to this late evening routine, and you will most likely find it a particularly relaxing time for both of you. Our bet is that she will feel extra secure because you are doing such a good job of anticipating her needs.

3. My two-week-old son wakes up every two to two and a half hours from 7 P.M. on, expecting to be fed. I am breast-feeding him so I am the only one who can feed him. I'm really exhausted and am wondering if all this is normal.

Your experience is entirely normal. First of all, nursing by itself makes a woman feel more tired than usual. This, coupled with your lack of sleep, could hardly leave you feeling any way *but* exhausted. Unfortunately, though, fatigue can lead to increased anxiety, stress, and depression and often leaves new mothers feeling quite desperate and inadequate. Fatigue can also put you into the vicious cycle of doubting the decisions you are making for your baby.

There are several ways to alleviate fatigue during this postpartum period, but you won't eliminate it until your baby is sleeping through the night. First, have one or two naps a day. Second, decrease at least by a half the normal expectations you have of yourself. Third, if you have enough milk, start expressing and freezing it so that you can occasionally have a six-hour stretch when you don't have to attend to the baby. This uninterrupted sleep will go a long way.

Babies are predictably unpredictable during the first few weeks of their lives. Two-to-three-hour wake-feed cycles are normal and help the nursing mother build up her milk supply. When your milk supply is well established and your baby is thriving, these stretches between feedings will become larger. Since your baby is two weeks old, it is not too early to establish your late evening focal feeding time. You can also familiarize yourself with what constitutes good sleeping habits and start to define realistic sleeping goals for your baby.

4. How long can I let my three-month-old cry in the middle of the night?

This is an important question, as all parents want to know if there is a time limit they should set on their babies' crying. Actually, we don't advocate letting a young baby cry a long time, but the exact amount of time is individual and depends on the baby and the set of parents. An easygoing, quiet baby who cries for a minute straight may be crying for a long time, whereas an active, vocal baby may *need* to cry for five to ten minutes or so as a regular means of winding down. Parents also vary in their ability to tolerate a crying baby. One set of parents may need to go to their baby after thirty seconds of crying, while another set of parents may wait five minutes until they even start to measure time.

For these reasons, we can't give you a specific time limit for your baby's crying, but we do think you should learn to decipher what your baby's cry means. Crying or complaining from fatigue is a different message from crying from pain. Focusing on the level of distress, then, will guide you in determining the length of time you should allow your baby to cry without intervening. As the months go by, you will become more confident in interpreting the significance of your baby's cry.

5. My five-week-old daughter falls asleep frequently after taking only one breast. I have trouble waking her for the second, and I know that if she doesn't have it, she will wake up in an hour, wanting to nurse again. What can I do to encourage her to take both breasts at a single feeding?

This is a common problem for the young infant, and it usually disappears by a couple months of age. Young babies find nursing so comforting that they often fall asleep after being changed, wrapped up, and offered the first breast. This can happen when their minimum milk and sucking needs have been met, but before their tummies are full.

There are several strategies you can try to get your baby sufficiently awake before offering the second breast. Try changing her in the middle of the feeding (before you offer her the second breast) instead of changing and readying her before the feeding. Also try unwrapping her. Sometimes, the effect of not being cozily wrapped in a receiving blanket wakes a baby. You might also try stimulating your baby by jiggling, tickling, or otherwise entertaining her. Also realize that five minutes of vigorous sucking is usually sufficient to empty a breast; if she is sleepy, don't let her stay on the first breast too long. Finally, there may be no immediate solution. Sometimes you just have to wait for babies to grow out of this habit.

6. My three-month-old son started sleeping until six-thirty or seven every morning when he was six weeks old. Four days ago he developed a bad cold and we have had to get up with him every night since. How can we get him to sleep through the night once he feels better?

Young babies are especially uncomfortable when they get a cold. Besides the normal discomfort associated with a cold, their primary self-comforting acts such as nursing or sucking their thumbs or pacifiers are disrupted during a respiratory illness. Therefore, when your baby has a cold, you must expect that he will be up at night from this discomfort. This is not the time to worry about sleep habits; attend to him when he needs you.

Provided you have not reestablished the habit of nursing your baby in the middle of the night, he will go back to his old pattern of sleeping through the night once he is feeling better. This usually involves no effort on your part. If you have started feeding him again in the middle of the night, you can try weaning him as soon as he is well. Go to him the first night he cries, comfort him, and then leave him to settle down on his own. If this approach doesn't work two nights in a row, review our method and start over, step by step, including reestablishing the focal feeding (if you have already given it up).

Sometimes, babies get one cold after another. This is especially a problem when there are older siblings who are in contact with illness through their school friends. What starts out as a short illness can lengthen into a month or two of colds, ear infections, and sleepless nights. These times are desperate for parents, but let us reassure you that you can get your baby back on the track of sleeping through the night. Wait until the sequence of illness is finished before you start retraining him.

7. My four-week-old usually sleeps well at night, getting up only once to nurse. I get him to sleep after his evening and 2 A.M. nursing by walking around the room with him on my shoulder. He falls asleep after about ten minutes and I put him down. Is there any problem with this?

You are lucky that your baby sleeps so well already, but we feel that you are building trouble for yourself by walking him to sleep. By consistently letting him fall asleep on your shoulder, you are compromising his ability to fall asleep by himself. This can lead to problems later on, as it is a difficult habit to break. A better pattern would be to wrap your baby snugly in a receiving blanket, hold him only briefly, and put him into his crib awake. His fussiness is likely due to fatigue and should last only a matter of minutes.

8. Our six-week-old daughter has colic. She cries a lot, often for several hours in a row. Otherwise, she seems just fine. She eats well and is growing. Our pediatrician tells us that there is nothing wrong with her and that she will outgrow her colic in a couple of months. Our neighbors are full of advice on ways to comfort her, none of which work, and imply that if we could relax with her, she would feel better.

Her crying seems to be the worst in the late afternoon, at bedtime, and in the middle of the night, although she isn't completely predictable. We often have to walk her for up to two hours to get her to fall asleep in the evening, and usually for another hour or so to get her back to sleep after her 2 A.M. feeding. Our lives and our sleep have been so disrupted that my husband and I are both wondering if things will ever get back on an even keel. Do you have any suggestions?

Your daughter definitely fits the classic description of a baby with colic. This is one of the most frustrating experiences for new parents, and unfortunately there is no easy solution to it. This is a time when your confidence as a parent is put to a real test. Intellectually, parents can understand that they are in no way responsible for their baby's discomfort, but the process of caring for a colicky baby remains an emotionally (and physically) draining experience, and one that is bound to promote self-doubt.

The best advice we can give is to look to the future. In fact, we can tell you from our personal experience that colic in no way affects or predicts a baby's future disposition or sleeping habits. One of our daughters, who had severe colic until twelve weeks of age, is now a well-adjusted, happy seven-year-old who sleeps more soundly than just about anyone else we know.

Because your baby's colic is worst at bedtime and after her 2 A.M. feeding, she is probably not now a candidate for sleeping through the night. Until she outgrows her colic, don't attempt the focal feeding and stretching techniques described in the text. You should instead continue to use whatever techniques you have found most successful in comforting her through her bad spells.

In the meantime, though, you can start building good future sleeping habits by incorporating our basic principles into your lives (see the introduction). Confident parenting and an appreciation for the power of routines will carry you a long way. Colic is a self-limiting condition, but if you aren't careful, old habits can continue long after the colic has disappeared. Therefore, encourage your baby to fall asleep on her own at other times of the day, when she isn't uncomfortable. You can also reduce the number of continuous hours she sleeps during the day, so she'll be able to sort out day from night and sleep more at night. In addition, introduce her to a security object, and spend some time making her crib and bedroom pleasant. All of this will go a long way toward making her a good nighttime sleeper once she outgrows her colic.

Once your baby does turn the corner (usually at about three months of age), you can begin the focal feeding and stretching techniques of our method. She will still be young enough at this point to easily get into the habit of sleeping through the night. Be careful to discontinue any night-time comforting routines you have fallen into (for example, walking, rocking, nursing her to sleep at bedtime or in the middle of the night). These will be much easier to eliminate now than when she is older.

9. Our son, who is three and one half months old, started rolling from his front to his back about two weeks ago. He hasn't learned to roll back to his stomach, though, so every time he gets onto his back, he is stuck. The real problem comes in the middle of the night. He is only comfortable sleeping on his stomach, so when he rolls over he can't get back to sleep. This happens several times a night, and either my husband or I have to get up and roll him back onto his stomach. He falls back to sleep immediately, but is invariably up again in a couple of hours. This is getting quite tiresome for us, but we don't know what else to do. Any suggestions?

It sounds as if your son is going through the first of what may be several developmental stages that can disrupt his sleep. Eventually he will learn to roll back to his stomach on his own, but in the meantime it is an exasperating problem.

Our first preference would be to leave him. There is no harm in having him sleep on his back, and it will allow him to learn to get back to sleep on his own resources. It may take several days of listening to him fuss, but after that he will feel fine in either sleep position.

If you are unwilling to wait out the situation and prefer to help your baby roll over during the night, go ahead. When you go to his room, though, simply reposition him and leave immediately. If you interact with him in any other way, you risk increasing his nighttime dependence on you.

10. I have tried waking my three-month-old daughter for a late evening feeding, but I have a difficult time getting her to nurse at this time. She is cranky when I wake her up, and all she wants to do is go back to sleep. At most she has just a few gulps of milk. What should I do?

First of all, don't expect your baby to be as alert and hungry at night as she is during the daytime. Because you are waking her (instead of waiting for her to wake you), it is normal that on some nights you will find that she isn't very interested in eating. And as the nights go on, you will probably find that your daughter is hungry some evenings and takes a substantial feeding. By the time a baby is three months old, it isn't as important how much milk she takes as that you are giving her the chance to eat, and in the process are resetting her internal clock. Even if she only takes a few sips of milk before drifting off to sleep again, she will probably be able to postpone her normal 1 to 2 A.M. feeding for at least a couple of hours. From that time, then, you can use our stretching techniques described in the text until she is sleeping through the night.

11. My four-and-a-half-month-old started sleeping through the night when she was about two months old. A few nights ago, however, she started waking up around midnight, wanting to nurse. She isn't sick, but she complains when I try to put her back in bed after a short nursing; if it were up to her, I think she would nurse for hours! Since she is my third child, I haven't had the time to walk or rock her to sleep, and she has always been good about getting herself to sleep (sucking her thumb)—except now, at midnight. She has been such an easygoing baby that I'm totally perplexed by this new waking pattern. What can I do to get her to sleep through the night again?

It sounds as if your baby is waking because she is hungry. It is common for babies to have a growth spurt at about this age, thereby increasing their caloric needs. Also, since you are the busy mother of three children, it is possible that your milk supply is down by the end of the day. This is a common situation, but the timing is unfortunate because the evening is the time when your baby's feeding must be large enough to hold her through the night. In your baby's case, it sounds as if this isn't happening.

Your solution, then, will have to be based on giving your baby enough nourishment late in the evening. Although it may sound backward to you, we suggest that you start waking her at about 11 P.M. for a feeding (or right before you go to sleep) for the next several nights. It is important that you not wait for her to wake you at midnight so that you stay in control of this feeding, thereby making it easier for you to eliminate it at a later time.

Late in the evening, then, pick your baby up and nurse her, but not for longer than a normal feeding. If you suspect that she isn't satisfied, either you can offer her some more milk that you expressed earlier in the day or you can give her some formula. If your pediatrician agrees, you might even want to offer her some cereal or other solids. Then put her in her crib. We're willing to bet that she will sleep through the night.

Once you are ready to stop picking her up in the late evening, use this supplemental feeding technique at dinnertime or whenever you put her down for the night. Also keep a close eye how hungry she is during the day and ask your pediatrician if she is ready to start a regular diet of solids.

Chapter Two

FROM FIVE TO NINE MONTHS

My baby is eight months old now and he is adorable in every way. At least almost. In the last month he has been waking every night and I have had to nurse him off and on all night long. I've always nursed him to sleep at bedtime but now that he wakes so much during the night I have to nurse him then, too. In desperation, I let him sleep a good part of the night in my bed. I feel like a zombie more and more during the day. I'm so confused because he was sleeping through the night until he was seven months old.

—*First-time mother*

THE GOLDEN AGE OF BABYHOOD

The time between five and nine months of age is a wonderful period of growth and contentment for most babies. By and large, parents have recovered from the initial adjustments to having a newborn and can now enjoy the newest family member, who is both appealing and thriving. This is a time when babies make tremendous gains physically, intellectually, and socially. It is difficult to imagine a creature more appealing than a six-month-old chortling and squealing with pride over her latest accomplishment.

Motor skills advance rapidly during this time, allowing a baby much greater freedom to inspect and explore her surroundings. Babies learn to sit up, crawl, and pull themselves to a stand, and some even take a few steps. By nine months of age, babies can skillfully grasp and pick up small objects with their thumbs and forefingers. They are physically much stronger than they were only a few months ago, and much more in control of their bodies.

Along with increasing dexterity and mobility, a baby's intellectual growth spurts at this time. She is curious, using her new motor skills to explore and learn about spatial relationships, and experience at first hand the physical characteristics of different objects. Eye-hand coordination improves, and through repetition she learns concepts such as cause and effect and object permanence. She begins to develop a memory and a sense of timing and by nine months of age may understand and carry out simple directions.

By and large, the five-to-nine-month-old is a wonderfully sociable person. She smiles easily and enjoys interacting with people. She learns certain behaviors by imitating what she sees, and her self-awareness grows every day as she explores her body and its image in the mirror.

With these huge developmental steps, however, come new fears. The world is no longer as simple as it once was, and the baby has a lot to sort out. One fear that often crops up at this time is a fear of unfamiliar people. It can be quite inconvenient or embarrassing for the mother who is trying to introduce a friend to her baby who refuses to stop screaming or explain to Grandma why Susan won't sit on her lap, but it isn't a cause for genuine concern. In fact, such displays are really proof of the baby's new ability to discriminate between people. And as she continues to mature, she will certainly outgrow this "stranger anxiety."

Another common fear for a baby of this age is being separated from her parents or usual caretaker. Appropriately enough, this usually coincides with the baby's new mobility and ability to physically separate herself from them. Suddenly, having crawled into the next room in search of a new discovery, she might turn around and find herself alone. Frightened by the surprise of not seeing her parents, this translates into a more universal fear of them leaving *her* or not being there when she needs them. Again, this is a perfectly normal and universal developmental stage, and it occurs only when the baby is mature enough to recognize herself as an individual separate from her parents.

With the exception of these fears that sometimes crop up as early as six months of age, the five-to-nine-month-old period is a relatively easy and contented time for parents and babies alike. Many parents report that the pieces of their lives are falling back into place and that they feel a real sense of confidence and well-being. The intensity of the newborn period is over, and new challenges of toddlerhood are in the future. By now the baby's sleeping and eating patterns are less connected and more predictable. By five months of age, most babies eat four to six times a day, and this may drop to three to four times once she is nine months old. Daytime nap and nighttime sleep times usually fall into a regular schedule. As at any age, sleep needs vary enormously from baby to baby, but at this age anywhere from thirteen to fifteen hours per day is common.

You also should be aware that this is the time when night-waking problems can first show up. Although statistics vary from study to study, it has been estimated that about one third to one half of babies don't sleep through the night, even if they have done so previously. As depressing as this may sound, though, there are lots of things you can do to encourage your child's nighttime independence. Our philosophy has been borne out by Dr. Isabel Paret, who, in a recent study of the relationship between night-waking and mother-infant interaction in nine-month-olds, concludes that babies who sleep through the night also share other characteristics such as being able to fall asleep on their own, having an attachment to a transitional (security) object, and quite possibly thumb-sucking. There also seems to be a correlation between the first steps toward weaning and sleeping through the night. Taken as a whole, this presents a profile of the more independent and self-reliant baby being more likely to sleep through the night. This is not to say that you shouldn't have a close relationship with your baby or that you should stop breast-feeding. Encouraging your baby to master those steps toward independence that are within her grasp, however, may well take more love and understanding than holding her back. In this chapter we will show you the appropriate steps for the five-to-nine-month-old.

Naps

Naps are an important part of almost every baby's day. As newborns, most babies spread their sleep out pretty evenly over twenty-four hours, but by the time they are five months old, they sleep primarily at night, with two one-to-two-hour naps. A common nap schedule for the five-to-nine-month-old who sleeps through the night (from 7:30 to 6:30) is 9 to 10:30 A.M. and 1:30 to 3 P.M.

But because individual sleep needs vary enormously, there are no set rules for how many hours your baby should spend napping. Just make sure that her daytime naps don't interfere with her nighttime sleep. If, for example, your baby isn't ready to fall asleep at night when you want her to, or if she wakes too early in the morning, these are good indications that you should cut down on her daytime napping. You can do this by simply waking her up after a set amount of time.

On the other hand, if you have a baby who doesn't want to nap at all during the day, or perhaps for only twenty minutes at a stretch, try to have her rest in her crib for at least forty-five minutes once or twice a day. This will give her time to relax, unwind, and collect herself for the rest of the day. If she isn't interested in sleeping during this time, you can give her quiet toys to play with.

Most parents also find it best not to let their babies get accustomed to an elaborate sleep ritual at nap times. You should be able to put your baby in her crib awake and have her fall asleep by herself. Your time during the day is probably too busy to spend a lot of time getting her to sleep, and you can save your special time of books and songs for evening.

THE FIRST APPEARANCE
OF SLEEP-DISTURBING HABITS

If your five-to-nine-month-old baby has never settled down into an easy sleep routine, it is most likely the result of habit. Most experts agree that by this age, continual problems in either falling asleep or staying asleep through the night are the result of conditioned behavior, not physical need. Sleep-disturbing habits that have commonly developed by this age include being unable to fall asleep alone, sleeping in the parents' bed, wanting to feed during the night, and wanting attention in the middle of the night. For reference purposes, we treat these problems individually, but in reality they often occur in combination. For example, it is rare to find a baby of this age who sleeps with her parents but who doesn't expect to eat. Or a baby who has become used to falling asleep on her father's shoulder may also routinely wake up at 3 A.M. expecting attention. Therefore, it is up to you to sort out your baby's habits and approach them in a logical sequence. Some problems are so interrelated that solving one will automatically alleviate the other. In any case, rest assured that at this age your baby is still quite receptive to a new routine. Your confidence and consistency, combined with your usual loving care, will go a long way in helping her form new habits.

In any of these situations, the traditional advice of "letting your baby cry it out" will work. If you carefully monitor the situation (from behind the scenes), your baby will not be harmed by crying. In most cases, the baby is as cheerful as ever the next morning. She may cry for up to several hours the first night or two, but after that her crying time will sharply decrease if you don't go to her. We realize, however, that many parents feel uncomfortable with this approach, and we have therefore devised the following gentler and more gradual guidelines and methods. The only time that we don't see an alternative to the "cold turkey" approach is in the case of the "trained night crier."

How to Help Your Baby
Fall Asleep Alone

In order to achieve overall good sleeping habits, your baby must learn to fall asleep by herself. Babies who always fall asleep with parental assistance come to depend on it. They get used to being walked, rocked, or nursed to sleep. Not only is this inconvenient for the parents, but the baby herself suffers. She doesn't develop the simple but essential ability to fall asleep!

This habit can be a problem for the parents of a five-month-old, but it can be even more serious for a nine-month-old. At about nine months of age, a baby first develops the ability to fight sleep. Before this, she always fell asleep when she became tired. But now she can become overstimulated or learn that putting off sleep gives her extra attention from her parents. She also learns to manipulate her parents into more elaborate procedures to help her fall asleep. Conversely, if she falls asleep by herself, she can take the extra time she needs in her crib to wind down. Her transition to sleep is gradual, natural, and independent.

Therefore, like so many other habits that we discuss, it is best to nip this one in the bud. The problem isn't likely to correct itself but usually only gets worse and harder to correct later on.

GUIDELINES FOR GETTING YOUR BABY TO FALL ASLEEP BY HERSELF

1. Encourage your baby to become attached to a security object such as a teddy bear or blanket before you try teaching her to fall asleep on her own.

2. Introduce a soothing, fun bedtime routine that lasts for a set period of time (five to fifteen minutes is fine for this age group). Hold your baby in your lap with her cuddly love object as you "read" an infant book together or sing a song. Then tell her that it is bedtime and put her into her crib with her snuggly.

3. Say good night and leave the room. If she cries, go into her room, say something reassuring, and leave quickly. Don't get her out of her crib.

4. You should expect your baby to protest for three or four nights. She'll get over it quickly, though, if you are consistent. While some babies may babble or make happy sounds as they fall off to sleep, other babies need to cry for a minute or two every night as they wind down. An experienced

parent recognizes this complaining as her baby's way of releasing herself from a stimulating day.

5. If your baby is used to being breast- or bottle-fed to sleep (as opposed to having her milk earlier in the evening), try feeding her an hour earlier or keeping her awake while she feeds. She may protest being put to bed awake, but not out of hunger. She will soon learn to rely on her inner resources to fall asleep.

6. If your baby is used to falling asleep in your bed and is then later carried to her crib, read our suggestions for moving your baby out of your bed in the next section.

How to Move Your Baby out of Your Bed

Sometimes, a parent's bed can be the best place for comforting a frightened or sick child. As a general rule, however, we agree with Dr. Brazelton and other experts who feel that sleeping without parents fosters a young child's sense of independence and self-reliance. Most young children learn to appreciate the comforting and secure aspects of their own bed and prefer sleeping there. So if, like most adults in our society, you value your nighttime privacy and don't want your baby in bed with you, don't feel guilty. You are entitled to sleep without your child and carry on an adult relationship, if you so desire.

It is also important to realize that there is nothing inherently frightening about sleeping alone, especially for the child who has been doing so from birth or just a few months of age. Therefore, if your five-to-nine-month-old has gotten used to sleeping in your bed, break the habit now—before she begins her first bout of separation anxiety. If her habit is firmly ingrained, it might take her two to three weeks to complete the transition to her own crib. If she has been sleeping in your bed for only a short time (during an illness or a vacation or because of some other upset), getting her used to her own crib again shouldn't take more than three or four nights.

GUIDELINES FOR MOVING YOUR BABY OUT OF YOUR BED

1. Don't expect immediate results. This process will require patience and consistency and may involve a few sleepless nights.

2. Make sure your baby's crib is comfortable and inviting. A pleasant bedroom, a night-light, proper temperature, and crib toys can all make your baby happier in her own bed.

3. Start reorienting your baby to her own special place by first insisting that she nap there during the day. Then, after she has made that adjustment, have her spend the night in her crib, too.

4. Try introducing a transitional object for your baby (babies who sleep with their parents often use them as transitional objects and aren't attached to anything else). You can encourage this attachment by holding and cuddling your baby at "sleepy times" with one chosen blanket or stuffed animal. In this way, you teach her to associate sleep and comfort with this object. Count on this taking at least one to two weeks.

5. If your baby complains about being left in her crib alone, keep coming in to reassure her and stroke and comfort her until she falls asleep. Do this at reasonable intervals, giving her a chance to settle on her own. If this doesn't work and she continues to protest vigorously, it is okay to stay with her in *her* room, but only as a last resort. (This may be particularly important if your child is experiencing a bout of separation anxiety; also see our section on developmentally related sleep problems.) Pull up a chair and doze or lie down next to her crib. This should reduce her feelings of abandonment and ease her transition to life in her new crib. But in any case, *do not* lift her out of her crib. This could counteract any advances you have made.

6. When she wakes up in the middle of the night (as she undoubtedly will) and cries because she isn't next to you, go to her and reassure her. Again, don't pick her up, but if you must, lie down next to her crib to reassure her. Go back to bed as quickly as possible. Repeat this if you feel that you are making progress; if you're getting nowhere, your only option may be to let her cry it out.

7. Once you have made the decision to move your baby into her crib, don't let her work her way back into your bed before her new habits are firmly established. If this happens, you are teaching her that crying longer

and louder is the best route back to your bed. You will have gained nothing and possibly lost ground.

8. We know that this retraining period is frustrating and difficult for both you and your baby, but no matter how tempted you are, don't substitute one bad habit for another. For example, don't start giving your baby a bottle to take to bed as a replacement for sleeping with you.

How to Wean Your Baby from Nighttime Feedings

Provided your baby is growing well, you can be sure that she no longer needs nourishment during the night. If she consistently demands to eat during the night after five months of age, she is demonstrating an act of training rather than physical need. Once you start her on solid foods (usually between four and six months), four to six nursings or bottles are sufficient. This can easily be accomplished during the daytime, between the hours of 7 A.M. and 7 P.M. (or whatever fits your schedule). Or, if you are still exclusively breast- or bottle-feeding your baby, she should still be able to sleep ten to twelve hours at night without a feeding provided her milk intake is adequate during the day. (One common indication that a baby is ready for solid foods is that she *stops* being able to sleep through the night. In this case, her caloric needs are not being met and she wakes up hungry. Introducing daytime solid meals often alleviates the problem.) Once you make up your mind to wean your baby from nighttime feedings, her body will quickly compensate to meet all her caloric requirements during the day.

Dr. Barton Schmitt of the University of Colorado refers to this type of waking as "trained night feeding." For ease of discussion, we have further subdivided this situation into perpetual nighttime nursing, once- or twice-a-night nursing, and once-a-night bottle-feeding. Since all these behaviors fall into the category of habits, keep in mind that as such, they are correctable. It is much easier to change a behavior that is based simply on habit rather than on developmental or psychological need.

The Perpetual Nighttime Nurser

The feeding and sucking habits of breast-fed babies are closely linked with their sleeping habits. Therefore, some of these habits may need to be modified to get your baby sleeping through the night. Keep in mind that even though we offer suggestions for changing some of the circumstances surrounding the way you breast-feed, we encourage you to continue nursing your baby as long as you like. For many women, breast-feeding is one of the most gratifying experiences of mothering an infant. But weaning your baby from nighttime feedings will in no way compromise your daytime and evening milk supply. Your breasts will make the adjustment over a period of days.

You may be perplexed and annoyed at yourself for getting into the jam of feeding your baby all night long. But before you are too hard on yourself, realize that your qualities that contribute to your baby's excessive feeding demands (and your fatigue) also constitute some of the best in motherhood. According to Dr. Schmitt, you are likely more generous, more selfless, and less opinionated than the average mother. You tend to put your children's needs before your personal needs. But you may also be less secure in your relationship with your baby and worry that you will be compromising her trust in you if you let her cry for even a few minutes.

If this profile rings a bell, it is time to find ways you can offer your baby more guidance. Being the adult in your relationship requires you to lead as well as protect. Good luck!

Preliminaries

1. Reclaim your bed for yourself. Perpetual nursers tend to spend the night or the early morning hours in their mothers' beds, allowing easy access to the breast and decreasing the amount of "conscious" attention the mother must give. If your baby is used to sleeping in your bed, first work on getting her to sleep in a crib in her own room before attempting to wean her from nighttime feedings. For suggestions on how to do this, see our section "How to Move Your Baby out of Your Bed."

2. Next you will need to tackle daytime feeding intervals. Babies who feed continuously at night also tend to feed fairly continuously during the day. By five months of age, your baby should certainly be able to go three or four hours between most nursings (late afternoon or early evening is a time when many babies seem to nurse more frequently). If she can't, this is an indication that she needs more nourishment, probably solids. Also, by spacing out her nursings, she should be able to increase the size of each feeding and therefore feel satiated for a longer time. This will also allow her last nursing of the day to be more substantial, which will, one hopes,

help her sleep through the night (and also convince you that she has had enough milk to sleep through the night).

3. Falling-asleep patterns have to be changed, too. Your goal is to be able to put your baby to bed awake and have her fall asleep by herself. She should not have to depend on nursing to fall asleep. You can practice this in the daytime by shifting your daytime nursings to right after your baby has awakened from her naps and to other wakeful periods of her day and evening. This way, she will begin to dissociate nursing and sleeping. Also, your baby will enjoy interacting with you as she nurses, if she is alert. For other suggestions, see our section "How to Help Your Baby Fall Asleep Alone."

4. Try not to use your breasts as a pacifier. Frequently, a nursing mother offers her breasts at various times of the day and night as a means of comforting rather than nourishing. This is part of the overall experience of breast-feeding, but practiced to an extreme, as in the case of the perpetual nighttime nurser, it can stand in the way of a good night's sleep. While we are fortunate that our bodies work in multiple ways to comfort and nourish our babies physically and emotionally, we can also use other means of comfort. Five- to-nine-month-old babies are socially receptive and respond to hugging, talking, walking, and being distracted in playful ways. During the day you can try lying on the floor together singing songs, or lying close together playing with an engaging baby toy. In addition to all the comforting acts you can offer, it is important to realize that babies benefit tremendously from developing their ability to comfort themselves. Although you can't make your baby suck her thumb, it is probably the most dependable, autonomous, and universal act of self-comforting. You can, however, try to introduce her to a love object such as a blanket or stuffed animal. Any of these can help your baby cope better in the middle of the night and comfort herself back to sleep.

Before you attempt to wean your baby from nighttime feedings, give yourself several weeks to incorporate these points into her life. We believe that it may be too traumatic for a baby who is accustomed to being nursed around the clock to be abruptly weaned from all nighttime feedings, so you can first modify her daytime napping, feeding, falling asleep, and self-comforting patterns as we have suggested. The gradual approach may be best for the mother, too, especially if she is used to being indispensable to her baby. Sometimes, mothers need to be weaned gradually from their need to be needed, too!

Preparation

Make sure that you have moved your baby out of your room at night. It is important that she have a warm, cozy sleeping area separate from your room. Your baby is old enough to be aware of your presence and will insist on interacting with you if you are sharing a room.

You will need to enlist the help of someone else during the time that you are training your baby to sleep through the night. The length of the training period will vary according to how many preliminary steps you have followed, the number of feedings a night your baby is used to, your baby's age and temperament, and how motivated and consistent you are. Frequently all you need is three or four nights, but it may take as long as two weeks. Commonly, when babies and children reach a milestone in their development, parents witness the phenomenon of two steps forward, one step backward. Don't expect overnight results.

NIGHT 1

Step 1: (early evening) Feed your baby a good amount of solid food and nurse her before putting her to bed.

Step 2: Put your baby to bed *awake* with her love object after having gone through the bedtime routine you have introduced.

Step 3: Wake your baby up at about 11 P.M. and nurse her. We call this the *focal feeding* time. It is important that you be in control of this feeding, so make sure that you are waking your baby *(not* your baby waking you). You are probably curious about why we advocate waking and feeding an older baby when you are trying to achieve just the opposite, getting her to sleep through the night. We do this for two reasons: first, it puts *you* in control of the situation, and, second, it gives you a focused time from which you can "stretch" her through the night without nursing. Once your baby has been sleeping from the focal feeding time until the early morning for about four weeks, you can abandon this late evening feeding.

Step 4: Father or helper, it is your turn! It is important that you intervene at this point instead of the mother because the baby associates her mother so closely with nursing. So for a few nights, at least, the baby should not see her mother when she first wakes in the middle of the night. Go to her only after she is really complaining. Pick her up with her love object and comfort her. If necessary, offer her a bottle of water. Make sure that her love object is with her while you comfort her.

Step 5: When your baby has settled down, put her back in her crib with her love object. Be reassuring and loving, wind up a music box or mobile, and leave the room. Don't linger!

Step 6: Your baby will either fall back to sleep or start crying again.

IF YOUR BABY FALLS BACK TO SLEEP	IF YOUR BABY DOES NOT FALL BACK TO SLEEP
If your baby falls back to sleep without any further assistance, this is a good indication that she will be easy to wean of her nighttime feeding.	If your baby has not fallen back to sleep and is crying, go to her. (If she is not crying, don't go to her.) Be brief and don't pick her up or let her out of her crib. You can be loving and reassuring by hugging her if she is standing in her crib or simply stroking her. Then leave. If she continues to cry, wait five minutes before you go to her again. Again comfort her, but don't get her out of bed, entertain her, or feed her. Continue this either until she falls back to sleep or for a full hour. If she doesn't fall back to sleep by the time an hour has passed, feed her as in Step 7.

Step 7: The next time your baby wakes up, let her fidget or cry for five minutes to see if she will fall back to sleep by herself. If she doesn't, provided four hours have passed since her focal feeding, it is finally time to feed her. Mother can nurse her or father can give her a bottle, depending on your preference. If you nurse her in your bed, be sure to put her back into her crib as soon as you are finished. *Don't* let her linger in your bed. This feeding should

carry her over until 7 A.M. If it doesn't, repeat steps 4 to 6 until morning.

DAY 2

This is the time to evaluate your experience from Night 1, removed from "the heat of the night." Exhaustion predisposes all of us to self-protection and bickering in the middle of the night. Therefore, it is important for you and your spouse to discuss and share your objectives during the day. Try to be confident in your approach. Before you start your second night, review all our preliminary points. This is a gradual approach, so you don't have to worry about being too abrupt with your baby.

NIGHT 2

Steps 1 and 2: Repeat as on Night 1.

Step 3:   Wake your baby for her focal feeding as you did on Night 1, but this time wait an hour longer (wait until about midnight, provided you're not too exhausted yourself). You want to stretch her as long as you can from this late evening feeding.

Steps 4 to 7: Repeat as on Night 1.

DAY 3

You now have the benefit of two nights' experience. Although you are likely more exhausted than ever, you probably also feel less intimidated by the process of nighttime weaning. If your baby is eating and nursing well during the day, you can feel confident that her need to nurse at night has been the result of behavioral training rather than caloric need. Over the next several days you will see her thrive as she gains autonomy and the ability to comfort herself during the day as well as the night.

NIGHT 3

Steps 1 and 2: Repeat as on Nights 1 and 2.

Step 3:   Repeat as on Night 2. Pick up your baby at about midnight for her focal feeding. Once she is sleeping through the night until 6:30 or 7 A.M., the focal feeding time can be more relaxed, and any time between 10 P.M. and midnight will do.

Steps 4 to 7:   Repeat as on Nights 1 and 2.

DAY 4

Congratulations on your success! Most of you will have achieved at least a six-hour nursing-free nighttime stretch. By Night 4, most babies adjust to not feeding all night long. Others may need several more nights of your consistent attention.

If your baby develops a cold or some other problem crops up, you can try again in a few weeks. Make sure that in the meantime you have adopted all of our preliminary points. If you haven't, you diminish your chances of succeeding with our method. Good luck when you try again.

Those of you whose babies have slept through the night until at least 5 A.M. need to reinforce your accomplishments with our final checklist.

The Final Checklist

1. Continue the focal feeding for two to four more weeks. This is in keeping with the gradual process of this method.

2. If your baby is waking at 5 A.M. and insisting on nursing, use the same method for nighttime weaning to stretch her until 6:30 to 7 A.M. It doesn't really matter if she is actually sleeping after 5 A.M., but you want her to be able to entertain herself.

3. Make sure you continue to put your baby to bed awake at nap time and bedtime. Let her get to sleep on her own.

4. If your baby reverts to nighttime waking, comfort her, but don't feed her.

The Once- or Twice-a-Night Nurser

Like the perpetual nighttime nurser, the baby who insists on nursing once (or sometimes twice) almost every night after four months of age is exhibiting a conditioned behavior. Physically, she is able to go through the night without feeding, but she had become accustomed to eating in the middle of the night. Unlike the perpetual nighttime nurser, though, she has probably mastered longer feeding intervals during the day and is less likely to share her mother's bed on a routine basis.

Once you have decided to eliminate this nighttime feeding, if you feel comfortable simply letting your baby cry it out, go ahead. No harm will come from letting her cry until she falls asleep, and she will quickly stop expecting a feeding when she awakens. Listening to your baby cry for a long time can be extremely difficult, though (it might take up to several hours, several nights in a row), so if you prefer a more gradual approach, you can follow our night-by-night suggestions. In either case, be sure to incorporate our preliminary suggestions into your baby's life.

Preliminaries

Before you attempt to wean your baby from her middle-of-the-night feeding, give yourself a head start:

1. Put your baby to bed awake (at nap time and at night). You want to develop her ability to fall asleep alone, without your intervention. This will be particularly helpful in the middle of the night.

2. Encourage your baby to become attached to a love object if she isn't already.

3. Make sure that your baby is eating well during the day, including a solid diet appropriate for this age group.

4. Don't bring your baby to bed with you during this retraining period.

NIGHTS 1 AND 2

Nurse your baby as usual for her one middle-of-the-night feeding. But instead of nursing her to her heart's content, or until she falls asleep, time her to four minutes on each breast. Then put her back to bed. If she cries, comfort her without picking her up or feeding her again. Check on her at five-to-ten-minute intervals if she continues to cry, but limit your contact as much as possible. Your goal is have her fall asleep on her own.

NIGHTS 3 AND 4

Nurse your baby when she wakes up in the middle of the night, but this time reduce her to three minutes on each breast. Then put her back to bed.

NIGHTS 5 AND 6

Now reduce your baby's middle-of-the-night nursing time to two minutes on each breast. Be sure you time her carefully.

NIGHTS 7 AND 8

These are the last nights you will nurse your baby in the middle of the night. Give her only a minute on each side and quickly put her back to bed.

NIGHTS 9 AND 10

If your baby still cries to be fed in the middle of the night, give her two to four ounces of diluted formula or breast milk in a bottle (half water, half milk). We suggest that the father or other helper give your baby this middle-of-the-night bottle, as she associates her mother so strongly with nursing. If she rejects the bottle, at least you will know that she isn't hungry.

NIGHTS 11 AND 12

If your baby is still waking in the middle of the night, offer her water only and put her back in her crib. If she cries, check on her every five to ten minutes, reassure her, but don't pick her up. Leave quickly. Repeat this as needed until she falls back to sleep.

After twelve nights of this regimen, most babies will be skipping their middle-of-the-night feeding. *Congratulations!* If your baby is still waking up, though, your next step is to comfort her while you let her cry. Go to her when she cries, but don't pick her up, not even for a bottle of water. Tell her that everything is okay but that it is the middle of the night, and time for sleep. She may not understand your words but will intuitively pick up on their meaning. Repeat this as necessary, every ten minutes or so, until she falls asleep. Make each visit as brief as possible. If this is too difficult to do as a weaning mother, enlist the help of the father or other helper for a few nights. This process might take another few nights, after which time your baby will finally be sleeping through the night.

The Nighttime Bottle Habit

The nighttime bottle habit, like other nighttime feeding patterns, is often part of a process that develops from early infancy. Whether you nursed or bottle-fed your baby in the early weeks and months matters little; the route to the nighttime bottle habit is fairly typical. As the baby gets older and continues to wake up in the middle of the night, the parent combats his or her exhaustion by finding the shortest route back to bed. What was initially concern for the baby's nutrition becomes an act of nighttime expediency. In the process, the baby's stomach becomes primed to expect this bottle every night.

The easiest if not the quickest method for weaning your baby from this practice is to gradually withdraw the nourishment; over a period of about two weeks, your baby's stomach will adjust. If you want faster results and you feel that you and your baby are better suited to the "cold turkey" approach, go ahead and let her cry it out. This will in no way harm your baby and within a few nights she won't expect her middle-of-the-night bottle.

In either case, whether you wean your baby from this feeding gradually or over just a couple of nights, you will have to be sure you break her habit of falling asleep with a bottle. If she falls asleep with her last memory being that of sucking a bottle of milk, she is conditioned to depend on a bottle to fall back to sleep when she surfaces in the middle of the night. Without it, she becomes agitated and cries. To change this pattern, make sure you put your baby to bed *awake*, without a bottle. This way, she will develop other ways of settling herself down to sleep. Sucking her thumb or a pacifier or holding a special blanket or stuffed animal—are all fine. Although your baby may cry at bedtime for several evenings, you can at least be sure she is not crying out of hunger.

The following two-week method will show you how to gradually wean your baby from her middle-of-the-night bottle.

NIGHTS 1 AND 2

When your baby wakes in the middle of the night, give her a full eight-ounce bottle of three-fourths milk, one-fourth water.

NIGHTS 3 AND 4

Continue to dilute your baby's bottle a little bit more—half milk and half water. This time give her only about six ounces.

NIGHTS 5 AND 6

Continue to give your baby a six-ounce bottle, but dilute it to one-third milk, two-thirds water.

NIGHTS 7 AND 8

Continue with the same dilution ratio of one-third milk to two-thirds water, but only give four ounces altogether. Don't bother to measure too carefully. You are actually giving your baby very little milk at this point— about one and a half ounces.

NIGHTS 9 AND 10

Now give your baby a total of three ounces, with the proportions one-third milk to two-thirds water.

NIGHTS 11 AND 12

You are now down to a total of two ounces, with only half an ounce of milk, the rest being water.

NIGHTS 13 AND 14

Give one ounce water only (no milk).

NIGHTS 15 ON

From now on, you won't be giving your baby a bottle at all. If she still wakes up and cries in the middle of the night, go to her room and try to settle her down *without* picking her up. Leave quickly.

If for some reason this gradual method has not worked for your baby, your best option is the cold-turkey approach. You may also accelerate or decelerate the two-week process, depending on your own needs and other factors such as illness, vacations, and so on.

How to Retrain Your Nighttime Crier

The term "trained nighttime crier," also used by Dr. Schmitt, describes the baby who wakes up at least once every night and cries until she gets attention. Once a baby reaches five months of age, she is physiologically able to sleep through the night, and her consistent waking is a learned behavior. The night crier is different from other nighttime wakers in that she doesn't wake up for food. Instead, she cries until mom or dad comes in to pick her up and walk, rock, or play with her.

This behavior pattern can develop for a variety of reasons: the parents are light sleepers and respond to their baby's first whimper; the baby had colic and crying has persisted; the parents have always walked, rocked, or nursed their baby to sleep; or one of the parents insists on a good night's sleep, thereby compelling the other parent to run to the baby before she has a chance to settle herself down. In any case, every time the baby whimpers or cries at night, she has been rewarded with ample attention. This behavior, then, is reinforced.

Another possibility is that your baby is a combination nighttime waker; that is, she wakes most nights for attention and some nights for a feeding. However, feeding is usually secondary to the other needs such babies have developed in the middle of the night. For this reason, we have grouped these combination nighttime wakers with the trained night criers. You should, however, review the other methods to extract whatever points apply to your own situation.

If your baby has developed this type of nighttime waking pattern, be sure that you always put her into her crib *awake*, both at bedtime and nap time. She must be able to fall asleep on her own (with the aid of a blanket, thumb, or pacifier, if she so desires) before you can expect her to fall back to sleep again when she surfaces in the middle of the night. For more hints, see our section "How to Help Your Baby Fall Asleep Alone."

The solution for this type of waking is both the simplest and the most difficult method of all: you must let your baby cry it out. When you are ready to embark on this method, you might want to let your neighbors know what you are doing. That way, they won't be worried when they hear your baby crying in the middle of the night.

NIGHT 1

When your baby wakes up crying in the middle of the night, go to her as usual to check on her. Do not get her out of her crib. Say something loving and brief like "We're all sleeping, darling; good night," and leave the room. You can expect that a five-to-nine-month-old who has never slept through the night will cry up to an hour or two before falling off to sleep. The absolutely worst thing you can do is go to her and pick her up after listening to her cry for an hour or so. If you do this, you are teaching her that the reward for crying for a long time is being picked up. It is okay to go peek through the slit in the door to make sure that she is okay, but don't let her see you. If you can't restrain yourself after thirty minutes or so has passed, try the "Go back to sleep, darling" routine a second time. Again, don't pick your baby up or entertain her in any way. Leave the room immediately. If you have to do this a third time, again use the same guidelines. Good luck, because we know that listening to your baby cry is one of the hardest things to do. But remember, you are not harming her at all. Retraining your baby to sleep through the night will be easier for both you and your baby if you are confident that your method and goals are fair and realistic. Let us reassure you: they are.

NIGHT 2

Follow the same procedure as on Night 1. You may or may not find that her crying is reduced.

NIGHT 3

If you have been consistent, your baby's crying should taper off substantially by the third night. If there is no change, increase the length of time between visits to check on her. Remember, crying won't harm her.

NIGHTS 4–10

Babies vary in the length of time they need to learn to sleep through the night. While it is common for a baby to sleep through the night on the fourth night of this program, some babies may take ten days or longer to learn new nighttime habits. The length of time your baby will need will depend on her age (usually, the older the habit, the harder it is to break), her temperament, your temperament, and your consistency. Illness and environmental factors such as cramped sleeping quarters can also interfere with sleep and therefore influence how quickly your baby learns to sleep through the night.

DEVELOPMENTAL FACTORS
THAT CAN DISRUPT SLEEP

Sometimes, a baby's sleep is disturbed for developmental reasons, not because of habit. Whether these developmental conditions are psychosocial or physical, they are different from habit-related problems in that they can crop up suddenly, and at any time. A baby who has been sleeping through the night beautifully for several months can suddenly enter a new developmental stage that will disturb her sleep. The positive side of this type of sleep disruption is that, if properly handled, it can disappear as quickly as it came up. Provided no new habits are formed in the meantime, once the developmental issue is resolved, the sleep disruption will pass.

Often, a baby who is already suffering from a habit-related sleep disruption will enter a new developmental stage that will only intensify her sleep problem. In this case, parents must sort out what is happening, consider the developmental issue first, and, once that is resolved, work on correcting the habit. For many parents, this is the most perplexing part of all, especially since your approach is very different for developmental sleep disruptions. A habit can be ignored, but a fear cannot.

The primary psychosocial developments of the five-to-nine-month-old age group that can disturb sleep are stranger anxiety and separation anxiety. Many babies begin to exhibit these behaviors as early as six to eight months of age, although they usually don't reach their peak until the first birthday. Common physical developments that can disrupt sleep at this age are learning to sit and pull to a stand (active babies tend to practice these skills in the middle of the night, even when half asleep) and teething. It isn't necessary, however, to let these developmental issues evolve into long-term sleep problems.

Stranger and Separation Anxiety

As a baby matures and her awareness grows, she will develop certain fears and anxieties that may temporarily disrupt her sleep. But unlike habit-formed situations, developmental stages should not be looked on as problems to be avoided. Rather, they are healthy steps toward maturity and independence that every child goes through and learns from.

When a seven-month-old becomes frightened by an unfamiliar person, we say that she is suffering from stranger anxiety. Or, when an eight-month-old cries every time her mother leaves the room, we call this separation anxiety. But because psychology is an inexact science, particularly when concerned with the behavior of someone who can't talk, it is impossible to pin down with any certainty *why* these situations are so upsetting to a child. Some people feel that the fears are emotionally founded; that is, they are based on the baby's strong attachment to her parent. Others link these fears to the baby's cognitive growth, in particular her memory and her ability to distinguish between people. It is interesting to consider these different theories, but in the final analysis, we can only speculate on the cause of separation and stranger anxiety. And while we certainly can't eliminate these fears, there are certain things we can do to minimize the effect they have on the rest of a baby's life, in particular her sleeping habits.

If your child is all of a sudden having trouble falling asleep or has begun waking and crying in the middle of the night, try to figure out if this behavior is coming from stranger or separation anxiety. If she is basically happy and relaxed during the day, her sleep disruption is probably due to something else. But if she cries pitifully when she sees a stranger, when you leave her with a baby-sitter, or even when you leave the room for a minute, developmental fears may well be at the root of her sleep problems.

If this sounds familiar, your solution will have to focus on alleviating the fears and therefore involve the way you treat your baby during the day as well as the night. In general, try to be sympathetic without becoming overprotective. This is a fine line to draw, but she will pick up on your attitude and respond accordingly. If, for example, she senses that you are worried about leaving her, or if you nervously whisk her out of your friend's arms as soon as she begins to cry, chances are she will become even more fearful. This can turn into more intense sleep disruption during the night. But if you are relaxed about her daily encounters and confident when you leave her with a familiar baby-sitter, she will sense this, learn to adjust to your comings and goings much more easily, and eventually return to good sleeping patterns.

Of course none of this is absolute. Some babies just seem to recover from separation or stranger anxiety much more easily than others. But in any case, this is not the time to test your baby's strength. The following guidelines will help you minimize anxiety-related sleep disruption.

GUIDELINES FOR MINIMIZING ANXIETY-RELATED SLEEP DISRUPTION

1. If you are using a new sitter, always have her arrive while your baby is still awake and perhaps have her participate in some household/caretaking activities before bedtime. Even better, arrange for her and your baby to have a "getting to know you" session for a few hours during the afternoon or on the weekend when you are around. This is important because one of the most common causes of sleep disruption for a baby during these months is the unfortunate experience of waking up to find an unfamiliar sitter. She is likely to continue waking every night at the same time for several nights or even weeks, anxious to see if you are home.

2. If you can help it, don't suddenly begin a full-time work schedule. It is much better to build up your time at work slowly, thereby letting your baby get used to your absence and her new daycare arrangements gradually.

3. If you are planning a vacation, try to take her along. A sudden or prolonged separation from you could be very hard on her.

4. Make your baby's bedtime especially pleasant. When you start to leave her room after having placed her in her crib, tell her in a relaxed voice, "We're here, we love you, and we'll see you in the morning." When she starts to cry, go to her and repeat what you just said. Do not take her out of her crib, as this could be the start of a new habit. Remember, your goal is to build up her self-confidence and make her more self-sufficient during the night. Help her lie down and get comfortable again, reorienting her to her security object. Leave quickly. Keep repeating this until she feels reassured enough to fall asleep. On alternate trips to comfort her, you can substitute going into her room with calling to her. If your baby is in really great distress (you will know the difference), you can pull up a chair next to her crib and sit by her and talk or sing to her as she falls off to sleep. Just don't pick her up.

5. Treat middle-of-the-night wakings the same way. If she wakes up in great distress, go to her immediately to show her that you are there and to comfort her, but don't prolong your visit or pick her up. You want her to get herself back to sleep, because you will simply be substituting one problem for another if she becomes used to being walked, rocked, or

nursed to sleep. This adjustment process will probably take several nights, after which time she should return to normal sleeping patterns.

Because most babies don't reach the peak of their separation and stranger fears until they are a year old, what you have witnessed so far is likely only the tip of the iceberg. The next several months will be an ongoing adjustment and learning process.

Gross Motor Development

The period between five and nine months of age is full of many gross motor achievements; during this time, most babies learn to sit, crawl, and pull themselves to a stand. The process of learning all of these skills involves so much repetition and focused energy that many babies tend to practice their new achievements at night, too, even when half asleep! A baby's need to lie down and go to sleep does not necessarily take precedence over the conflicting need to practice sitting, crawling, or standing.

The best news about this type of sleep disruption is that it usually lasts for only a couple of nights. Once your baby feels comfortable with her new skill, she will no longer feel the need to practice it at night.

Therefore, your best approach may be to help your baby practice her skill during the day. The faster she masters it, the faster she'll be able to sleep through the night again. Keep your practice sessions short and low-key; overstimulation won't help her sleep.

GUIDELINES FOR OVERCOMING SLEEP DISRUPTIONS WHEN YOUR BABY FIRST PULLS HERSELF TO A STAND

Learning to pull up to a standing position is probably one of the most sleep-disruptive gross motor achievements. This is because most babies learn to get up before they learn to get back down again. As a result, a baby can find herself caught standing, frightened and holding on to her crib railing for dear life, but unable to ease herself down to a safe sitting position. This often happens at night, either when the baby is trying to fall asleep or in the middle of the night, during a light sleep phase. In fact, this process of popping up without being able to get back down will often be repeated several times during a night, sometimes as often as ten or twenty times!

If your baby is going through this trying phase, try playing standing/sitting games with her during the day. Any kind of "up we go, down we go" or "all fall down" game, where you hold your baby's hands and show her how to get to a sitting position, will help. During the night, go to her when she cries to see if she is stuck in a standing position. Gently break her rigid standing position by placing your arm across the back of her knees, thereby forcing her to bend to a sitting position. Hold her hand as she collapses. She will eventually learn that she has to bend her knees to get down. Repeat this as many times as necessary until she finally falls off to sleep. The next night will probably be a little easier, and after that your baby will be much more secure in getting herself up and down independently.

One final note: During this process, be sure to leave your baby's room quickly each time you get her down from a standing position. Any prolonged contact during the night could turn into a new nighttime habit. This would be the last thing you'd need after finally conquering her sleep disruption.

Teething

Almost all babies experience the normal growth process of teething during the five-to-nine-month age period. (Some babies start teething at as early as three months, and others as late as a year.) A baby's teething timetable seems to follow an inherited familial pattern that has no developmental significance. In other words, if your baby is early or late teething, it means nothing. Also, tooth eruption is only rarely affected or delayed by illness or other causes.

Teething is one of those normal growth processes that are shrouded in misconceptions. Our culture has promoted teething as the culprit for fever, convulsions, diarrhea, and even death for over two thousand years. According to Penelope Leach, in her book *Babyhood,* Hippocrates wrote, "Teething children suffer from itching of the gums, fever, convulsions, and diarrhea. . . ." As late as the 1800s, according to Leach, one of Britain's registrar generals' reports ascribed more than five thousand infant mortalities directly to teething. Opinions have changed drastically over the last century, but sleep difficulties, crying, and "nonspecific" crankiness, as well as a range of health problems, are still attributed to teething.

Improved medical knowledge of infection and disease processes in the twentieth century has enabled us to dispel the myth that teething causes illness. We now know that symptoms of illness are caused by infection or other disease and that teething is not the cause. Still, there is a lot of disagreement about the effects of teething. While some pediatricians say that normal teething causes little more than itchy or swollen gums and perhaps increased saliva production, others feel that it can be a more significant problem. Many mothers attribute complaints such as runny nose, slightly elevated fever, and loose bowels to teething.

One way of interpreting these symptoms is to look at a baby's behavior during teething. Frequent mouthing of toys and teething objects and rubbing or massaging gums on a parent's hand or finger are possible sources of germ transmission. Others speculate that teething actually may reduce resistance to infection, while not directly causing it. This is because teething may create mild stress for the body, and increased internal or external stress is believed to predispose one to illness. Another valid point of view is that teething in no way predisposes a baby to illness. Rather, it may be the decreasing level of maternal antibodies between the ages of four and six months, coinciding with the beginning of teething, that makes the baby more vulnerable to infection.

Even though there is such a wide range of opinion concerning the effects of teething, we caution you against attributing nonstop crying and excessive crankiness to teething. If your baby seems unusually unhappy, you should first consult your pediatrician to rule out other causes. Teething may cause mild fussiness and discomfort. Rarely, it may cause severe pain, and often this pattern is familial. Like so many other aspects of human development, there is a wide spectrum of possible responses. In addition, the range in an infant's threshold to discomfort varies from individual to individual and from culture to culture. To gain perspective on the degree of discomfort a baby might experience from normal teething, keep in mind that everyday life, too, causes mild fussiness.

Teething, of course, is often targeted as the reason for a baby's sleeping difficulties. It is likely, though, that teething pain is most acute immediately prior to tooth eruption, when the gums look red and swollen. Therefore, if a five-to-nine-month-old baby has chronic sleep problems, or has never slept through the night, this cannot be attributed to teething. Teething might contribute to the problem on a short-term basis, but it is certainly not solely responsible for it.

GUIDELINES FOR OVERCOMING OCCASIONAL SLEEP DISRUPTION CAUSED BY TEETHING

If your baby wakes up crying in the middle of the night and you are pretty sure that she is about to cut another tooth because her gums are inflamed, there are a couple of things you can try. We feel that the best approach is to offer physical comfort and a reassuring "Go back to sleep, darling." If this doesn't work and you are convinced that she is uncomfortable, you can talk to your doctor about possible medication. Keep in mind, though, that teething will continue for months and medication can be regarded as only a temporary solution. If your baby starts to wake up more than a few times over a period of a week, it is time to reevaluate the role teething is playing. She may have an underlying illness (such as an ear infection) that is causing her to wake up. Or there may be nothing wrong with her and she may just be enjoying your company. In this case, you will need to discourage this nighttime attention.

If your baby is waking early in the morning and is too cranky from teething either to get herself back to sleep or to entertain herself as she normally does, we suggest that you use the same approach as for middle-of-the-night waking. Since this is an occasional situation, you can take her out of bed, but don't let this turn into a habit.

SITUATIONS THAT CAN DISRUPT SLEEP

The third type of sleep problems a child can develop are situational. These problems form a distinct category because they are not related either to habits or to a child's individual development. Rather, they occur as the direct result of a distinct situation and as such are self-limited. Once the situation is resolved, so are the sleep problems (provided, of course, that no new habits have cropped up in the meantime). The most common situations that can disrupt the sleep of a five-to-nine-month-old are illness and travel.

Illness

Illness is an unfortunate but universal cause of sleep disruption. Colds, ear infections, fever, pinworms, diaper rash, croup, gas, and allergies are just a few of the possible health-related causes for night-waking in this age group. Babies who have older siblings or who are in daycare are much more likely to get sick than are babies who are not constantly around other children. The season of the year also seems to contribute to increased frequency of colds and other viral infections.

When ill, a baby must not only cope with feeling lousy but also get along without her usual primary means of self-comforting. A cold will almost always impair her ability to suck her thumb or pacifier, as well as inhibit nursing or bottle-feeding. Babies understandably get cranky and frustrated at their inability to suck. When this happens, sleep disruption of various kinds and to various degrees is common. Unless a baby experiences repeated illnesses that make her wake up regularly over a long period of time, she will usually resume her normal sleep patterns when she feels better. Most of the time, no special effort on the part of the parent is necessary.

If your baby is sick, the most important thing you can do is give her all your loving care. This is the time to attend to her all night long, if necessary, and to make plenty of exceptions to your regular routine. Some distinctions should be made, however, between the care of a seriously ill baby and the care of a baby who has a minor ailment. First, if your baby is really ill (high fever or other worrisome symptoms), check with your pediatrician to see what you should do. If you want, you can set up a portable crib in your room and have her sleep close by you (or, if she has an extra bed in her room, you can sleep there). This isn't necessary, and she may just sleep right through the night, but if you are quite worried about her, this will allow you to check on her frequently during the night.

On the other hand, if your baby just has a cold, we suggest that you keep to her normal sleep habits as much as possible. There is no need to move her out of her crib. A cold-water vaporizer or humidifier will help moisten her nasal secretions so that she can breathe through her nose more easily. This way, she can comfort herself with her thumb or pacifier.

GUIDELINES FOR OVERCOMING SLEEP DISRUPTION CAUSED BY ILLNESS, A MEDICAL PROCEDURE, OR HOSPITALIZATION

Always wait until your baby's illness has passed before you make a consistent effort to change any undesirable sleep habits. Then, when you move her from your bed or room or firmly insist that she not bother you at night, you can feel confident that you are doing the right thing. If you aren't succeeding after a week or so, check back with your pediatrician. Sometimes, babies can have a relapse of their previous illness, and parents are confused as to what is wrong.

An outpatient medical procedure or hospitalization can often disrupt a baby's normal sleeping patterns. As with an illness, give your baby a chance to settle back into her old routine on her own before resorting to stricter tactics. Fear and separation anxiety are large components of these sleep problems, and your baby will need extra reassurance for a while. For the first night or two, go to her when she cries, comfort her, but do not take her out of her crib once you have tucked her in for the night. She needs not only your love and encouragement but also a consistent reminder that her bed is a safe and wonderful place to sleep. If she doesn't respond to this approach after a few nights, she may have become overly dependent on your nighttime attention. In that case, see our sections on alleviating habit-related sleep disruption.

Travel

Travel is a common cause of sleep disruption in this age group, mostly because it disturbs a baby's routine. By the second half of the first year, a baby has developed enough memory to anticipate regular features in her daily routine. Once her routines and familiar landmarks are changed, especially at sleeping times, she can be thrown off and become more susceptible to sleep disruption.

Although babies are creatures of habit, they also thrive on new stimuli. Traveling and vacations can be a marvelous time for you and your baby if you have realistic expectations. By and large, babies tend to behave the same away from home as they do at home. So if your baby is easygoing at home and goes to bed without problems, chances are good that she will do the same in new surroundings. But if your baby often demands special attention at night, sleeps lightly, or gets upset easily, she may test your patience while you travel. If you have had a hard time settling her into good sleep habits, you may be better off waiting to travel until she is older.

In order to minimize your baby's chances of sleep disruption while you travel, we suggest you do the following:

GUIDELINES FOR MINIMIZING SLEEP DISRUPTION WHEN YOU TRAVEL

1. Bring your baby's security object and several familiar crib toys with you.

2. Without being overly rigid, try to keep your baby as close to her normal nap time and bedtime schedule as possible. If you are traveling a long distance, the time change may throw her off a little, but she should adjust in a few days.

3. If possible, don't use baby-sitters while you are away from home. But if you must, give her lots of time before bedtime to become acquainted with her sitter.

4. If you don't have an extra room for your baby to sleep in, try putting her in the farthest corner of your room, or preferably in an alcove, hallway, or bathroom. Many parents find themselves shortchanged on morning sleep if they share a room with their baby (and vacation is often the time you covet that extra sleep most).

All in all, traveling with your baby can be enjoyable if you are relaxed and flexible, but still keep to comforting nap time and bedtime routines whenever possible. The occasional missed nap or late bedtime takes on little importance, provided you are having a good time.

GUIDELINES FOR OVERCOMING SLEEP DISRUPTION CAUSED BY TRAVELING—ONCE YOU RETURN HOME

Usually, parents know if their baby is having sleep problems well before a vacation is over. Often, though, they don't appreciate the full extent of the "damage" until they are back home, finally without the worry of disrupting others.

If your baby is having trouble settling down at night when you return home, your first step should be to reorient her to her bedroom and regular bedtime routines. You can be firm and consistent and at the same time reassuring. If she doesn't fall asleep easily, go to her, talk to her calmly, but don't get her out of her crib. You don't want to start any new habits that you will regret later on.

Take care of waking problems in a similar way. She may be feeling some separation pangs if she became used to sleeping near you during the vacation. On your first night home, you should go to her immediately to reassure her, but on subsequent nights give her a few minutes to try and settle herself down first. When you go to her room, give her lots of verbal reassurance and reorient her to her cuddly love object. Leave her room quickly. You may repeat this process as many times as necessary, but be sure not to get her out of her crib. Over a number of nights, if she still isn't sleeping through the night, gradually reduce your interaction with her by calling to her from your room. Your voice may be all that she needs to feel comfortable enough to fall back to sleep.

QUESTIONS/ANSWERS

1. Our family lives in a small one-bedroom apartment. Our three-year-old son sleeps in the bedroom, we sleep in the living room, and our six-month-old son sleeps in an alcove between the living room and the bedroom. Our baby cries at least once every night, at which time I run to see him so he won't wake anyone else in the family. My doctor told me that the only solution is to let him cry it out, but I'm afraid he will get our three-year-old up. I'm also concerned about my husband's sleep, as he has to be at work by 7 every morning, and about what my neighbors will say when they hear the baby crying. What can I do?

Yours is an especially common problem for people who live in small quarters. What has happened is that, through your consideration for your family, you have trained your baby to be a nighttime crier. Inadvertently, you have reinforced his nighttime crying habit by never allowing him the chance to learn to settle back to sleep on his own. In order to get on top of the situation now, you must overcome your hesitation to allow your baby to disturb the rest of your family. The problem won't go away by itself and may only get harder to correct as your baby gets older. In the long run, your family will be much better off if you deal with the situation now.

Actually, we don't think that the retraining process will be as difficult as you might think. If you are consistent, your baby should learn to sleep through the night in just three or four nights. He may need to cry for up to two or three hours on the first night, but after that his crying time should diminish rapidly. On the second night, he will probably cry for only a half hour or so, and on the third night, he will probably cry for only ten minutes before settling down to sleep. In any case, don't worry. No harm can come from crying. If it makes you feel better, you can peek at him every twenty minutes or so and then check him again when he finally is asleep.

In order to minimize disrupting the sleep of your three-year-old and your husband, plan your training program to begin on a Friday night. This way, everyone can recoup his or her sleep the next day, if necessary. Also advise your neighbors of your plan, so they won't worry when they hear your baby cry. If possible, arrange for your three-year-old to sleep somewhere else for at least the first night, and possibly the second night as well. Grandparents or a close friend are good people to help you out. When your older child comes home on the third night, don't worry about the baby waking him up. A baby's crying rarely bothers a sibling as much as a parent, and your baby will probably cry for only a few minutes if you have consistently avoided giving him nighttime attention.

Once your baby is sleeping through the night, we suggest that you put both children together in the bedroom. As long as you continue not to interfere with them in the middle of the night, they will sleep and happily entertain themselves in their own beds. Most likely they will enjoy each other's company.

2. How long can I let my eight-month-old son cry in the middle of the night?

The length of time you should allow your baby to cry in the middle of the night depends entirely on *why* he is crying. If he is suffering from separation fears or is sick, don't let him cry more than a minute or two. But if you have determined that he has developed a nighttime-waking habit, and you feel comfortable letting him cry it out, go ahead and do it. In this case, there is no such thing as letting a baby cry too long. As unbearable as it may sound, you may have to listen to your baby cry for several hours on the first night. No harm will come, provided you check on him at regular intervals. When he first wakes up, first briefly go to reassure him, without picking him up. Then continue to peek through the crack in his door every fifteen to twenty minutes to make sure that his foot isn't stuck in the bars of his crib or that he doesn't have some other physical problem (but don't let him see you). As long as you don't reward his crying by giving him attention or picking him up, the length of time he cries on successive nights will sharply decrease.

3. My eight-month-old son sleeps nine hours a night and has two forty-five-minute naps during the day. Is this enough sleep for a baby of this age?

Your baby seems to need less sleep than the average baby his age, but his sleep pattern certainly falls within normal limits. Provided that he is healthy and thriving, don't concern yourself with the amount of time he sleeps. As long as you or something around the house isn't interfering with his sleep (for example, waking him to go to a sitter every morning, or too much evening stimulation), he will sleep as much as he needs to. In fact, the only complication associated with a child who needs only a little sleep falls onto the parents. Obviously, if a baby requires more daytime attention, this leaves the parent fewer hours for other things.

Given your constraints, the best thing you can do is determine reasonable nap times and the length of time your baby should spend in his crib at night. Even though he may not spend his full crib time sleeping, you can encourage him to entertain himself during these times. At nap time, if he sleeps only forty-five minutes, you can encourage him to spend an additional fifteen minutes playing by himself. At night, you can try putting him to bed a little later than the baby who requires more sleep, perhaps at eight-thirty or eight forty-five. Then, when he wakes up at five-thirty after nine hours of sleep, encourage him to play independently in his crib until six or six-thirty. Provide lots of fun, safe crib toys for nap times as well as this early morning session. The closer realignment of your baby's sleeping schedule with yours is a successful compromise for everyone.

4. My five-month-old baby wakes up every night and cries for her pacifier. I go and put it in her mouth and go straight back to bed. Although I am up for only a minute, I am getting tired of this nightly ritual. What can I do?

We recommend that you stop getting your baby her pacifier for two main reasons. First, this type of dependence on a parent, even for something as simple as locating a pacifier, rarely improves with time. It is much more common for this type of pattern to accelerate, so that you may soon find yourself getting up several times a night, not just once, and what started out as a fairly innocuous situation becomes increasingly bothersome. Therefore, we suggest that you allow your baby to find another way of comforting herself to sleep. She may cry for a few nights, but she will soon learn to get through the night without you.

And second, before you become absolutely convinced that the loss of the pacifier is what causes your baby to wake up and cry, think of other possibilities as well. We know of a six-month-old who started a similar waking pattern. Coincidentally, her mother started her on good solid feedings, and she no longer woke up at all. Apparently, her waking problem had started because she needed to eat more during the day, not because she couldn't get her pacifier into her mouth! This is an example of how sometimes you have to look beyond the immediate situation for a solution.

5. My six-month-old baby sleeps thirteen hours a night. I put her down at 7 P.M. and I go to her at eight in the morning. She just lies there happily sucking her thumb. She also sleeps two hours in the morning and two hours in the afternoon. Does she sleep too much?

Your baby sleeps a lot, but within the normal range for someone her age. Because babies vary tremendously in their sleep needs (as do adults), there are no rules for how much time an individual baby should sleep. Also remember that your baby may not be sleeping the entire time that she is quiet in her bed. So as long as she continues to thrive physically, emotionally, and socially, consider yourself lucky that she sleeps and entertains herself well in her crib. If you are concerned that she is too placid, don't be. Let us reassure you that easygoing babies such as yours can grow into wonderfully assertive children!

6. My nine-month-old baby uses her bottle as a love object. She shows no particular attachment to any other object (blanket, teddy, or doll) and insists on having her bottle constantly. Of course she needs her bottle to get to sleep at night, too. I am concerned about the long-range consequences of her bottle (food) being her primary means of self-comforting. Do you have suggestions for decreasing this bottle use?

Many babies are attached to their bottles, and this attachment often grows with age. Like so many other things, this can become a problem if allowed to go to an extreme. If your baby has a bottle with her virtually all of the time, this is excessive. It can disrupt her normal daily activities, including playing and eating other foods, and can promote tooth decay. Therefore, we definitely agree with you: it is time to cut down on her time with a bottle.

One way you can do this is to encourage her to bond to another security object (include it in her nightly bedtime ritual, and tuck it into bed with her). Limit her to four or five bottles a day. If she wants to get down and crawl around with the bottle, just put it away until later. When she gets upset, give her all your love, but don't offer her a bottle at the same time. At nighttime, give her the bottle in your arms before you put her to bed. Then, put her in her crib with her new love object. Or, if you prefer to ease her out of her nighttime bottle habit, you can either give her a bottle of water or use the gradual milk–water dilution schedule outlined in the text. In either case, the bottle should gradually lose its appeal.

7. My six-month-old baby wakes up crying every evening at eleven. I have been feeding him at this time since he was born. Although he insists on being fed at this time, he sleeps well the rest of the night and doesn't wake up until 7 A.M. How can I eliminate this feeding?

Let's compare your baby's pattern with that of a baby who is wakened by his parents at 11 P.M., as in our "stretching" method. Both eat, and so their stomachs are primed to feel hungry. Both receive some secondary gains of playful interaction with their parents. (Usually, parents have not gone to bed before this feeding, so there is no sleep disruption for them.) The only difference is that your baby is rewarded for crying.

Therefore, the easiest way to help your baby give up this late evening feeding is to regain control of it. For two weeks, pick up your baby at 10 P.M., *before* he has a chance to wake on his own. Feed him and put him quickly back to bed. After two weeks, when you are firmly in control of this feeding, you can just abandon it. Most likely, he won't wake at this time again.

Since your baby is waking in much the same way as a trained night feeder, you can also try the gradual weaning approach elaborated in the text. Or you can try the "cold turkey" approach, which is probably the shortest way to get your baby off this feeding. One of our pediatrician friends let her baby cry it out for two nights and on the third night, she slept through until her usual 7 A.M. waking.

Regardless of the method you choose, you need to make sure that your baby is eating well in the evening before bedtime. The late afternoon/early evening is the time of day when a mother's milk supply is often at its lowest. Since your baby is six months old, it may be time to get him on solid food, if he isn't already, especially at this time of day. A full stomach should help him make the transition to an uninterrupted night without feeding.

8. My eight-month-old daughter had an operation for an intestinal problem (intussusception) three weeks ago. She was hospitalized for only five days, but the experience seems to have made a real change in her personality. She used to be so happy and easygoing, but now she cries a lot, especially when I leave the room or put her to bed. Unfortunately I was

sick with the flu while she was in the hospital, and I couldn't be with her for two days. My husband's work schedule allowed him to visit her only during the evenings. Could this time in the hospital without us be the cause of her problems? How can I get her over this crisis and back to her usual sunny disposition and good sleeping habits?

Your baby is suffering from normal separation anxiety, triggered by her hospital experience. Hospitalization can be a frightening and disorienting experience for a baby. Besides not feeling well, a baby suddenly finds herself in an unfamiliar environment with new faces and strange smells. Under the best of circumstances this would be a lot for a baby to contend with. But given the fact that you and your husband were not always available to comfort her, and that at eight months of age she is subject to separation fears anyway, her new behavior is totally understandable.

Your immediate goal is to rebuild your daughter's self-confidence and trust in you. Don't worry too much about what has already happened, but instead focus your attention on making her feel more secure. As we discuss in our section on separation anxiety, you will have to walk the fine line between being sympathetic to her distress and becoming overprotective. Try to spend as much time as you can together, building back to her normal prehospital routines. Leave her only with baby-sitters she knows and is comfortable with. If her crying and clingy behavior bothers you, try not to let it show. Your relaxed attitude will go a long way in calming her down, too.

At nap and bedtimes, give her lots of reassurance within the boundaries of her old routines. Go back to her old bedtime rituals and focus on her security object to encourage her old independent sleeping habits. For several nights, at least, go to her as soon as she cries in the middle of the night, reassure her that you are there, but don't pick her up or feed her. This is not the time to start a new habit that you will only regret later on.

We feel sure that within a couple of weeks of your loving and consistent care, you will see the return of your daughter's happy and well-adjusted behavior.

9. Our eight-month-old has never learned to sleep through the night. It seems that she is always up for one reason or another. She has had a couple of colds, and for a while she was teething, and now I'm not exactly sure why she keeps waking up one or two times a night. All I know is that

I'm exhausted. I'm at the point where I'm ready to let her cry it out, but my husband, who has been helping me take care of her in the middle of the night all along, doesn't agree. But he doesn't take care of her during the day and doesn't understand how draining it is to be on call twenty-four hours a day. He thinks that we should keep going in and helping her fall back to sleep. The other night we had a terrible argument about it. I'm so desperate that I don't know how I can go on like this. I know what I have to do, but I need my husband's support. Do you have any suggestions?

The first thing that you should do is find time to have a relaxed discussion with your husband. It's important for you to reach an agreement and solve your daughter's night-waking problem together. If the two of you don't back each other up, you'll find it much harder to succeed in getting your child to sleep through the night. Perhaps it would help to speak to your pediatrician or review this book together before you go ahead with a plan. You also have to communicate to your husband that having your baby cry for a few nights is far less harmful to her than the long-term effects of a sleep-deprived mother! Good luck.

As you help your child build independent sleep habits, it's important to keep in mind that she will continue to surface during the normal course of her sleep cycling. Like other babies who sleep through the night, she has to learn to get herself back to sleep without help from anyone else. For further suggestions, see our section on the trained night crier.

Chapter Three

FROM TEN TO EIGHTEEN MONTHS

Becoming a Toddler

The Importance of Patience
Naps—Making the Transition to One Nap a Day

Sleep-Disturbing Habits

How to Help Your Toddler Fall Asleep Alone
How to Move Your Toddler out of Your Bed
How to Wean Your Toddler from Nighttime Feedings
  The nighttime nurser
  The nighttime bottle habit
How to Retrain Your Nighttime Crier
How to Defer Your Early Morning Riser

Developmental Factors That Can Disrupt Sleep

Separation Anxiety
Nightmares
Learning to Walk
Teething

Situations That Can Disrupt Sleep

Illness
Hospitalization or Outpatient Medical Procedure
Travel
Moving

Questions/Answers

I wish someone would give me some advice to help me sort this whole situation out. I went to my pediatrician and he said the reason my son doesn't sleep through the night is that I am overprotective. He says that my son doesn't have the problem, but that it's me. He says that I just have to let him cry it out. His words just made me feel angry at him, as if I'm not loaded down already with fatigue and frustrations. I need a lot of support right now, and some more concrete suggestions.

—*Mother of ten-month-old*

BECOMING A TODDLER

Developmental growth continues at its breakneck pace between ten and eighteen months of age, with babies making enormous physical, intellectual, and social gains. At eighteen months, a toddler is hardly recognizable as the baby of only eight months ago, he is so much more skilled and independent. Looks can be deceiving, though, and the toddler may appear to be more capable than he really is. Not still a baby, not quite a child, the young toddler is in an in-between stage. More often than not, his experience and common sense lag far behind his physical prowess.

By far the most obvious of the budding toddler's gains is his new mobility. Practicing being upright and learning to walk (and run!) often occupy much of his day. For some babies, this is an intense and frustrating time. Parents often find that their baby is crankier and more difficult than usual in the few weeks before he takes his first steps. Once the skill is mastered, however, he can relax and turn his attention to other matters. In addition, the new walker almost always has the advantage of being a sound sleeper. Active toddlers are normally so tired by nap time and bedtime that they sleep better than they've ever slept before.

Although not as apparent as his physical gains, the young toddler's intellectual growth is also impressive. By the time he is eighteen months old, his language may be developed to the point where he has a speaking vocabulary of ten to twenty-five words, and he certainly is able to understand far many more words than that. He is very interested in what other people do and learns from imitating their behavior. The world is his laboratory, as he experiments with objects and the effects his actions can have. He understands basic concepts such as cause and effect and is learning to generalize from them. His memory develops, as does his ability to think and plan ahead.

This is a slow and emerging process, though. A baby doesn't become a reasonable and logical person overnight, and oftentimes he displays a strong-willed determination before he has the sense to know what he is doing. It is easy for parents to read adult significance into these first signs of independent thought, when in reality the baby's experience level doesn't justify it.

Separation and stranger anxiety usually reach their peak during these months, as babies continue to work out their relationship to their parents and other less familiar people. There are many explanations for why a baby gradually becomes better able to separate from his parent or usual caretaker. Perhaps it is his improved memory and ability to think to the future that makes him feel more sure of his parents' return. Or perhaps, as some people think, it is his ego development, or ability to think of himself as a separate individual, that makes him feel more secure when they are gone. In any case, separation anxiety does subside, and unless poor habits have developed in the meantime, so do related sleep disturbances.

During these months, parents are often put to the test. They must encourage their baby's independence and growth, comfort him when he is feeling insecure, and maintain control when he is acting unreasonably. This is all a part of the young toddler's "in-between" stage; one minute he is asserting his independence, and the next minute he is suffering from a new bout of separation anxiety, clinging to his parent for dear life.

One of the most exciting developments of this age group is the baby's emerging ability to think beyond what is physically present. When this happens, often between fifteen and eighteen months, the baby is no longer tied to concrete reality and his imagination takes hold. Like so many developmental stages, this one has its negative as well as positive side. Some babies experience their first nightmares during these months, perhaps as the result of a frightening daytime experience. This is usually not a significant problem, though, and it becomes less disturbing as the child begins to differentiate his dreams from reality.

As is true with all age groups, individual sleep needs vary greatly between the ages of ten and eighteen months. Most babies, however, sleep between thirteen and fourteen hours a day. Although the number of hours an individual baby needs to sleep cannot be changed, parents can organize their baby's day so that he is sleeping at convenient times. Most ten-month-old babies have a regular, predictable schedule, and are sleeping through the night. Temporary night-waking is not uncommon, but, properly handled, it won't develop into a regular pattern. At this age a child is still young enough to form positive sleep habits that will last a lifetime.

The Importance of Patience

There is no doubt about it, taking care of a toddler can be an exasperating business. In most cases, the toddler's physical mobility exceeds his common sense, and monitoring his nonstop curiosity can be exhausting. One minute he is happily playing with his toys, and then suddenly he develops an intense interest in the electrical outlets. A new type of temperamental "testing" behavior often emerges at this time. Throwing sand in the park, or food from his high chair at home, is not uncommon.

As trying as these situations can be, parents are much better off trying to maintain a calm, patient approach. In fact, one of the fastest ways to undermine your confidence and joy in being a parent is to frequently be impatient and huffy with your toddler. Although your ten-to-eighteen-month-old will probably not test your patience to the extent that he will when he is two, *this is the time* for you to start working on your patience skills. Although many parents sail through this wondrous and joyful age, far too many others lay the foundation for future power struggles.

Like other skills, patience is something you can get better at. Once you recognize that you want to change the way you respond to your child, you can practice a new approach. Removing your child from a situation, or an object from your child, in a firm but friendly way is preferable to losing your temper or hitting your child. Don't expect to respond to your child in a calm, consistent, and patient fashion all the time, but you can expect this positive pattern to emerge if you set goals for yourself.

Training yourself to respond to stressful daytime situations with your baby in a positive and patient fashion will go a long way in helping you change an undesirable nighttime situation. Parents are often at their worst at the end of a long day or in the middle of the night and cope less well with their babies' insistence on attention. If you can combine firmness with the calm, pleasant attitude that you have adopted in the daytime, you will be much better able to manage your child's sleep habits.

Naps—Making the Transition to One Nap a Day

Many ten-to-twelve-month-old babies are still napping twice a day, once in the morning and once in the afternoon. Nap times vary as sleep needs and life-styles vary, but a fairly typical nap schedule for this age group is 10 to 11 A.M. and 1 to 3 P.M. Somewhere between twelve and fourteen months (give or take a few months on either side) you will notice that your baby is awake for more and more of his morning nap, or that he isn't sleeping at all at this time. This is a signal that he is ready to give up this nap.

Some toddlers are able to cheerfully wait until after lunch at 12:30 or 1 P.M. until they take their nap, but most start to fall apart at 11 A.M. They have entered the awkward stage where two naps a day are too many and one nap isn't enough. For the next month or so, they will need an early lunch or snack before a long midday nap. Since they will probably be waking earlier than usual in the afternoon, they may need to go to bed earlier in the evening, too, while they are making this adjustment.

With the enormous increase in physical activity associated with learning to walk, many babies who have cut down to only one nap a day may temporarily need two naps again. After a month or so, when practicing walking no longer takes up so much of their days, they will again be ready to nap only once a day.

Since sleep needs vary enormously, there is no set number of hours your child should be napping a day. You should, however, make sure that his daytime sleep does not interfere with his nighttime sleep. You can help minimize bedtime problems by ensuring that your toddler's afternoon nap does not start too late in the afternoon and that he is not sleeping too long in the middle or late afternoon.

If you have a child who resists napping during the day and seems to require only a little daytime sleep, try to have him rest in his crib for at least forty-five minutes every day with some toys. This will give *both* of you time to relax, unwind, and renew yourselves for the rest of the day.

SLEEP-DISTURBING HABITS

If your ten-to-eighteen-month-old has never settled into an easy sleep routine, it is most likely because of habit, not physical need. You shouldn't be discouraged, though. Even if these habits have persisted from early infancy, your baby is still young enough to settle into a good sleeping pattern.

There are several reasons for you to tackle the problem now. First, we can't emphasize enough the importance of good sleeping habits. In the next several months solid habits will go a long way in minimizing your baby's almost inevitable temporary sleep disruptions caused by develop- mental factors, such as separation anxiety or learning to walk. Second, it is generally true that habits only get harder to change with time. You'll have a much easier time making a change now than later. Third, some babies learn to climb out of their cribs as early as eighteen months old, making it much more difficult to control them at night. And finally, the ten-to- eighteen-month-old is so active that he is truly spent by nap time and bedtime. His fatigue and need to sleep should help you in reshaping his sleeping habits.

The most common sleep-disturbing habits at this age include being unable to fall asleep alone, sleeping in a parent's bed, wanting to eat during the night, wanting attention during the night, and demanding a parent's attention too early in the morning. Although we discuss each problem individually, it is clear that these sleep habits almost always over- lap by the time a baby starts his second year of life. For instance, a baby who sleeps in his parent's bed almost always nurses himself to sleep. A baby who cries every night for attention also probably has not yet learned to easily get himself to sleep at bedtime. Therefore, if your baby has any of these sleep problems, you may want to consult several of our discussions on sleep-disturbing habits. As you develop your strategy from our sugges- tions, you will find that correcting one habit often helps another. If you approach changing your toddler's sleep routine with conviction, consis- tency, and a goal in mind, combined with your usual good humor, you'll find the task much easier.

Before we embark on our specific discussions, there are three final points that we would like to emphasize. First, the traditional advice of letting your baby cry it out will work for any of these habits. We offer alternatives, though, in case you prefer a gentler approach. Second, no matter what method you choose, we always advise against picking your baby up out of his crib when he is distressed in the middle of the night. It is always preferable to comfort him while he remains in bed. This is especially important in this age group, as he approaches the time when he will be able to climb out of his crib. He is much less likely to think of this as an option on his own if you haven't built up this association for him. Having a night-wandering toddler is a situation best avoided. And third, but equally important, during any adjustment period, do whatever you can to bolster your young toddler's confidence. If you are trying to change an undesirable sleeping pattern, make a special effort to have positive interaction with him during the daytime.

How to Help Your Toddler
Fall Asleep Alone

As a baby gets older, his demands for help in falling asleep both at bedtime and at nap time begin to take on new dimensions. When he was little, rocking, walking, and nursing him to sleep somehow seemed more appropriate (and more successful, too). Beginning in the second year of life, parents find that their efforts are met with increasing resistance. In fact, statistics indicate that between 25 and 50 percent of babies have trouble going to bed in their second year of life. There are many reasons for such problems, not the least of which is the parents' mismanagement of bedtime. The young toddler, who loves his parents' company so much, is naturally sad to give them up at bedtime. More often than not, he has learned that his crying gets results.

GUIDELINES FOR HELPING YOUR TODDLER FALL ASLEEP ALONE

1. Encourage your baby to become attached to a love (security) object such as a stuffed animal or blanket. This attachment is particularly helpful for this age group.

2. If you haven't done so already, get your baby used to a fun, wind-down bedtime routine. This can last anywhere from five to twenty minutes, depending on your other commitments at this time. After looking at a book together, hold him and snuggle with his love object. Then tell him it is bedtime, put him in his crib with his love object, say good night to him and his stuffed animal friend(s), and leave the room.

3. If your baby cries, go to his room, say something reassuring, and leave quickly. Don't get him out of his crib and don't reenact any lengthy bedtime ritual.

4. If your baby is used to getting to sleep with your assistance, you should expect that he is going to protest during this new adjustment period. If you are firm, good-natured, and consistent, he will take only from three days to a week to get used to your new expectations. If he continues to cry and complain, even after you have consistently put him to bed on his own for a week, keep in mind that many babies cry as a natural means of releasing themselves from a stimulating day. This may be your baby's regular means of achieving a transition to sleep.

5. If your baby is accustomed to falling asleep at the breast or with a bottle, this is an opportune time to change this habit. Make this feeding a little earlier, so that he is still awake. Because of the usual toddler's fatigue, and because he is decidedly less opinionated than the two-year-old, he'll adjust quickly to having this comforting feeding a little earlier. He may initially protest being put to bed awake, but at least you will know it is not from hunger. His ability to rely on his own resources to fall asleep will ultimately make him feel a lot more secure.

6. If your baby always falls asleep first in your bed and is later carried to his own crib, read our guidelines for moving your baby out of your bed.

How to Move Your Toddler out of Your Bed

Ten to eighteen months old is a sensitive time for many babies. It is the time when separation fears often reach their peak, and babies can be their most clingy, especially at bedtime. To make matters worse, babies often become quite opinionated and determined at this age, and may well resist sleeping in their own crib, especially if they never have slept there before. Given this background, it is understandable why some parents relent and allow their baby to share their bed.

Although some parents don't object to having their baby sleep in their bed, others find that this practice becomes increasingly difficult as the baby grows into toddlerhood. Because the active toddler requires relentless parental supervision during the day, most parents legitimately need a break by the time evening arrives. This break never seems to come when the baby sleeps with them. If you are in this position and are starting to crave some independent time, it is normal to feel torn. It doesn't mean you love your baby any less because you want him to sleep in his own crib, in his own room. It also doesn't mean that you have done the wrong thing by your baby up until now. But once you feel confident about your new goal of nighttime independence, you'll be able to help him through the transition to sleeping happily in his own crib.

Also keep in mind that your young toddler is often in a state of conflict between his desire for independence and his genuine need for you. As his parent, it is up to you to help him move toward independence in a smooth and careful way, including sleeping in his own bed. The road to independence isn't always easy, but in the case of an independent sleeper, it will be well worth everyone's effort!

If your baby's habit of sleeping in your bed has been firmly ingrained since early infancy, it may take you up to several weeks or a month to complete his transition to his crib. On the other hand, if you have only temporarily brought your baby to your bed because of an illness or a frightening experience he had, he'll need only a few days to feel comfortable and secure again in his own crib.

GUIDELINES FOR MOVING YOUR TODDLER OUT OF YOUR BED

1. As with the five-to-nine-month-old baby, getting your toddler used to sleeping in his own crib requires patience, consistency, and a commitment to your goal even if it involves a few sleepless nights in the process. Immediate results may be within the reach of a few of us, but not most of us!

2. Create an inviting sleep environment for your toddler. If your baby has been sleeping in your bed, you may have neglected making his crib and own room a comfortable and interesting place to be. Also, it is important for your toddler to have positive associations with his bed and bedroom. Try not to use his crib as a place for "time out" or punishment.

3. First orient your toddler to his crib by having him take naps there. After he has made the transition to sleeping there during the day, you can then start the training process of getting him to sleep in his crib during the night.

4. If your toddler doesn't have a firm attachment to a transitional (love) object, try to help him develop this bond. While he is still sleeping in your bed, bring his stuffed animal, blanket, or whatever he has chosen to bed with him. Always cuddle and comfort him with his love object, especially

when he is tired. Your goal is to teach him to feel secure and comforted by this object as he falls asleep. Count on this taking a few weeks.

5. Once you are confident that your baby is sleeping happily in his crib at nap time (and hopefully is "glued" to a love object), you can take the big step and put him to bed in his crib. Before you make this step, you must be convinced of your long-term commitment to having your child sleep in his own place. When he protests, you don't want to take him out of his crib and bring him into your bed, thereby teaching him that crying is the entry ticket to your bed.

6. Put your baby into his crib after winding him down with his regular bedtime routine. Say good night and leave the room. If he cries, go to him and reassure him but don't get him out of his crib. You can continue to check on him as many times as you need to, but try to give him enough time between your visits to settle on his own. If this doesn't work and he keeps up the crying, as a last resort you can consider staying with him in *his* room. You may feel compelled to do this if he is feeling separation anxiety (and see the section on developmentally related sleep problems). Stay with him until he falls asleep, and then leave.

7. When your toddler wakes up a few hours later or in the middle of the night, and he cries upon discovering that you are not there, go to him and reassure him. Even though you are comforting him, do not take him out of his crib. If you feel you need to stay with him until he falls back asleep, lie down next to his crib and doze there until he is again asleep. Repeat this process as many times as necessary, and for the next few nights. After a few nights you should start to wean him from your nighttime presence. Instead of staying, go to him briefly, reassure him, and leave. It is often a good idea for parents to take turns offering this middle-of-the-night reassurance.

8. This may be a difficult process for you and your baby, but remember how secure he will feel once he completes the transition to his own bed. During this time try not to introduce any other habits that will be difficult to break such as a bottle in bed.

How to Wean Your Toddler from Nighttime Feedings

A healthy ten-month-old baby does not need to eat in the middle of the night; he can easily go ten to twelve hours a night without a feeding.

So if your toddler is waking and insisting on feeding, he is doing this out of habit, *not* caloric need. Even the occasional bottle or nursing may cause him to wake in anticipation of a feeding. Fortunately, since this waking pattern is based on habit alone, it is much easier to correct than one that is caused by psychological or developmental need.

As with the five-to-nine-month age group, we have further subdivided what Dr. Barton Schmitt calls the "trained night feeder" into the bottle-fed night feeder and the breast-fed night feeder. We make this distinction because the breast-fed toddler's sleeping, sucking, and eating habits are so closely tied to the mother and therefore require a somewhat different approach.

The Nighttime Nurser

During the ten-to-eighteen-month period, a baby who has habitually nursed once a night may come to expect a second or sometimes continual nighttime nursing. It is at this point that the weary, sleep-deprived mother becomes truly torn. She often feels committed to continue nursing her toddler, but her toddler is demanding more from her than just nursing: more nighttime nursing, more time in his parent's bed, more fuss going to bed, and often more daytime attention. If this pattern sounds familiar, let us reassure you that your baby will continue to thrive when you eliminate his nighttime feeding. And it is important to do it now, before you have an even more determined two-year-old on your hands! By all means, continue to nurse during the day if you wish; just be consistent about not nursing at night anymore. Remember, weaning your toddler from night-time feedings will not only help you get more rest and ultimately help you be a more patient mother, it will also help your toddler feel more secure as he gains confidence in his ability to be separate from you.

Before you attempt to wean your baby from nighttime feedings, it is especially important in the older baby to incorporate some of the following preliminary points into his daytime as well as nighttime habits.

In most cases, it is best to wean the nighttime nurser gradually. Most babies who are weaned "cold turkey" do fine and seem relatively untraumatized by the whole process. But this may not be true of the parents! Many parents suffer intensely when their babies cry, even if the baby is not being harmed. The gradual approach also gives the mother the opportunity to wean herself from her twenty-four-hour need to be needed. By all means, though, if you feel you are up to the "cold turkey" approach, don't worry about harming your baby. He will make the adjustment quickly and will not hold it against you.

Preliminaries

1. Reclaim your privacy and bed for yourself. Your toddler is likely spending a good part of every night and early morning in your bed. Sharing your bed with your toddler may eliminate your need to wake up and attend to him (babies often nurse while their mothers doze in bed), but neither of you will achieve a good night's sleep until he stops feeding in the middle of the night. If you are waiting for your toddler to give up these nighttime nursings on his own, chances are he will not, particularly if he is sharing your bed. He needs you to make that decision for him. So before you wean your baby from his nighttime feedings, first help him to feel comfortable and happy in his own crib. To do this, see our section "How to Move Your Toddler out of Your Bed."

2. Next, analyze your baby's daytime eating habits. The young toddler who nurses off and on all night long often has eating or weight problems. If he eats well during the day and also nurses throughout the night, he may become obese. At the other extreme, some nighttime nursers eat like a bird and prefer to be on and off the breast throughout the day as well as the night. When this happens, the baby may not be getting adequate nutrition. In either case, it is best to teach your young toddler good eating habits. Make sure that his meals are well rounded and space out his nursings to at least three-to-four-hour intervals. He will be much healthier, as well as better able to sleep through the night.

3. Help your toddler learn to fall asleep on his own. You can eliminate a habit of falling asleep on the breast by nursing your toddler at wakeful periods of his day, such as when he awakens in the morning, after nap time, and around dinnertime. He will enjoy his alert interaction with you, too. Once he learns to dissociate nursing and sleeping, he will be able to develop the resources to fall asleep by himself. For other suggestions, see our section "How to Help Your Toddler Fall Asleep Alone."

4. As your baby matures, try to use your breasts less and less as a pacifier. Because of the added stress of this transitional age, the nursing toddler will often seek to nurse for comfort alone. Although this is okay some of the time, it is wise to find other ways of comforting your toddler. Young toddlers are especially receptive to being distracted in playful ways and by

being comforted in a parent's lap with hugs, rhymes, and songs. Since toddlers are also able to comfort themselves, encourage him to bond to a love object, if he hasn't already. A love object can provide him with the extra security he needs as he starts to explore his world and spend more time away from you. This attachment to a blanket or stuffed animal will also help him comfort himself back to sleep without a nighttime nursing when he surfaces in the middle of the night.

Preparation

Enlist the help of the baby's father or someone else during the period you are training your baby to sleep through the night without nursing. This is important because as a nursing mother it is difficult to take care of a baby in the middle of the night without feeding him. If getting up in the middle of the night presents a hardship to the father who has to be at work the next morning, we suggest you start this weaning process on a Friday night so that he can recoup sleep during the weekend days. By the time Monday rolls around, your baby will be well on his way to being weaned from nighttime feedings. The total length of the training period will vary, though, according to the number of preliminary steps you have followed, the number of feedings a night your baby is used to, your and your baby's temperaments, and how motivated and consistent you are. You may need only a few nights to eliminate these nighttime feedings. On the other hand, you may need several weeks to a month to complete the transition to an uninterrupted night's sleep. Also, toddlers sometimes slip back to their old waking habits after a week or ten days. If you are prepared for this phenomenon of "two steps forward, one step backward," you shouldn't be discouraged by this temporary setback.

NIGHT 1

Step 1: (early evening) Give your toddler a good dinner. If you are still nursing him at the end of the day, do so before or right after you have given him dinner, before he gets sleepy.

Step 2: Start your bedtime routine. As part of your baby's wind-down process, you might give him a bath. Put him in his pajamas and then start his bedtime routine. After you brush his teeth, you can look at a book together, sing a song, or cuddle together with his prized love object. Then bid him good night with lots of kisses and leave the room. If he has trouble at this point, refer to our suggestions in "How to Help Your Toddler Fall Asleep Alone."

Step 3: Wake your toddler at about 11 P.M. and nurse him. This is the *focal feeding*. We recommend this feeding as part of the retraining process for two reasons: first, it puts *you* in control of the situation (you wake him before he has the chance to wake you), and, second, it gives you a focused time from which to "stretch" your toddler through the night without an additional nursing. Once your baby is sleeping from the focal feeding time until the early morning and you are confident that this is his established pattern, you can abandon the focal feeding altogether. If you are consistent, it should take from two to four weeks. Since you will be in control all along, you will find that your baby won't wake up on his own once you decide to stop picking him up for this feeding (see Question 7, Chapter Two, for a discussion of what can happen if your baby controls this feeding).

Step 4: Father or helper, it is your turn! It is important that you go to your baby when he first cries instead of the mother. Remember, your baby strongly associates his mother with nursing; it will be easier on him if he doesn't see her when he first wakes in the middle of the night. Wait until he is really complaining before you go to him. Then pick him up and comfort him with his love object. If necessary, offer him a bottle of water. After the water, try to comfort him once again with his treasured love object or a pacifier or his thumb, if he uses either.

Step 5: Put your baby back in his crib with his love object. Tell him it is time to go back to sleep, wind up his music box or whatever else signals to him that it is sleepy time, and leave the room. Don't linger.

Step 6: Either your baby will fall asleep on his own after this nighttime encounter or he will start to cry.

IF YOUR TODDLER FALLS BACK TO SLEEP	IF YOUR TODDLER DOES NOT FALL BACK TO SLEEP
If your toddler falls back asleep without further fuss, this is an excellent sign that he is going to be easy to wean from nighttime feedings.	If your toddler starts to cry after you leave the room, give him at least five minutes before you go back to him. (If he is just being noisy and not crying, don't go to him at all.) Be brief and don't take

him out of his crib, even if he is standing up and hanging on. You can be loving and reassuring by hugging him as he stands in his crib or by simply stroking him. Gently help him lie down, reorient him to his love object, tell him again lovingly but firmly that everyone is sleeping now and that you are going back to bed. Continue this either until he falls asleep or for a full hour. If he doesn't fall back to sleep within an hour, feed him as in Step 7.

Step 7: The next time your baby wakes up, let him fidget or cry for at least five minutes to see if he will fall back to sleep on his own. If he doesn't fall back to sleep and a minimum of four hours has passed since the *focal feeding* (you can adjust this waiting period according to the number of times a night your baby is accustomed to nursing and what seems like a reasonable spacing for the first night), it is finally time to feed him. Mother can nurse him or father can give him a bottle, depending on your preference. Because his biggest association is most likely being in bed with mother, it is best to nurse him somewhere else, such as in his bedroom. Then, when you have finished feeding him, put him back in his crib with his love object. This feeding should carry him through until 7 A.M. If it doesn't, try repeating steps 4 to 6 until morning. Remember, your goal is to break him of the habit of nursing all night long, but for the time being you can still comfort him in other ways.

DAY 2

The day after is the time to review your first night's experience with your spouse or helper. Parents are generally much too tired and self-protective to plan a strategy during the middle of the night. Therefore, share your objectives during the day and make sure that you agree on your approach and goal. Try to be confident and positive before you start your second night. Keep in mind that this is a gradual approach, so you don't have to worry about being too abrupt. Remember, too, that your toddler's transition to sleeping through the night will be easier if you continue to incorporate our preliminary points.

NIGHT 2

Steps 1 and 2:   Repeat as on Night 1.

Step 3:   Wake your baby up for his focal feeding as you did on Night 1, but this time wait a little later, perhaps until eleven-thirty or midnight. Since you want to stretch him as long as possible from this late evening feeding, you increase your chances of his sleeping longer the later you pick him up. But remember, you must pick him up before he has a chance to wake on his own. His previous habits will guide you in determining the actual time of his focal feeding.

Steps 4 to 7:   Repeat as on Night 1.

DAY 3

You now have the benefit of two nights' experience. Although you may be more exhausted than ever, you probably feel less intimidated by the whole process of nighttime weaning. If your toddler is eating and nursing well during the day, you can feel even more confident that he is ready to give up these nighttime feedings. Also, if your toddler is happy during the day, this is another good indication that he is not suffering any ill effects from his new nighttime habits. Over the following days and weeks, you will see him thrive as he gains autonomy and the ability to comfort himself during the day, as well as the night. Keep in mind that changing something as big as sleeping habits is a process and does not always yield instant results. There may be setbacks, but as long as you are firmly committed to your goal, your baby will eventually make the transition to sleeping through the night.

NIGHT 3

Steps 1 and 2:   Repeat as on Nights 1 and 2.

Step 3:   Repeat as on Night 2. Pick up your toddler at eleven-thirty or midnight for his focal feeding. Once he is sleeping through the night until 6:30 or 7 A.M., you can relax the focal feeding time and pick him up any time between 10 P.M. and midnight.

Steps 4 to 7:   Repeat as on Nights 1 and 2.

DAY 4

Congratulations on your success! Most of you will have your older babies and toddlers sleeping at least a six-hour nursing-free stretch. In particular, those toddlers who are accustomed to only one nursing in the middle of the night often make the transition to sleeping through the night in these few short days of retraining.

On the other hand, if your toddler is not responding to our method and if his daytime behavior is showing signs of stress, you can try again in a few weeks. In the meantime make sure that you have adopted all of our preliminary points, that there are no other major stresses in his life, and that he is not, and has not been recently, ill. In order for you to increase your chances of success with our method, you must consider all the other influences in your baby's life. Good luck when you try again.

Those of you whose babies have slept through the night until at least 5 A.M. can reinforce your success with our final checklist.

The Final Checklist

1. Continue the focal feeding for several more weeks, or until you and your baby are both ready to give it up. This is in keeping with the gradual process of this method.

2. If your toddler is waking at 5 A.M. and insisting on nursing, use the same method for nighttime weaning to stretch him until 6:30 to 7 A.M. It is not important whether he actually sleeps after 5 A.M., but you want to help him learn to doze, comfort, and entertain himself until

you are ready to start your day. For further suggestions, see our method for the early morning riser.

3. Continue to encourage self-sufficiency at nap time and bedtime by putting your baby in his crib awake. Let him get himself to sleep.

4. If your baby reverts to nighttime waking, comfort him, but don't feed him.

The Nighttime Bottle Habit

The nighttime bottle habit, like other trained night-feeding habits, is usually part of a process that starts in early infancy. Occasionally, though, a nighttime bottle habit develops later on in response to some new situation (see our section on situations that can disrupt sleep). In either case, parents continue to give their babies nighttime bottles because it is easy. In the short run, there is less effort and less lost sleep in getting up, getting a bottle of milk from the kitchen, handing it to the baby in bed, and heading straight back to bed than there is in eliminating the bottle. In most cases, babies want only one bottle a night, and often this is either late at night or early in the morning, further reducing any inconvenience to the parents.

In the long run, though, this is not a good habit to encourage. Not only does it cause sleep disruption, it also begins to pose other problems in the second year of life. Tooth decay is rampant in children who take bottles to bed with them, whether the bottle has milk or juice. This in itself is a serious problem, as it can necessitate extensive dental work. In addition, nighttime bottles may make a baby urinate much more during the night, making it almost impossible for him to stay dry. This isn't a concern in the ten-to-eighteen-month-old group, except that some babies wake up when they are wet. And if the child continues to have a bottle at night when he is older, he may develop a bed-wetting problem.

The easiest way to wean your toddler of the nighttime bottle is to gradually modify the habit over a week or two. This gives his stomach the chance to adjust to decreasing amounts of milk, so that he won't feel hungry. However, if you want faster results and you feel confident that you and your baby are suited to the "cold turkey" approach, by all means go ahead and try it. In this context, letting your baby cry will in no way harm him; within a few nights to a week he will no longer expect his middle-of-the-night bottle.

Regardless of the method you choose, you must first help your toddler overcome his habit of falling asleep with a bottle at bedtime. If he falls asleep with his last memory being that of sucking a bottle of milk, he is likely conditioned to depend on a bottle to get himself back to sleep if he awakens in the middle of the night. To change this pattern, give him his last bottle of the day in your arms. (This discourages your baby from using the bottle as a security object.) Then put your toddler to bed *awake* and give him the opportunity to learn other ways to settle himself down to sleep. Sucking his thumb, using a pacifier, and holding his treasured blanket or stuffed animal are all alternatives to sucking a bottle in bed. Although your toddler may cry at bedtime for several evenings, you can at least be confident that he is not crying out of hunger. He'll adjust quickly if you are firm, but friendly, in enforcing his new bedtime routine.

Our two-week gradual dilution method outlined in Chapter Two is equally appropriate for weaning your toddler from his middle-of-the-night bottle. You may also try accelerating or decelerating the process, depending on your needs and other factors such as illness and vacations. You can feel confident that you are doing the right thing by weaning your toddler from his nighttime bottle habit now. He does not need this bottle and, like any of the trained night-waking habits, it usually gets harder to break as he gets older. Good luck and try to be consistent, regardless of the pace you choose.

How to Retrain Your Nighttime Crier

Trained night crying, another sleep disorder classified by Dr. Schmitt, refers to the baby or toddler who wakes solely for attention. Like the other sleep-disturbing habits that we discuss, this is a learned behavior. In this case, the baby has learned that when he cries, his mother or father comes and entertains him.

It is important for parents of a nighttime crier to understand how this behavior develops. There are any number of possibilities: the baby had colic and the parents didn't change the way they cared for their baby after the colic subsided; the parents picked up their baby every time he *started* to wake up or fidget, never allowing him to learn how to resettle himself; the parents replaced a nighttime nursing or bottle habit with the attention that creates a trained night crier; the parents were either light sleepers or afraid someone else might be disturbed by their baby crying; or the parents believe that their baby should never cry.

If your toddler has developed this type of nighttime waking pattern, your goal is to retrain him to be independent in his crib for at least ten to twelve hours at night. You want to help him learn to use his inner resources, combined with such aids as his treasured love object, a pacifier, his thumb, or crib toys, to help himself get back to sleep in the middle of the night. And perhaps most importantly, before you embark on our method to wean your toddler from nighttime attention, *you* must be convinced that he does not need you during the night. If you are not, you will not succeed.

Many trained night criers are what we refer to as combination nighttime wakers; that is, they wake up for both attention and food. Since feeding is almost always occasional and secondary to the other needs, we think that the combination wakers respond best to the method we have developed for trained night criers. However, if you have a combination nighttime waker, you should review the other methods to extract the points that are relevant to your own situation.

Preliminaries

1. The initial process of retraining your baby should take from five to ten nights at this age, but you will need another month or two to consolidate this new sleeping pattern. Try to be consistent during these subsequent months because your toddler can relapse into a night-waking pattern.

2. Your baby must learn to fall asleep *on his own* at nap time and bedtime. If you are in the habit of walking, rocking, or nursing him to sleep, shift these activities to wakeful times of his day. For further suggestions, see our section "How to Help Your Toddler Fall Asleep Alone." Once you have achieved this goal, you will be ready to proceed with our method.

The most effective method for eliminating trained night crying is to let the baby cry it out. As uncomplicated as it seems, it is one of the most difficult methods for parents to use. Some parents feel that withdrawal of nighttime attention is tantamount to withdrawal of love. But as long as you are loving and bolster your child's sense of well-being during the day, he will not suffer at all from a few nights of purposeful middle-of-the-night crying. Remember, you are not letting him cry when he truly needs you (such as during an illness). Chances are that he will not stop his quest for nighttime attention *on his own.* He needs you more than ever at this age to take charge and reshape his nighttime habits. Good luck!

One last tip: advise the rest of your household and neighbors of your plan before you start this method. They may wonder why your baby is crying.

Step 1. Before you put your toddler to bed, tell him, "We [I] love you, but we plan to sleep through the night tonight. We'll always check on you to make sure you are fine, but then we are going straight back to bed." Conveying these words or some similar message helps your toddler understand that you are taking a firm stand, even if he does not understand all the words. He certainly will understand your tone of voice.

Step 2. When your toddler wakes up in the middle of the night, go to him as usual to check on him. Do not lift him out of his crib. Say something brief but reassuring like "We love you, we are all sleeping, and I am happy to see you are fine. Good night, darling," and leave the room.

Step 3. You can expect your toddler to cry for a long time if he has been accustomed to your nightly attention since early infancy. Go check on him every thirty minutes or so by *briefly* telling him he is fine, reorienting him to his love object, and then leaving. You can alternate this procedure with peeking into his room through the doorway to make sure he is okay. It is better for him not to see you so he doesn't have the opportunity to engage you. The worst thing you can do is to lift him up after he has cried for an hour or so. If you do this, you are teaching him that he has to cry for a long time in order to be picked up. Good luck. Although it is not easy, remember your method and expectations are fair and realistic. Feel confident that your whole family will benefit from your weaning your baby from regular nighttime attention.

Follow the same procedure as on Night 1. You may or may not find that his crying is reduced.

If you have been consistent, the amount of time your toddler cries this third night should be less. From now on, check on him only from behind the door where he can't see you. Try not to be disheartened if he is still crying as long as on the first two nights. In many cases, this is the last night of crying, but depending on your child's temperament and past waking patterns, it may take him longer to get by without your attention.

NIGHT 4

Repeat as on Night 3 if your child is still crying for you in the middle of the night. Remember, don't interact with him at all during the night.

NIGHTS 5 TO 10

By the fifth night, most toddlers are sleeping through the night. Congratulations if your baby has finally settled down. If he hasn't, don't be discouraged. Remember, you and your child are individuals with unique temperaments and other influences, all of which contribute to the rate at which he will learn new sleep habits. As long as you are consistent in your method, your baby will eventually learn to be independent throughout the night.

How to Defer Your Early Morning Riser

Early morning rising is one of the most common forms of sleep disruption in the ten-to-eighteen-month age group. Even with the common hurdles such as colic, parental inexperience, and frequent colds, most babies are able to sleep through the night by the end of their first year of life. That is, once down for the night, they don't wake up for a feeding until the morning. But for many parents, the next morning comes too soon, when they are confronted with their bright, sunny little person at 5 A.M. Unlike the middle-of-the-night waker, the early morning riser is rested, and ready to get up, eat, and start the day. Because he can make up his sleep needs during naptime, the young toddler doesn't suffer from sleep deprivation at all. Only his parents suffer, as this early morning waking pattern can undermine their ability to carry on a busy daytime schedule.

If you have an early morning riser in your family, the first thing you should do is evaluate his overall sleeping and eating habits. If he is waking unacceptably early every morning, one of the following suggestions may make a big difference:

1. Make sure that your child isn't waking because it is too light in his room. If you haven't already, invest in some roller shades or other window coverings that block out light.

2. Regulate your toddler's bedtime. If he normally goes to bed at seven-thirty, try keeping him up until eight-thirty or even a little later to see if this makes a difference. Your goal is for him to be good and tired so that he will sleep a minimum of ten hours, or even longer. Don't give up too soon, as it may take several days before you notice a difference.

3. Nap times may require some adjusting, too. Try decreasing the length of the afternoon nap by cheerfully waking your toddler up after an hour and a half or so. If he is in daycare, or cared for at home by a sitter, be sure to check on his schedule. You don't have to be precise in scheduling the afternoon nap, but the idea is to ensure that your toddler has lots of time to play between his afternoon nap and bedtime. You want him to be tired and ready for a good sleep.

4. Never overlook the importance of eating well during the daytime. If your toddler is eating well, you can at least be sure that his waking patterns are not due to hunger.

5. Wean your toddler from a bottle-in-bed habit if he has one. It is important that he not associate his dozing or wakeful time in his crib with a bottle.

If the above suggestions don't help your baby sleep later in the morning, your next approach is to add an early morning deferral method to the preceding points. Parents can inadvertently reinforce an early morning waking pattern by going to their toddler as soon as he awakens in the morning. This doesn't give him the chance to learn to settle himself back to sleep, doze, or entertain himself with his crib toys. If the toddler has finished sleeping for the night, there is no way parents can insist that he sleep longer. On the other hand, it is perfectly reasonable for parents to assume that their toddler can learn to be independent in his crib, even if it is for as little as fifteen to twenty minutes. Like other sleep-disturbing habits, most toddlers have acquired this pattern of waking over the long term, since infancy, and have learned to need their parents immediately upon awakening.

The purpose of this method is to help your toddler learn to first accept, and later enjoy, independent time in his crib in the early morning.

(We have arbitrarily chosen six-thirty as the earliest acceptable waking time, but this is all highly individual, so adjust the times according to your own household.)

Early Morning 1: When your toddler wakes at 5 A.M. (or whenever) and starts crying for you, go to him and tell him firmly but lovingly that you are going back to bed because it is still sleep time. Orient him quickly to a few crib toys (that you should have placed in his crib the night before) and his love object and leave the room. Do not take him out of his crib at this point. He will probably start to cry since he has come to expect your immediate attention. Instead of going to him this time, go back to bed just as you said you were doing. Let him cry for fifteen minutes. If he doesn't settle down, walk into his room with a great big smile, signaling to him that you are ready to start your day, and a cheerful "Good morning." Don't give him any indication that it has been rough on you counting the minutes go by in bed, as you listened to him cry.

Early Mornings 2 to 5: Repeat as in Early Morning 1. Make sure you are consistent and wait at least fifteen minutes before you get him out of his crib and allow him to start his day.

Early Mornings 6 to 10: Do the same as you did the first five mornings, except eliminate that first resettling visit. From the time he wakes up and cries or calls for you, wait a full fifteen minutes until you go to him to get him up for the day.

Early Mornings 11 to 14: Your goal now is to defer him another fifteen minutes, for a total of thirty minutes. (If you have been consistent the first ten days, you may not even have to use any further deferring strategy. Your toddler may have started to resettle himself on his own until 6:30 or 7 A.M. On the other hand, some toddlers will require a *consistent* effort for a month before they adjust to the new early morning routine.) From the time your toddler wakes up, wait a full fifteen minutes before you go

to him. Then go and briefly resettle him, and go back
to bed. Wait another fifteen minutes until you go in to
cheerfully start the day.

Early Mornings 15 to 21: Now wait a full thirty minutes before you go to
him in the morning. After three weeks of this consis-
tent deferment, your toddler should certainly start to
internalize this shift in his daily schedule. He may still
cry momentarily when he wakes up at 5 or 5:30 A.M.,
but he will likely settle into a playing or dozing pattern
after several weeks. If you continue to maintain the
later bedtime, the shorter nap time, and the regular
early morning deferment, your toddler will learn to stay
happily in his crib until your family has reached a compromise on what is an acceptable rising time.

DEVELOPMENTAL FACTORS
THAT CAN DISRUPT SLEEP

All babies are vulnerable to occasional sleep disruption from developmental factors. Like anyone else, babies and young toddlers often become
more insecure at night. They are especially prone to attacks of separation
anxiety and may have their first nightmares, perhaps reenacting a confusing or frightening daytime experience. New motor achievements can also
take their toll during these months; the frustration and excitement associated with learning to walk sometimes interferes with sleep. Finally, teething can pose a problem for some children.

Even the baby who has always slept like a log may now have a few
difficult nights. In the long run, though, his solid sleeping habits will
certainly prevail. On the other hand, the baby who has consistently had
problems sleeping through the night is likely to have an even harder time
when one of these issues surfaces. Parents will have to analyze their own
child's sleep disruption in light of their past experiences and devise an
appropriate strategy. In most cases, it is best to deal with a new developmental issue before trying to correct a long-standing habit.

Separation Anxiety

Almost all young toddlers have trouble separating from their parents,
during the day as well as the night. For most children, separation anxiety

is an ongoing process lasting several months or even years, waxing and waning according to the particulars of their lives as well as their temperaments. As inconvenient as it may be, separation anxiety is definitely a normal part of growing up.

Of course not all children experience separation anxiety to the same degree. Usually these fears are most intense somewhere around the first birthday, but there is no exact timetable. So don't be worried if your easygoing fourteen-month-old suddenly won't let you out of his sight during the day and has trouble separating from you at bedtime. By the same token, don't be overly confident if your one-year-old has never been concerned by your comings and goings. There is no way to predict exactly when or how intensely an individual child will develop a new fear.

It does help, however, to recognize that your baby is vulnerable to separation anxiety during these months. With this in mind, there are a few things you can do to minimize the effect it will have on his life and his sleeping habits.

GUIDELINES FOR MINIMIZING ANXIETY–RELATED SLEEP DISRUPTION

1. Always prepare your young toddler for your departures. If you sneak out on him, he will only become anxious about being deserted by you.

2. Always try to use a familiar baby-sitter, especially at night. Waking up to find a stranger can be especially upsetting to children of this age, and disrupt their sleep for weeks. If you are using a new baby-sitter, always have her arrive before your baby goes to sleep. Leave enough time for her to get to know your baby before you leave for the evening.

Some parents find it helpful to establish a regular weekly night out. If you find a regular, dependable baby-sitter who comes at least once a week, you not only have a chance for a regular adult evening but may also help alleviate your baby's separation anxiety. He is much more likely to feel comfortable separating from you if it is part of his normal routine. The same goes for the daytime: if a baby is used to being cared for by one of his parents all of the time, you may do yourselves both a world of good by establishing a regular, predictable babysitting schedule, even if only once a week.

3. Try to be confident when you leave your baby. If he senses that you, too, are worried, he will only become more frightened. Remember, the only way for your child to learn that you always return is to see it happen,

over and over again. Your confident manner will help him through these difficult times.

4. If you can arrange it, try not to suddenly begin a full-time work schedule at this time. Unless your ten-to-eighteen-month-old is used to your being away from home all day, this is a big adjustment for him. It will be easier on him if you start back to work part time, and only gradually build up your time away from home.

5. Try to include your young toddler in your vacation plans. This may not be the ideal, restful vacation you have been dreaming of, but a sudden, extended separation from you might be quite stressful for him.

6. Do what ever you can to bolster your baby's confidence during the day. Games such as peekaboo and baby hide-and-seek sometimes help a baby understand that you are not permanently gone when you are out of sight.

7. Make sure that your baby is sleeping in his own bed. By bringing him into your bed at night, you are simply reinforcing his fears of separation. In effect, you are telling him that sleeping alone is a frightening experience and that he needs you at night.

8. At nap time and bedtime, make sure your baby falls asleep by himself. He will have a hard time getting himself back to sleep in the middle of the night if he learns to depend on you now. You can do this most effectively by making bedtime a relaxing and fun time for both of you. A specific routine often works best, with lots of time for hugs and kisses. When you put him in his crib, make sure he has his security object. Leave his room with a smile and a reassuring "Good night, darling; we'll see you in the morning."

9. If your baby protests when you leave his room, give him several minutes to calm himself down. You don't want to be overly responsive, thereby giving him the message that he is right to be frightened. When you decide that it is time to go in to his room to reassure him, be calm and brief. Don't pick him up out of his crib. Continue this until he falls asleep on his own.

10. If your baby wakes up again and cries for you before morning, again go to him to reassure him, but be as brief as possible, and again, don't pick him up. Instead, reorient him to his security object. On the first night you might want to go to him right away, but after that, give him a few

minutes to settle himself down first. If he continues to cry, wait at least fifteen to thirty minutes before going to visit him again. You can also try calling to him, without actually going into his room. This way, you will slowly be building up his confidence and independence during the night.

11. When your baby has finally slept through the night on his own, give him lots of kisses and praise the next morning. Let him know that you are proud of him.

Because the struggle for independence and learning to separate from parents is such an ongoing process, your baby may well have reoccurrences of separation-related sleep disruption over the next several months. But if you are consistent about reinforcing good sleep habits and sensitive to your baby's day-to-day needs, actual sleep disruption will continue to diminish. By about eighteen months of age, most babies are over the worst of their separation anxiety.

Nightmares

Sometimes, a baby's fears can show up in the form of nightmares. Besides fearing separation from his parents, a young toddler may also fear animals, trucks, motorcycles, or any number of things. Like adults, children dream about what is most familiar or important to them. Their dreams are reflections of their daily lives and feelings and may, on occasion, take the form of a nightmare when those feelings or experiences are frightening.

Unlike adults, though, babies are unable to sort out their dreams from reality. And at this age, they don't have the vocabulary to express what is bothering them. For these reasons, a nightmare may be an extremely upsetting experience for a young child.

Most people associate a baby's first nightmares with his emerging imagination. While a young toddler may experience an occasional upsetting dream, nightmares become much more common over the next year or so, as the child's experience and imagination continue to grow. For that reason, we deal with nightmares in more detail in Chapter Four. Night terrors, a different and much less common event, are discussed in Chapter Five. In the meantime, though, we offer the following suggestions to help you deal with your young toddler's occasional bad dream.

GUIDELINES FOR DEALING WITH NIGHTMARES

1. If you hear your child moaning or complaining in his sleep, there is no need to wake him up and comfort him. If you let him stay asleep, he will probably get over the dream quickly. If you wake him in the middle of a dream, he is more likely to remember it.

2. If your child wakes up with a sudden scream, by all means go to comfort him. If he is verbal enough, he may mumble something about a big dog, or truck, or whatever it was that frightened him. At this age, it doesn't pay to try to reason with your child or to explain that the dream was not real. Simply reassure him as best you can with hugs, kisses, and your calm presence.

3. If your toddler is prone to frightening dreams, keep a night-light on in his room and keep his door open. These may help him feel more secure.

4. Never belittle your child's bad dream or dismiss it as "just a silly dream." His fears may seem insignificant or illogical to you, but they are important to him. He will feel much more secure if he knows that you are taking him seriously.

Learning to Walk

Like other major physical milestones, learning to walk often interferes with a baby's normal sleeping habits. For many babies, practicing walking becomes the focus of their lives, with little time and interest left over for such mundane activities as eating and sleeping.

Sleep disruption can begin several weeks before a baby takes his first steps. Parents often find that their baby is crankier and more demanding during this frustrating and intense time. He may have a hard time settling down to sleep and also awaken easily from a nap or in the middle of the night. Usually, though, this period doesn't last too long. Most children get back to normal within a few weeks, as soon as they feel somewhat comfortable toddling around. Provided your child has had good sleeping habits until now, he will certainly settle back to his old routine. In the meantime, you can't rush his development and make him a competent walker any sooner than his body is ready for it. You can, however, try the following suggestions to improve his night's sleep.

GUIDELINES FOR HELPING YOUR BABY OVERCOME SLEEP DISRUPTION
WHEN HE IS LEARNING TO WALK

1. Make sure that your baby's bedtime is especially comforting and pre-dictable. If necessary, spend more time than usual getting him ready for bed so that he can wind down from his day's activities. Do not engage him in any roughhousing or physical play at this time. A bath and gentle rocking are both good ways to help him relax. When you put him in his crib, be sure he has his treasured love object.

2. If your baby wakes up in the middle of the night and seems too tense to fall back to sleep, try comforting him in his crib by getting him back into his favorite sleep position and gently rubbing his back or head. It is best not to pick him up out of his crib.

3. If your baby is continuing to have trouble sleeping through the night for several nights in a row, examine his daytime nap schedule. He might be sleeping too much or too late in the day. If he is still taking two naps a day, it might be time for him to give up one of them.

4. A final word of caution: during this time of sleep disruption, be careful not to initiate any new habits that you will regret later on. If you start nursing your baby in the middle of the night or begin to give him a bottle in his bed, you will be replacing a self-limited developmental condition with a more long-term problem.

Teething

Between the ages of ten and eighteen months, babies may cut as many as eight teeth: the upper and lower first molars and the upper and lower cuspids. As we explained in Chapter Two, teething pain may occasionally disrupt a child's sleep, but it shouldn't pose a major problem. If your child's gums are swollen and red, you may be correct in attributing new crankiness to teething pain. But if your child has a well-established pattern of waking and crying in the middle of the night, teething isn't the culprit. Teething may cause increased saliva production or mucus in the bowels, but it won't cause diarrhea, a fever, runny nose, red throat, or other symptoms of illness.

If your child seems uncomfortable and is having trouble sleeping at the time that he is cutting new teeth, first rule out illness. We don't advise you to use aspirin or acetaminophen on a regular basis, but an occasional dose can help alleviate his pain. He may also get some comfort from chewing on his fingers or a pacifier, and during the day you can give him a frozen teething ring.

As always, keep in mind the possibility of starting a new nighttime habit that you will regret later on. Handled properly, teething shouldn't cause more than a few nights of minor problems.

SITUATIONS THAT CAN DISRUPT SLEEP

At one time or another, almost all children experience temporary sleep problems that are related to specific situations. Depending on the situation, these problems can be short- or long-term, but most of the time they are self-limited. Once again, a solid foundation of good sleeping habits proves invaluable in helping children through these times. Provided that no new habits develop or that new separation anxieties do not surface, the sleep problem will disappear once the situation is resolved.

If, on the other hand, your child has never had reliable sleeping habits, these situations might be even more disruptive. This is not the time to change old habits, but once the situation is resolved, don't delay any longer in getting your toddler on the right track.

Situations that commonly disrupt sleep in the ten-to-eighteen-month-old are illness, hospitalization, travel, and moving to a new home. We cover other situations, such as a new sibling and divorce, in Chapters Four and Five.

Illness

Illness is a universal cause of sleep disruption. Colds, ear infections, fever, pinworms, diaper rash, croup, and allergies can all temporarily interfere with your child's sleep. Toddlers often get sick because of their regular, frequent contact with other children. Toddlers who have older siblings or who attend daycare are exposed even more to common colds and other viral infections. In our experience, children seem to get sick more during the cold weather when they spend long stretches of time indoors.

If your toddler is sick, the most important thing you can do is give him all your loving care. He needs you now, both because he isn't feeling well and because, if he has a head cold, he isn't able to comfort himself by sucking his thumb or his pacifier. He may also be sensitive enough to be somewhat frightened by his illness or the discomfort he is feeling. So attend to him through the night, if you must, and don't worry about upsetting his usual sleep routines.

Once you are sure that your baby is completely recovered from his illness, it should only take a few nights to get him back into his old sleeping routines. Don't be surprised if he is more demanding than usual in the beginning, but if you reinstate your old bedtime rituals and make your expectations clear in a nice way, he will respond within a few nights. If for some reason your toddler doesn't resume his old sleep patterns after several nights or a week, check with your pediatrician. Children can have relapses of an illness, thereby confusing their parents as to the cause of their sleep problems.

Hospitalization or Outpatient
Medical Procedure

Hospitalization or even an outpatient medical procedure almost always disrupts a toddler's normal sleep habits. Since this is an age when a child is so susceptible to fears and separation anxiety, even minor procedures can cause sleep disruptions. Hospitalization is particularly traumatic for a young child.

If your child has to go into the hospital for an illness, an operation, or even a simple outpatient procedure, make every attempt to stay with him at all times, around the clock (often parents or other friends and relatives can split this time). In the face of so much newness (and quite possibly pain), he needs the constant reassurance of your presence.

Once he is home again, expect him to need extra reassurance for a while. From talking to parents whose children have been hospitalized, we have found that toddlers can take from a month to six weeks or even longer to regain feelings of security at bedtime and nighttime. The length of time your child will take to settle down will vary according to his previous habits, his temperament, the reason for his stay in the hospital, and your ability to attend and reassure him.

Once your child is well and *completely* healed from any surgical procedure, you can start to help him resume good sleeping patterns and in so doing help him become his old, happy self. For the first several nights, go to him whenever he cries and comfort him, but do not take him out of his crib. He needs all your love, including your confident, consistent reminder that his crib is a safe and wonderful place to sleep. Once you have regained *your* normal easy self-assurance as a parent, your toddler will relax and feel much more secure, too.

If your toddler does not respond to your approach after he is fully recovered, he may have become overly dependent on your regular nighttime attention. If you suspect that this has happened, see our sections on alleviating habit-related sleep disruption.

Travel

In our experience, toddlers are more likely to have trouble sleeping when traveling than are other age groups. Babies are more flexible because of their dependence on their parents; the change in their environment figures little if their care remains constant. Preschoolers, on the other hand, have language, some ability to reason and anticipate, and the ability to integrate new experiences into the rest of their world. This leaves the toddler somewhere in between, at a much less flexible stage in his development. Perhaps because he is undergoing such rapid cognitive and physical growth, he needs the security of his routines and familiar landmarks. When a child of this age travels, he is especially susceptible to being thrown off at sleeping times.

As a general rule of thumb, you can expect your toddler to behave the same away from home as he does at home, or worse. Therefore, if he normally demands a lot of attention at night, sleeps lightly, gets upset easily, or pushes continually for limits, you will find traveling with him difficult. If you can help it, you would be wise to wait either until he is a little older or until his sleep problems are resolved.

On the other hand, if your toddler goes to bed easily, stays asleep through the night, and is generally easygoing, he will likely adapt well to new surroundings. Sleep problems don't usually arise unless some new traumatic event occurs while he is away from home. The occasional missed nap or late bedtime takes on little importance, provided you are having a good time.

Our following checklist will help you minimize your toddler's chances of sleep disruption while you travel:

GUIDELINES FOR MINIMIZING SLEEP DISRUPTION WHEN YOU TRAVEL

1. Bring your toddler's love object, a familiar blanket, and several crib toys with you.

2. If you are changing sleeping places frequently, we suggest that you bring along a familiar playpen or portable bed for sleeping. Your toddler

will be reassured by having his bed travel with him and will welcome its comforting sight.

3. Without being rigid, keep your toddler to his regular routines as much as possible. If you are traveling a long distance by air, the time change may throw him off, but he will adjust in a few days.

4. *Do not* try to change any of your toddler's habits while you are away from home. If he is used to having a bottle in bed, or nursing in the middle of the night, or has any other habit you want to change, wait until you have returned home and your toddler is resettled into his old routine.

5. Don't use baby-sitters while you are away from home, unless your toddler has a reasonable amount of time to become acquainted with his baby-sitter before he is left.

6. Have realistic expectations. A toddler will invariably balk at being rushed through breakneck, adult schedules. Try to be as relaxed and flexible as possible.

GUIDELINES FOR OVERCOMING SLEEP DISRUPTION CAUSED BY
TRAVELING, ONCE YOU RETURN HOME

New sleep disturbances can begin on vacations when families share a room and are hesitant to disturb each other or someone else in the room next door. What begins as an expedient way to keep your toddler asleep so that his night waking won't disturb others can easily turn into new night-time expectations. If your toddler has become accustomed to sleeping in your bed, resists bedtime, or has developed a new middle-of-the-night feeding habit, you will have to correct the situation as soon as you are resettled at home. For specific suggestions on how to deal with the situation that best fits your toddler, see our sections on sleep-disturbing habits.

If your child is having trouble settling down either at bedtime or during the night when you return home, your first task is to reorient him to his bedroom and regular bedtime routines. Some separation pangs are normal, especially if he became used to sleeping near you during the vacation. You can help him adapt quickly to his at-home sleeping arrangements by comforting and reassuring him in his own room (not yours). Develop a comforting routine that gradually reduces your bedtime/night-time interaction and that does not provide any secondary gains such as food or playtime. Do not take him out of his crib. Simply give him verbal reassurance and quickly reorient him to his cuddly love object. If he still isn't sleeping through the night after several nights or a week, you may have to resort to letting him cry it out (see our section on the trained night crier). Good luck!

Moving

Moving is frequently rated (somewhere after death and divorce) as one of life's most stressful experiences. Fortunately, though, you can protect your child from many of the adult concerns that build stress at moving time if you plan ahead and follow a few simple guidelines:

GUIDELINES FOR MINIMIZING SLEEP DISRUPTION WHEN YOU MOVE

1. Never attempt to change any of your toddler's habits immediately preceding or during the resettling period. For instance, if you are moving to a bigger house or apartment because you are expecting another baby, now is *not* the time to move your toddler to a big bed. Similarly, right after moving is not a good time to stop a bottle habit or any other habit you might want to change. Your toddler needs a sense of continuity between his old and his new living quarters, and his regular patterns will help him through that transition.

2. While you are preparing to move, try to do your packing when your toddler is either asleep or out of the house. Besides getting in your way, he may become troubled by all the disruption in his household. If possible, make childcare arrangements so you are free to pack and move without your toddler hampering your efforts. When he comes home, make a special effort to play and be cheerful with him. Keep to his regular routine, especially at bedtime, as much as possible.

3. Wait for the last possible moment to dismantle your toddler's room and pack his belongings. When you arrive at your new home, set up your toddler's room first. The faster he is settled in his new home, the less likely he will experience any sleep disruptions. When you arrange his new room, try to reconstruct as many familiar landmarks from his old room as possible.

4. If you are moving nearby, you might consider moving your toddler's possessions gradually, over a period of days. This will give him time to get used to the idea of moving.

5. Make every effort to keep track of your toddler's treasured love object. Since moving is so stressful, you may forget or lose track of something as

"minor" as a blanket or stuffed animal. But this object is not minor to your toddler, nor are the consequences of its loss minor to you. So treat it as one of your most precious valuables!

6. Keep in mind that your toddler will pick up on your attitude. If you feel stressed, so will your toddler. Conversely, the greater effort you make to be as pleasant and relaxed as possible, the more relaxed your child will feel about your move. Try not to be short-tempered with your toddler during the moving period.

7. If you are moving because of a separation, divorce, or death, obviously other major stresses will factor into the upheaval of moving. Still try to be sensitive to your toddler's needs, and offer him as much reassurance and continuity as you can. For further discussion on family change, see Chapters Four and Five.

QUESTIONS/ANSWERS

1. My thirteen-month-old son has recently started screaming at bedtime and wakes up frequently at night crying. He didn't have any sleep problems until about a month ago, shortly after I quit work. At that time we also had a close friend and her ten-month-old daughter move out of our house. They had lived with us for about two months while our friend was in the process of getting a divorce. What can I do to help him get over his crying and clingy behavior at bedtime?

As we mention frequently in this chapter, ten-to-eighteen-month-old children are particularly susceptible to separation anxiety. In your son's case, two major changes worked together to trigger this developmental anxiety: your quitting work and your friend moving out of your house. If your son had become attached to your friend and her baby, it is easy to understand why an abrupt departure would be upsetting. In his mind, if it is so easy for them to vanish from his life, you could possibly do the same.

There are several things you can do to help allay your child's fears. First, understand that whenever a mother makes decisions about career and family commitments, she is bound to feel torn. At the very least, most mothers go through a period of adjustment after quitting work and making the transition to staying full time with their children. If you are feeling such strains (as much as you may love being with your child), try to keep these feelings from your baby. He is certainly capable of picking up on your ambivalence. In your efforts to reassure your son, be as relaxed as possible and adopt a confident and firm manner at bedtime. If you have been overly attentive at bedtime (as many working mothers are, for the good reason that they don't see their children during the day), now is the time to make parting easier. He may be at a developmental stage where parting is difficult, but *you* are now entering an era (being at home full time with your child) that should make parting easy. Communicate this.

Second, your son needs to be in contact with your friend and her baby, so make every effort to go visit them. Tell him in simple language that they have a new house and that they sleep there now, but that you can visit frequently. If possible, follow up on these visits for at least a few weeks so that he can better integrate the change from them being a regular part of his life.

Sometimes, all your efforts don't seem to change clingy behavior once it starts. It has to run its course. However, clingy behavior need not persist in the form of nighttime sleep disruptions. Avoid traveling and any other major upheavals until your child has settled back into his former good sleeping habits. Be reassuring, but also make him feel safe and comfortable in his room at night by comforting him there. For more particulars, see our section on sleep disruptions caused by developmental anxiety.

2. My sixteen-month-old son wakes up almost every night for attention. I never feed him in the middle of the night; I simply pick him up and hold him for a while and then put him back to bed. I have tried not going to him at all, but his crying often turns into a breath-holding spell. This scares the living daylights out of me, so I try to accommodate him. I don't have any other ideas to get him to spend a night without me popping up. Can you help?

Although a breath-holding spell is indeed scary to watch, it is *not* dangerous. It is somewhat common in this age group and is perhaps the most controlling form of the toddler temper tantrum. Breath-holding occurs when the toddler is enraged either because he is not getting his way or because he has hurt himself. The usual mechanism is that he inhales his cry (instead of letting it out) and continues to hold this first deep breath until he loses consciousness or control, at which time the normal, involuntary breathing process resumes. There are three things parents must realize: (1) their toddler will always resume breathing on his own; (2) he is not oxygen-deprived long enough to suffer any brain damage; and (3) he has developed breath-holding as a learned behavior that has enormous power to direct and control the parents' attention to him.

We urge you to have a talk with your pediatrician about your son's breath-holding. After you are convinced that these spells don't represent a danger to your son's health, you will have to develop a strategy to deal with his demands. Because your son has become used to nightly attention, he fits into the category of a trained night crier (see that section). Your best approach is to let him cry it out during the night, and give him lots of loving support during the day. If you remain concerned about his safety as he begins to hold his breath during the night, it is okay to peek in on him, but try not to let him see you. After several nights of no nighttime attention, his crying spells will shorten and eventually disappear.

We know that this process is very difficult for parents, but don't cave in. His behavior is telling you that he needs you to set firm limits for him. As you may sense, you are not helping him by accommodating him, and you may actually be hindering his development. Parents often confuse their child's demanding behavior as a sign that the child knows what he needs and is best for him. This is not the case. He needs to be the child; he needs you to be the adult and be confident that you know what is best for him. He is still too young to put controls on his own behavior, so he needs your help and direction in learning self-control. We know it's hard to be unimpressed with breath-holding behavior, but your efforts will pay off. Good luck.

3. I am a forty-year-old single mother of a sixteen-month-old son. I have taken the last year and a half off from work and have been almost inseparable from him. After a trip back East, during which time he started waking up at night, I began letting him sleep in my bed every night. I love his company as I watch him peacefully sleep next to me. But I also feel torn about his being in my bed every night. Should I let him stay or should I make him sleep in his own bed?

Whether a child should share a bed with a parent on a regular basis is a complex, and we think, crucial, issue. On the one hand, we can understand your enjoying his company and wanting to share this close time. But on balance with the other implications of this arrangement, we feel quite strongly that the "family bed" concept is not a good idea, at least in our culture where independence is such a basic value.

Let us first consider the implications of this arrangement for your son's development. We are opposed to a child's sleeping with his parent on a regular basis at any time in his life, but particularly by the time he reaches toddlerhood. We discourage this practice for the newborn and young baby primarily because of the habits and expectations that are cultivated. But by the time a child reaches toddlerhood, the effects are stronger. By having your son share your bed every night, you are building his dependence on you, right at the time when other children in our culture are developing their natural and healthy tendencies to grow progressively more autonomous and self-reliant. By encouraging your son's dependence on you during the night, you are undermining this development and, perhaps, his self-esteem. Instead, we suggest that you try helping your son be the big boy he wants to be. Help him feel confident and happy about each independent step he takes on the developmental ladder. Sleeping alone in his bed is just one example of how he can begin to master his environment.

Added to these issues is the more obvious need for your child to develop a solid foundation of reliable, independent sleeping habits. As he grows, he will be much less susceptible to the occasional sleep disruptions that inevitably crop up if he has this strong foundation to fall back on. Growing up isn't always easy, but the process will be much less traumatic for the child who can independently sleep through the night.

It is also important for you to consider what *your* needs are at this time in your life. You may love your baby so much that you dread the inevitable separation that comes with growth and development. We encourage you to try to dilute some of the intensity in your time together. Let us reassure you that your bond and love will grow without you holding on so tight. The physical closeness between mother and infant changes, but the total sum of the relationship can remain as full. We also encourage you to reach out more for adult contact and support, and not to depend so heavily on your child for company. You might find welcome support in a single-parents organization or a parent-toddler co-op.

For all these reasons, we encourage you to get started now in helping your son readjust to sleeping in his own bed. The longer you wait, the harder it will get. By the time a child is eighteen months or so old, it is quite difficult and takes a considerable amount of time to change the firmly ingrained habit of sleeping with a parent. From a practical point of view, the less dependent he is on you at night, the more flexible his sleeping habits will be as he grows. So get going now to develop a strategy to get your toddler out of your bed. For guidelines, see our section "How to Move Your Toddler out of Your Bed." Remember to be consistent, to reassure him in *his* bedroom, and to make a special effort to bolster his confidence and emerging sense of independence during the day.

4. My eighteen-month-old son climbs out of his crib all the time, even in the middle of the night. He started to walk when he was nine months old and has always been a very active baby. He doesn't seem to sleep much, considering his level of activity. One of my neighbors suggested that I tether him at night so he can't climb out of his crib. What do you think I should do?

We feel that tethering a child is dangerous and a poor idea under any circumstances, and we advise you against it. A better solution for your son would be to either move him into a regular bed or bring down one of the sides of his crib so that it will function as a bed without constraints. Next, *carefully* accident-proof your son's room (for example, make sure the windows are impossible for a toddler to open and climb through, block off all electrical outlets, and eliminate any toys from his room that require adult supervision). Then, buy or borrow a baby gate (the kind with netting is much safer than one with crossed wooden rungs) and place it in his doorway every night after you tuck him in. This baby gate will confine him to his room but will not isolate him from the rest of the family the same way closing his door would. Try to enforce an approximately ten-hour stretch when your toddler can *independently* (so you can sleep too!) and *safely* amuse himself and sleep according to his own needs. In other words, all you have really done is enlarged his crib or sleeping space to the size of his room.

If he cries because he can't climb over the gate, go to him and tell him in a brief, friendly way that it is time for sleep, that he needs to stay in his room until morning, and that his door is open for you to be able to check that he is fine. If you continue to reassure him without taking him out of his room, he will come to accept the new limits you have defined for him.

In our experience, very active toddlers need these clear limits on their behavior and a comforting routine. A number of parents with active toddlers have reported to us that these children go to bed easily, without fuss. Perhaps this is because they use an extraordinary amount of energy to propel themselves through the day, and they are truly exhausted at bedtime. But many of these same children seem to have trouble resettling, dozing, or quietly entertaining themselves when they surface during the normal course of sleep cycling. This doesn't mean, though, that they don't need their sleep. Like any other child, they benefit enormously from good sleeping habits, even if they require more firmness and consistency from their parents.

5. Our eleven-month-old twins share a room. They have both been sleeping through the night since they were three months old, but about a month ago, one of them started waking and crying in the middle of the night. Since then, I have been placating her with a bottle every night (I quickly microwave and hand it to her and go back to sleep myself). I am afraid that if I let her cry she will wake up her twin sister, but I also don't want to continue this nightly bottle. What can I do to get her back sleeping through the night?

Your situation is not that different from having two different-aged siblings share a room. Usually one sustains a sleep-disrupting habit because the parents are afraid that this child will disturb the other one if they try to change that habit. With twins who have similar patterns, parents are even more likely to anticipate the potential of one disturbing the other.

In reality, though, a sibling (in your case, a twin) is rarely disturbed by the other child's waking. Most children are able to sleep through noise that would disturb an adult. Therefore, go ahead and wean your child from her nighttime bottle habit without worrying too much about disturbing her sister. Either the cold-turkey or the gradual-dilution approach will ultimately achieve the same result (see our section on the nighttime bottle feeder). Even though the cold-turkey method is quicker, in your case it might be wiser to try the dilution method first. This way the chances of one twin's disturbing the other are reduced even further.

6. My sixteen-month-old throws all her crib toys as well as her love blanket out of the crib whenever I let her cry in an attempt to enforce a bedtime. I have to go back into her room a number of times to put everything back into her crib. I also frequently end up taking her out of her bed to comfort her. What can I do to get her to go to sleep without this regular struggle? How can I keep her love object in bed with her?

The first thing you have to do is sit down and evaluate what is bothering your toddler at bedtime. If you are convinced that her bedtime comes at a time when she is normally tired, that she has had a regular, happy wind-down bedtime ritual, and that she is an otherwise happy, untroubled toddler, you have to consider the secondary gains she accomplishes by her bedtime behavior. Develop a strategy that combines your consistent, friendly, but *firm* manner with a nonnegotiable bedtime policy. Then stick to it.

As you put your daughter in her crib at bedtime, say something like "We love you. It is time to go to bed. We'll come check you later, but you may not get out of your crib until morning." Then, when she starts to cry, go check on her at twenty-minute intervals. Be brief and friendly as you reorient her to her love object and help her lie down. If she has thrown her crib toys out of her bed, don't make any effort to pick them up at this point (you can try tying her love blanket to one of the slats in her crib before you put her to bed). Then leave her room quickly. Act as unimpressed with her next temper display as you can. *Never* take her out of her crib as you quickly reassure her, since you have already told her that she must stay in her bed until morning. Continue to ignore the toys on the floor (you can pick them up the next day). After a week, or perhaps only a few nights, she will be convinced that you mean business, and her temper display should either vanish or decrease to the point that she may only cry for a minute as a means of releasing herself to sleep.

If she needs a second or third week to consolidate her new bedtime routine, change the way you check on her. Continue to reassure her at bedtime as you always do, but then wait to check on her again until she is back asleep (you can peak through the crack in her doorway). Sometimes your reappearances can compound her crying. In the meantime, during this retraining process, be sure to be relaxed and loving with your toddler during the day, making every effort to bolster her confidence and happy nature. You will succeed if you are consistent. Good luck!

7. We are both working parents with a thirteen-month-old daughter. We get home around six every evening and want to spend as much time as possible with her. We know she should be winding down her day at this time, but we get her revved up anyway and she often stays up until ten or even later. Is this okay?

Like all parents, working parents need time with their children. Therefore, when you arrive home late, bedtime can become a difficult question. You are correct to insist on having several hours a day to play and interact with your child. You also recognize that ten or eleven is too late a bedtime for a toddler as a steady diet. Also, working parents need to have some time in the evening to themselves, as well as with their children.

For these reasons, although a seven or seven-thirty bedtime may normally be optimal for a thirteen-month-old, we suggest that you compromise on eight-thirty. Try to hold off doing evening tasks, with the exception of dinner preparation, until your daughter is in bed. Also make an effort to establish a bedtime ritual that is relaxed and fun for both of you. You will then feel that your time with her is somewhat more productive, although condensed.

One of the things we all come to realize, whether we are working outside of the home or not, is that late afternoon and early evening is the most demanding and stressful time of day for all family members. New parents who work full time especially tend to feel that they must be superhuman. Realize, though, that your child will love you even if you reduce the time that you spend with her in the evening. All of you will appreciate good bedtime and sleeping habits as the months and years go by.

Chapter Four

FROM ONE AND A HALF TO THREE YEARS

The Emerging Child
The Young Child's Self-esteem
Naps
New Beginnings: From Crib to Bed

Sleep-Disturbing Habits
How to Enforce Bedtime and Help Your Child Fall Asleep Alone
How to Move Your Child out of Your Bed
How to Wean Your Child from Nighttime Feedings
The nighttime nurser
The nighttime bottle habit
How to Retrain Your Nighttime Crier or Middle-of-the-Night Attention Seeker
How to Defer Your Early Morning Riser

Developmental Factors That Can Disrupt Sleep
Bedtime and Middle-of-the-Night Fears
Nightmares

Situations That Can Disrupt Sleep
Illness
Hospitalization
Birth of a Baby Brother or Sister
Travel
Poor Diet and Food Allergies

Questions/Answers

I was standing in line at the supermarket and tears started pouring down my cheeks. I felt like a fool. I was crying for no good reason. I was just exhausted. My two-year-old hadn't slept through the night since she was born. At least I could figure out that exhaustion was causing my confusion and depression. I made an appointment right away with my pediatrician to discuss my child's sleep problems. Finally, my survival instinct took over. I had no other choice. It was either my child sleeping at night or my cracking up. It wasn't easy to force the issue with her, but I finally did it. We had a couple of rocky months, but she doesn't wake me up anymore. I'm beginning to feel like a normal human being for the first time in ages!

—*Mother of two-year-old*

THE EMERGING CHILD

The year and a half between eighteen and thirty-six months of age is a busy and full time for children, as they mature from toddlers to accomplished preschoolers. Development continues on all fronts, but the emphasis begins to change from physical to social and intellectual. Whereas the young toddler is consumed with learning and perfecting her motor skills, the older toddler and young preschooler focuses her energy on perfecting the mental skills to supplement this mobility.

Louise Ames and Frances Ilg of the Gesell Institute of Child Development have formulated an interesting model of the young child's development in which six-month stages of relative calm and equilibrium alternate with more difficult six-month unsettled periods of disequilibrium. According to this model, eighteen months is a difficult age. Subject to all the frustrations we described in Chapter Three, the one-and-one-half-year-old can be self-involved, unpredictable, and prone to sudden temper tantrums. Then, somewhere around her second birthday, everything seems to fall into place, and a happy and affectionate child emerges. This period of calm is likely to continue until the child is about two and a half, when new, and often more intense, challenges arise. Although our summary is oversimplified and of course subject to the variations of individual personalities and developmental timetables, we find this model extremely useful in providing an overview of the toddler's development.

At eighteen months, most children remain obsessed with mastering their large motor skills. In most cases, their emotional and intellectual development hasn't caught up with their physical prowess. Or, as Ames and Ilg say, "they think with their feet." An eighteen-month-old will run full speed ahead, but usually without a plan of where she is going, and without the common sense to know what to do once she gets there. If distracted along the way, she is likely to stumble and become frustrated by her own awkwardness.

As a child approaches her second birthday, things become easier. Physically, she is much more adept than she was just a few months ago, as she walks, runs, and climbs with ease. Her language skills are also much improved; her vocabulary may well be two hundred or three hundred words, and she is starting to put two or three words together in sentence form. All of this makes for a much happier, more easygoing child. She is the model of sociability, affectionate and fun to be with.

Then, just when you thought you had all your child-rearing problems solved, your perfect child approaches two and a half. Suddenly, you see what everyone means by the "terrible twos." Demanding, negative, and rigid, she can become extremely difficult to live with. Her love of routines, which has been growing over the last two years, may now evolve into rigid demands. The trouble, though, is that she often doesn't really know what she wants. Even when these demands are met, she still isn't satisfied. Unsure of herself, she becomes oppositional, setting up and exploring the extremes of any situation. Then she can't decide between her choices. All of this is quite frustrating for the child as well as the parents, and she may have frequent emotional outbursts, either shouting, striking out, or a temper tantrum.

Throughout these sometimes tumultuous months, the young child's mind and sense of herself as an individual develop at an almost incredible pace, as she continues to grow more and more independent. In fact, it is probably because she is working so hard to sort out her world and become less dependent on her parents that her outward behavior is so erratic. By the time a child is three, she will have had her time to think about the pros and cons of different situations and have the emotional maturity to be able to make simple decisions and stick to them. Because she has gone through the arduous work of figuring out where things belong, she will be able to relax a little and slowly become more accepting of variations and change. She has matured from the eighteen-month-old who lived completely in the present to someone who can understand the concepts of past and future time, and has a real appreciation for sequences and timing. Probably because she is becoming more sure of herself, she slowly becomes less egocentric and sometimes even concerned for the welfare of others.

Of course, every child is an individual and will develop at her own pace and according to her own temperament. An extremely easygoing child may sail through her entire third year without much difficulty, or a precocious child may be more difficult at two than she is at two and a half. The parents' interaction with their child and family dynamics can also have an enormous effect on a child's development. So don't expect your two-year-old to behave the same as your neighbor's child, or even the same as her older sister or brother did at that age. If you respect your child for being the individual she is, and strive to keep your interactions positive during the more trying times, you will be well ahead of the game.

During this year and a half, the average child's daily sleep requirements decrease from about thirteen hours to somewhere between eleven and twelve hours. Whereas a daytime nap is an important part of the average toddler's day, many children are ready to give up this nap by their third birthday. Therefore, the eighteen-month-old who sleeps eleven hours at night and two hours during the day may continue to sleep eleven hours at night when she is three, but without an afternoon nap.

For most eighteen-month-olds, bedtime is not an issue. By and large, the typical toddler is so tired at nap time and at the end of her busy physical day that sleep comes easily. But even the best sleeper may begin to have trouble settling for the night during the next eighteen months. She might call for her parents with specific demands or, even worse, climb out of her crib to present her demands in person. About a third of all two-year-olds wake up in the middle of the night expecting a feeding or other attention. This may come from either a well-established habit or an occasional fear or nightmare. One piece of advice for dealing with your toddler: unless she is sick, don't pick her up out of her crib when she cries for you, either in the evening or in the middle of the night. It is much better to comfort her *in* her bed because that won't build her association of getting out of bed when she has trouble sleeping. Many children learn to climb out of their cribs on their own, but if yours hasn't, count yourself among the lucky. Living with a night roamer is an experience you're better off without.

The Young Child's Self-esteem

Like so many other behaviors, sleep can be considered a reflection of a child's inner self. You can't expect a child who is insecure during the day to feel secure enough to sleep through the night on her own. Of course this doesn't mean that all sleep disruptions can be traced to feelings of insecurity. But if you want to change your child's nighttime behavior, one of the best places to start is by helping her to feel good about herself during the day.

There are a number of factors that contribute to your child's sense of self-esteem, including her ability to master developmental steps with a feeling of personal pride; her interactions with you, other family members, and other children her own age; and your ability to provide her with firm but nonpunitive limits for her behavior. By working on all these goals, you will be not only laying the foundation for good sleeping habits but, perhaps more importantly, helping her to build a foundation of self-esteem that will last the rest of her life.

First of all, self-esteem is closely linked to a child's ability to master each step on the developmental ladder. Your child should always feel a great deal of pride (and rightly so!) from each step along the way, whether this step be physical, social, or intellectual. Try not to fall into the common trap of involving your ego or your pride with her progress. Let your child feel good about herself, for herself, and not only through your eyes. For example, when your two-year-old first learns to sleep through the night alone, or is first toilet-trained, focus on her pride and accomplishment as well as your reaction to it. As well as saying, "I'm so proud of you," think about how she must feel: "You must really feel like such a big girl." As much as she might want to please you, she has to learn to please herself, too, in order for her positive self-concept to grow.

Another important part of building your child's self-esteem is helping her learn to be part of a community. For the two-year-old, this means learning to function as a team in the family unit as well as to mix socially with children her age on a regular basis. The more she is able to interact with a group (including both the family and her friends in either a play or a nursery school setting) in a positive way, the more her feelings of well-being will grow. Whenever your child's sleeping habits improve, help her to feel the success on two levels: the personal sense of accomplishment

that we speak of above and the sense of team accomplishment that benefits the whole family.

Finally, some parents mistakenly believe that their child's positive
self-concept can best come about through having totally free rein. On the
contrary, most experts feel that a child who is allowed to lash out at others
or whose behavior often spins out of control is feeling mostly confused and
insecure. She needs to know that you are there for her, for guidance as
well as love. In the same way that you teach your child not to throw sand
at the park, you can establish firm limits about acceptable bedtime and
middle-of-the-night behavior.

It is also important to examine the methods you use for enforcing
limits. Losing your temper and angrily snatching your toddler out of the
sandbox or spanking her when she wakes up in the middle of the night will
show her that you mean business, but it won't help either your relationship with her or her self-image. Of course you can't always be patient,
especially in the middle of the night, but when you are able to combine
patience with your firmness, you will be helping your child grow to be
more confident and well-adjusted.

Naps

Almost all eighteen-month-olds are well on their way to needing only
one nap a day. While many older toddlers will cheerfully wait until after
lunchtime to take their naps, others start to fall apart at eleven or twelve.
It doesn't really matter when your child's nap time is, provided it fits in
with the rest of her daily activities and doesn't interfere with bedtime.

By the time a child has reached her mid-twos, she is almost always
able to wait until twelve-thirty or one-thirty to take her nap. The time she
goes down every day should remain fairly constant, although the actual
amount of time she sleeps will be up to her. Length of nap times varies
considerably from child to child, but the average nap is about two hours
long at this age.

Some active two-year-olds recharge themselves after a twenty-to-
thirty-minute nap. If you have a child like this, you can't make her sleep
longer, but you can encourage her to stay in her bed and have a quiet time
for forty-five minutes every day. Supply her with books and toys and tell
her that she needs to stay in her bed until you come get her, or until the
record or cassette is over, or until the timer goes off. By the time she is in
her mid-twos, she has likely gathered enough language skills for you to
successfully communicate that she must have a midday quiet time every

day. Besides, it's important for *you* to have a break from your active two-year-old so you can give yourself a realistic chance of positive interaction with her for the rest of the day.

Children in daycare are often encouraged to have especially long afternoon naps. This helps caretakers regroup after a busy morning and also gives the child enough rest to stay up and spend time with her parents in the evening. Parents who work outside of the home often rely on a few precious evening hours together. Occasionally, though, this long afternoon nap (especially if it starts around two in the afternoon) can interfere with bedtime and nighttime sleep. If you have a two-year-old who just isn't tired by the time you would like her to go to bed, it's time to cut down on afternoon napping. If you are in charge, you can try putting your child down earlier in the afternoon or waking her after an hour and a half. If your child is in daycare, explain your bedtime problems to her caretakers and tactfully insist that she sleep less during the day.

Somewhere around their third birthdays, many children are ready to give up their naps. Just as your child went through a period of transition when two naps was too many and one nap was too little, she will now go through a similar adjustment. This time, one nap will be too many, but going without any nap will make her tired, cranky, and marginal in the late afternoon. When this happens to your child, move her dinner and bedtime earlier until she acclimates to going through the day without napping.

One of the most frustrating results (besides the crankiness) of giving up napping is that young children have a tendency to fall asleep in the car, playing, or watching their favorite television program in the late afternoon. Although the child usually doesn't enjoy being awakened, it is better to meet those consequences than to have a well-rested two-year-old who has just wakened from a nap at 7:30 P.M.! If, however, you find that your child repeatedly falls asleep in the late afternoon, you might want to be extra vigilant about a regular quiet period every day. Our bet is that she will fall asleep at least three out of seven days a week, indicating that she is still in the transition period, and in need of at least some daytime naps.

This transitional period may continue for up to several months, but don't worry. It is quite common, for example, for a child who has given up her nap to start needing it again once she starts nursery school. The newness and excitement of her day simply tire her out. As a general rule, don't rush your child to give up her naps. Her body knows what is best for her.

New Beginnings: From Crib to Bed

The move from a crib to a bed is quite a milestone for the young child; in our culture, it constitutes a form of initiation rite into childhood. Because of the feelings of security attached to this transition, it is important to make sure that your child feels positive and safe about the move.

Like everything else in development, there is no set age when you should move your young child into a bed. Somewhere between two and three years is a reasonable time, allowing for differences in development, personality, and life-style. Occasionally, parents have such problems with an older toddler climbing out of her crib that they see this as an opportune time to make the change to a bed. And once your child is three years old, you can be pretty sure that she is ready to graduate to a big bed. It is never good to rush this process, but if you delay much longer, she may feel crowded or resent being treated like a baby.

There are a number of things you can do to make this transition smooth and positive. If you are purchasing a new bed, bring your child along to help select it. This will make her feel like she is taking part in this process. No matter what bed you decide to use, it is usually a good idea to put it in your child's bedroom for a while, along with the crib, before she actually uses it. This will give her a chance to get used to the idea gradually. Then, as a first step, you can have her start napping in the bed to try it out. Again, depending on her response, you can proceed right away or over a period of weeks to having her sleep in the bed at night. Depending on your child, it may be a good idea to leave the crib in her room for another month or two, gradually phasing out its importance.

Creating an inviting bed and night table can also entice your young child. Let her help choose new sheets and pillowcases, if finances permit. You can also set up a bedside lamp, a hanging mobile, or an inexpensive clock-radio or cassette player near her bed. A few new stuffed animals can serve as accessories to your child's favored love object on her new bed. We also recommend that you keep a row of picture books handy for nap, bedtime, and early morning independent entertainment.

Since moving to a bed is a new beginning, it's important to get your child started on the right track from the very first night. Go through your normal bedtime ritual, making her as comfortable as possible. If she gets out of bed, take her firmly by the hand and put her right back in bed, without anger. Explain to her right from the start that she is not allowed out of bed until morning. She must understand that the new lack of physical barriers does not constitute an open invitation to get up and play or come to your room. (You can encourage her, however, to bring a toy or two to bed with her.) She will catch on fairly quickly if you are consistent and firm and give her lots of compliments when she does stay in bed. If you continue to have problems, you might find some helpful suggestions in our section on enforcing bedtime.

As a final note, there is one mistake so commonly made that we must point it out: don't suddenly move your child out of her crib so that your new baby can move in. A child's worst fears of being rejected in favor of a younger sibling can come true, in her eyes, if the new baby takes over her bed. If you plan ahead, you can move your older child out of the crib in time to leave it empty for a couple of months. This way, she is less likely to feel usurped and resentful toward the baby.

SLEEP-DISTURBING HABITS

Habit is the foundation of a good night's sleep. As much as we want to tell ourselves otherwise, and no matter how many excuses we conjure up to explain away our children's poor sleep, we still get back to the same premise: the child who is used to sleeping through the night on her own will probably continue to do so. On the other hand, the child who has never settled into a reliable sleep routine is much more likely to continue to be bothered by any number of nighttime problems. Of course any child can lose a few nights sleep when she is sick or has had a frightening experience. Once this situation is resolved, however, she will have her old sleep habits to fall back on. The child who has never developed these habits, however, remains at a loss. She goes from one crisis to the next.

This is where your confident parenting comes in. It isn't easy to step in and change a long-standing habit, but you can certainly do it. Don't keep waiting for your child's sleep to improve on its own. This may not happen for years, so the sooner you decide to take charge of the situation, the better.

Of course all family problems can't be traced to sleep deprivation, but there is nothing like chronic fatigue to strain relationships. Not only are all of you tired and cranky during the day, but after one and a half to two years of poor sleep, you really can't help feeling angry and resentful, too. No matter how much you love your child, it is only natural that you eventually begin to resent this person who is responsible for your constant fatigue.

The next step in this unfortunate but predictable pattern is guilt. And often, it is the most conscientious and adoring parents who find themselves in this situation. They feel guilty for a variety of reasons: they may sense that their child's behavior is unnecessary and feel somewhat responsible for it, they may feel bad because they continue to respond in a negative way to their children's demands, or they may wish that they had more energy to offer their children. In most of these cases, the children are advantaged, loved, and reasonably well adjusted. The parents have erred, though, in believing that their children need to express an opinion about every aspect of their daily lives, or they have erred by believing that their children will hold it against them for enforcing nighttime limits.

The importance of good sleep habits, then, can't be overemphasized. Until you are well rested, you can't even give yourself and your family a fighting chance at a happy life together. It certainly doesn't pay to feel guilty about what you've done so far or worry about what might have been. Instead, look to the future and start working now on developing good sleeping habits. Once you have, the other pieces of your life can fall into place.

The most common sleep-disturbing habits in the two-year-old include resisting bedtime and not being able to fall asleep alone, sleeping in the parents' bed, wanting to eat during the night, wanting attention during the night, and wanting attention too early in the morning. Although we discuss these problems individually, you should also be aware that they frequently overlap. For example, a child who sleeps with her parents may still be nursing in the middle of the night and may not have learned to fall asleep alone. Or a child who cries every night for attention probably has trouble falling asleep alone and has difficult bedtime habits.

Therefore, your best approach is to evaluate your child's sleep problems and carefully read all the sections that apply. As you gain an overview of the different problems, you will be better able to develop a strategy suited to your own child. You will also see how solving one sleep-disturbing problem frequently solves another.

Before you begin, though, there are two important positions you must maintain to smooth your child's transition to good sleep habits. First, do everything you can to bolster her self-esteem during the day. Because you will be setting clear limits at night, it is especially important for you to reinforce the positive implications of those limits with constructive and friendly interaction during the day, including providing plenty of fun activities for your child. Although not all children are demanding or regressive during a period of enforced change, some two-year-olds will do a lot of acting out. And no doubt about it, it is hard to be pleasant to a less than pleasant child. Be prepared, then, for this response, and make an extra effort to positively interact with your two-year-old during this adjustment. By bolstering your child's confidence during the day, you are giving her the foundation on which she can base her new nighttime behavior.

A second position you must adopt to help change your child's nighttime behavior is overall patience. If your child has built up her poor sleep habits since infancy, recognize now that it may well take several weeks or even months to get the results you want. But with conviction toward your goal, a planned strategy, and overall consistency, you will slowly see your results.

And finally, keep in mind that any of these habits can be changed by allowing your child to cry it out for a few nights. Many parents, however, have a difficult time with this approach, so, where appropriate, we offer ways of cushioning the blow.

How to Enforce Bedtime and Help Your Child Fall Asleep Alone

Getting a two-year-old to bed can be one of the hardest challenges in a parent's day. Under the best of circumstances, parents have to make a valiant effort to organize and then go through all the steps of dinner, bath, story, and bedtime. And as if having this daily task in the face of fatigue weren't enough, parents also have to contend with the other common interruptions and demands of family life that come up every evening. As difficult as it may be, however, we urge you to organize your efforts. If you approach your child's bedtime from a position of strength rather than weakness, you have a much better chance of succeeding.

Besides the parents' vulnerability at this time of day, normal two-year-old behavior characteristics contribute to bedtime difficulties. We have all heard of the terrible twos, a term that captures the oppositional or contrary nature of the two-year-old's behavior. Children seem to be especially prone to this contrary behavior when they are tired. It is little wonder that parent and child alike develop negative feelings about bedtime.

On the brighter side, there are plenty of ways to make bedtime a positive experience for both you and your child. And we encourage you to help her develop good bedtime habits now, during the twos, before she starts with the more elaborate delaying strategies that characterize the three-and-four-year-old age group.

Finally, before we list our preliminary guidelines, there is one point that we would like to emphasize. It seems so obvious, but many parents seem to overlook it: don't expect your child to fall asleep when she isn't tired. There is no better way to promote a negative association with bedtime and bedtime struggles than by regularly insisting that your child get in bed when she isn't ready for sleep. The first thing you should do, then, is figure out if your child really is tired when you are expecting her to fall asleep. The only way to do this is to look at her behavior. You can't assume that she needs the same amount of sleep as her brother or sister, or anyone else, for that matter. If she is happy and energetic with only ten hours of sleep a day, that's fine! At that point, the only thing you can do is try to adjust her schedule so that she is sleeping at the most convenient times. For example, if your child is both falling asleep too late in the evening and waking up too late in the morning, you can gradually advance her sleep schedule at both ends. Or if she is waking up at a decent hour but having trouble falling asleep at night, you can try cutting down on her daytime napping. You can't however, expect her to add one or two hours to her sleep time!

Many children, however, *are* tired at bedtime, but have trouble falling asleep for a variety of reasons. If this sounds familiar, read on!

Preliminaries

1. First, in order for you to successfully enforce bedtime, your child has to be able to fall asleep on her own. If she has never been able to fall asleep without your help, you are going to have to work on this "skill" at the same time that you teach her that bedtime is a nonnegotiable, inevitable event every night. Therefore, always put your child to bed awake. Unless she is sick, you should never rock, nurse, or walk her to sleep.

2. Help your child become attached to a love object such as a blanket or stuffed animal. If she doesn't have one, you can encourage this bond by cuddling her with the object at comfort and sleepy times or by talking up a certain stuffed animal as a friend. This attachment to a love object will help her feel comfortable enough to fall asleep alone.

3. If you haven't already done so, introduce a consistent bedtime ritual. Depending on your other commitments at this time of day, it can last

anywhere from ten to thirty minutes. Stick to the same wind-down steps every night.

4. Don't overlook the entertainment you may be offering your child when you respond to her delay tactics or forays out of bed. If you start out the evening being firm, then pleading, then reasoning, then angry, and finally screaming, that is worth the price of admission right there. And in many families, the first unsuccessful parent might then turn the stage over to the other parent, who then proceeds to run through his or her entire repertoire. No wonder the child won't go to sleep! If you want to get results, then, be boring. If you are even, consistent, and repetitive, it really isn't worth your child's time to stay awake.

5. Don't nurse your child at bedtime or during the night. This can interfere with her ability to learn to comfort herself as she falls off to sleep.

6. Wean your child from a bottle-in-bed habit, unless she is only taking water. You can either make her give up the bottle cold turkey or you can use our gradual-dilution method (see our section on the nighttime bottle habit).

7. Don't feed your child once you have started her nightly bedtime ritual. You don't want her to get into the habit of expecting food just before bedtime, nor do you want her to use requests for food as a way of delaying bedtime.

8. Don't start bringing your child a glass of water at bedtime, or you will find yourself repeating this waiter act nightly. Offer her water when she is brushing her teeth and then no more (unless, of course, she is sick).

9. Don't give your child choices about any issue that either delays or detracts from the process of winding down. If it is time for her bath, for instance, just tell her it is bath time, lead her to the bathroom, and help her into the tub. She is still young enough for you to move her through the steps of her bedtime ritual without allowing her to delay her bath by saying, "I'll come when I am finished building!" Even if she is pushing three and quite verbal, be firm, detached, and friendly about backing up your words with action.

10. Don't allow toilet-training issues to hamper your bedtime efforts. Sometime between two and three years, your child will probably be toilet-trained. Don't be concerned, though, if it takes another six months to a year (or even longer) for her to be dry at night. If your child is toilet-

trained during the day, take her to the toilet one last time before you put on a nighttime diaper and her pajamas. It can be after her bath, when she is brushing her teeth, or just before you tuck her in for the night. Our rule of thumb is to leave a child in diapers overnight for at least a month beyond the time she seems to need them. And if she should have an accident one night, don't scold her. This way, she will feel relaxed enough to sleep through the night, without fear of wetting her bed.

11. Unless you are a single parent or your spouse or housemate is unavailable in the evenings, get into the habit of sharing bedtime responsibilities. It is an awful lot for one person to do every night. If your spouse is resistant, keep bringing up this issue as something you need to share.

12. If your child is falling asleep first in your bed and you are then carrying her to her own bed, read our guidelines for moving your child out of your bed.

With these preliminary points in mind, you are now ready to proceed with our method:

Step 1: Go through all the usual steps of your child's bedtime routine, perhaps including a bath, brushing teeth, going to the bathroom (if applicable), putting on pajamas, laying out clothes for the next day, reading a story, and singing a song.

Step 2: Next, wind up your child's music box, or put on a cassette or record. Tell her that you will sit with her until the music box (or whatever it is) is finished and that you are then leaving the room. Make sure the time constraint is set by an object rather than by you, as she is less likely to dispute the limit-setting of an inanimate object! Even eighteen-month-olds can understand and respond to this kind of time limit.

Step 3: Tuck your child in with her love object; put on a hall, closet, or dim night-light; tell her that you will check on her when she is asleep, and then leave the room. If getting out of bed has been a problem, tell her firmly that she may not do this.

Step 4: If your child calls out to you, go to her *once* to quickly reassure her. Say something like "It's bedtime, you're safe, you have your [whatever she calls her love object], and we're here to protect you —so don't call out anymore." Then turn on your heels and leave the room. If she cries, wait ten to twenty minutes before you go to check her and say something simple like "Try to go to sleep, now. Mommy [or Daddy] will check on you later." If she continues to cry, check on her from the doorway at about twenty-minute intervals. Don't engage in any more dialogue with her and only go to pull up her covers once she is asleep.

Of course, it would be great if bedtime were all that simple. Read on if your child is constantly climbing out of her bed or crib.

Step 5: If your child jumps out of bed and chases after you as you leave the room or if she comes to you five or ten minutes later, take her quickly by the hand and lead her right back to bed. If you're angry, try not to show it (at least until you're alone) and don't engage in any lengthy dialogue. Say something to her like "We love you and love being with you, but it's bedtime now and you have to stay in your bed until morning." Make sure that you have established eye contact so that she knows that you mean business. Then leave. Repeat this as many times as necessary, but you can cut out your reassuring words after saying them once or twice. Just lead her back to her bed as quickly as possible.

Step 6: If your child's getting-out-of-bed problem is particularly severe, we suggest that you use a baby gate (or a Dutch door with the top half open) at the entrance to her room. You can say something to her like "We can't sleep when you keep coming to our room, so that's why the gate is there. You're safe; it's like having the door open. We can check on you and hear you." If she keeps calling to you or crying, go to her periodically to reassure her (every thirty minutes or so), but do not engage her in lengthy contact. Do not take her out of her room. Reassure her with "You're fine and you still need to stay in your own room. We'll check on you when you're asleep." If she finally falls asleep on the floor, you can then put her in her bed.

Step 7: If your child's bedtime problems are complicated by fears, don't dismiss them. Simply repeat the message that she is safe and that you are nearby to protect her. For further details, see our section on bedtime fears. Still insist that she stay in bed.

Step 8: In the morning, regardless of how difficult your child was the night before, comment on one positive aspect of her behavior the night before. What you are trying to do is encourage her positive feelings about bedtime. Even a child turning two will understand something like "Wow, you must really feel like a big kid falling asleep in your big bed all by yourself!" Don't mention the two hours that she spent crying or the fact that she fell asleep on the floor!

Repeat steps 1 to 8 as many nights as necessary until your child has caught on. As always, if you are consistent, bedtime should become much easier after a week or so. If you have been using a baby gate, you should be able to take it away after a couple of weeks.

How to Move Your Child out of Your Bed

If your two-year-old has been sleeping in your bed since she was a baby, it won't be easy to change her habit. The job won't be quite as hard if she has only recently begun to sleep in your bed, but still there are no instant, magical solutions. There are, however, lots of things you can try. The following guidelines will help swing the odds in your favor so that your child will eventually begin to prefer her own bed.

GUIDELINES FOR MOVING YOUR CHILD OUT OF YOUR BED

1. As always, be consistent and patient. Inviting your child into your bed one night and then evicting her the next just won't do! Once you take a stand, you have to carry through.

2. Define a realistic goal for yourself. If your child has been in your bed since infancy, it might be helpful to work out a two-month strategy for getting her into her own bed. Talk to your spouse or friends about your weekly gains. You'll gain extra insight by talking about your attitudes and strategies.

3. Make some concrete improvements in your child's room. It only makes sense that the more attractive she feels her room is, the more she'll want to spend time there. Some ideas for decorative and functional additions are new pillows, a few stuffed animals, interesting sheets, posters on the walls, a bedside lamp, a mobile, and a cassette or record player.

4. Start the whole process in motion by first having your child take her naps in her room. After she has taken her first nap there, congratulate her for being a big kid! Help her feel proud that she was able to sleep on her own. If she already sleeps independently in her room at nap time, you can still emphasize what a positive habit it is, even if it isn't a gain.

5. If your child hasn't done so already, encourage her to bond to a love object.

6. If you are breast-feeding, wean your child from all evening and night feedings. (See our section on the nighttime nurser.)

7. Try to focus on positive aspects of your child's sleep behavior. If she is carrying on in the middle of the night, don't say something critical the next morning like "I don't like the way you keep coming to my bed." No matter how hard it is to find a positive point on which to comment, say something like "How wonderful that you were able to comfort yourself with your blanket last night."

8. If you have another child who sleeps in his or her own room, you can try moving your child from your bed into her brother or sister's room. If she has had chronic sleep problems or she is experiencing any developmental anxieties or fears (a child in this age group will commonly say she is afraid of something in her room), she'll feel much more confident about separating from you at night if she has the reassuring company of a sibling. Don't worry about this child disturbing the other. Room-sharing problems usually take care of themselves within just a few nights.

9. If you don't have another child or you prefer to have your children in their own rooms, read on! You have to feel confident and really committed to the next part. At bedtime, tell your child something like "Tonight you are going to sleep in your own bed. I'm here if you need me, but you may not come into my bed." Even an eighteen-month-old will understand this message. Once you have said it, you have to stick to your word. Any comforting from this point on should go on in your child's room, even if you have to sleep in *her* room for several days. If you want, go ahead and set up a mattress or bed next to her for this interim period so you can be consistent without being totally sleep-deprived! After a few nights, you can start to wean her from your nighttime presence by reassuring her and then leaving her. If you have a spouse or other housemate with whom to share this task, take turns offering middle-of-the-night reassurance. The

trick is to be firm but equally reassuring that your child is safe and you are still there to protect her.

10. At the same time that you are being firm and reassuring, start a deliberate plan to build your child's confidence in a general sense. Make her feel good about herself during the day by providing her with opportunities to feel successful at her daily activities. Your child will feel more secure in her own bed if she feels secure and confident with herself during the day. Keep in mind that your child's sleep habits are not an isolated part of her development and can reflect as much about her feelings about herself as any other facet of her behavior.

How to Wean Your Child from Nighttime Feedings

All parents know that by the time their child is eighteen months old she doesn't need to eat in the middle of the night. They keep the habit going, however, because it takes an extra push of energy, motivation, and organization to eliminate it. Many parents in this situation hope that their child will magically wean herself from this feeding (or feedings) when she is ready. This line of logic, though, doesn't take into account what a habit really is: an unconscious, ingrained, repetitious act. If we take a look at how we change an adult habit, we quickly recognize that it requires lots of determination, a plan, and often a considerable amount of time. It certainly doesn't change by itself.

Childhood habits are no different. But since you are the adult in the relationship, it is up to you to supply the incentive that your child lacks. It is up to you to help your child overcome her desire for a middle-of-the-night feeding. We belabor this point only to emphasize that you can't be passive about it. If you don't take a stand, you are simply perpetuating your child's bad habit.

Nighttime nursers and children who depend on a nighttime bottle differ quite a bit. In fact, just about the only way they are alike is that they are both dependent on a nighttime feeding at a time when most of their peers have long since given it up. Because breast-fed children are so tied to their mothers, they often don't have any other way of comforting themselves during the day or night. Children who are still nursing at night also tend to spend considerable time in their parents' bed and become dependent on this nightly interaction. As a result, their sleep cycling may be physiologically less mature than that of their peers who have learned to sleep through the night.

Nighttime-bottle toddlers usually have a simpler, more limited attachment to their food source, and the ramifications are not as profound. The biggest challenge in weaning a child from the nighttime bottle habit is substituting the comforting aspects of this attachment with something else that won't interfere with a good (and independent) night's sleep.

The Nighttime Nurser

Nighttime nursing in a two-year-old is a complicated issue because of its emotional as well as physical components. Weaning your child from nighttime nursings may not be easy, but it is certainly possible. The following guidelines should help.

GUIDELINES FOR WEANING YOUR NIGHTTIME NURSER

1. It is very difficult to wean your child from nighttime nursings if she shares your bed and depends on you to fall asleep. Therefore, when you are constructing a strategy for your child, first consult our sections "How to Enforce Bedtime and Help Your Child Fall Asleep Alone" and "How to Move Your Child out of Your Bed." These suggestions, combined with the following points, will help your child achieve nighttime independence.

2. Although we are firm advocates of breast-feeding, we encourage you to evaluate the advantages and disadvantages of nursing in this older age group. First of all, for nearly all children, nursing is no longer nutritionally necessary at this age (this may not be true in other parts of the world). Second, if you haven't done so already, it is very difficult to draw the line between nighttime and daytime nursing. If you haven't been able to confine nursing to the daytime, your child has probably become dependent on your breasts for comfort around the clock. For these reasons, you may find that it is time to wean your child altogether. This is a personal decision, though, that no one else can make for you. But cutting off your milk supply is certainly the surest way to wean your child from nighttime nursings.

3. If you want to continue nursing your child once or twice a day, that is fine, but try not to nurse her when she is falling off to sleep. You want to break her association of sleeping and nursing.

4. Also focus on your child's daytime eating habits and make sure that she is getting adequate nutrition. Encourage her to eat healthful meals during the day, especially at dinnertime, so that she won't wake up in the middle of the night from hunger.

5. The easiest way to wean your child from nighttime nursings is to limit her middle-of-the-night contact with her mother. Therefore, when she wakes up and wants to nurse, it should be the father or someone else she is close to who comforts her. By the time a child is two years old, she has a clear sense of how far she can test her mother. This is complicated by the fact that a nursing mother often feels ambivalent about her role in nighttime nursing. Even though intellectually she may want to wean her child from these nighttime nursings, her emotional bond is powerful. Therefore, although the father may be an involved and loving parent, the fact that he doesn't have this physical attachment allows him to be more effective in managing nighttime waking.

6. So, it is your turn, father! When your child cries or asks to be nursed in the middle of the night, go to her right away in her room and say something like "I'm here to check on you and see that you are fine. Mommy is sleeping and won't be able to feed you anymore at night. We love you and will see you in the morning." Then leave her room. If she continues to fret and complain after you have comforted her several times, you can offer to stay a little while with her the first few nights of the weaning process. Try staying five or ten minutes and then leaving her room. If you are firm but reassuring, she will do fine. If your child has been in your bed all along and the separation is too abrupt, you can stay with her a little longer, but only in her room. You can consistently decrease the amount of time you spend with her over a period of two weeks or so. If your child asks or cries for mommy, give her a big hug and tell her that it is your turn to take care of her. This can also give your child the chance to balance her feelings of intimacy with her mother with new feelings of closeness with you.

We recognize that it is hard on some fathers to get involved at night if they are due at work the next morning. Unfortunately, though, there isn't an easier way to wean a two-year-old at night. You can, however, plan the first couple of crucial nights for the weekend so that you can recoup some sleep during the day. And after the first several nights, the mother can again participate (but not nurse!). In the beginning, though, the father has a definite overall edge: although the child trusts and loves him, his presence does not offer an association with nursing.

7. Two final but important considerations, as always, are that you be absolutely consistent once you start the weaning process (don't go back to nursing three hours or three nights later!) and also bolster your child's confidence during the day. In the morning, say something to her like "What a big kid you are that you don't need to wake Mommy to feed at night anymore." Don't forget that you have her drive for independence on your side. As she turns the corner, she will feel good about her growing independence.

The Nighttime Bottle Habit

A nighttime bottle habit is undesirable for several reasons. The most obvious disadvantage for you is that you have to get up during the night. Even if it only takes you a few minutes to get a bottle out of the refrigerator and hand it to your child, your sleep has still been disturbed. The biggest problem for your child, aside from the fact that she wakes up and can't fall back to sleep on her own, is the damage the bottle can do to her teeth. Pediatricians and dentists agree that sucking on a milk or juice bottle during the night is one of the best ways to promote cavities. And finally, if your child is drinking any type of liquid during the night, it will be much more difficult for her to stay dry until morning.

Once you decide to wean your child of her nighttime bottle habit, there are two tacks you can take: the cold-turkey approach or the gradual-reduction method. If you want fast results and you and your child are temperamentally suited to cutting out the bottle all at once, go ahead and do it. For those of you who prefer a gentler but slower approach, see the gradual-reduction method outlined in the nighttime bottle section of Chapter Two.

Part of your decision on how to proceed should be based on your child's individual habit. If your child is carrying around a bottle throughout the day, as well as depending on it at night, you have a far different situation from if your child is used to an occasional bottle at specific times. Like the child who is perpetually comforted by breast-feeding, she is using her bottle as a comforting device. In many cases, this dependence is so strong that it will be more difficult for her to adjust to part-time bottle use than to give up the bottle altogether. Therefore, she may be better off learning a completely new way of comforting herself. So if you do elect the cold-turkey route, encourage your child bond to another security object. She will continue to need some form of comfort when she falls asleep and when she surfaces during the night.

You should also know that the cold-turkey method will in no way harm your child. If you are consistent and continue to be loving and supportive in other ways, she will be able to get over her habit in just a few days. Be prepared to go and reassure her at night, but also be absolutely firm that there will be no bottles or drinks. To make things easier on your child, though, and to ensure your success, don't make your move to eliminate the bottle in the middle or on the heels of some big change in her life (such as starting daycare or moving to a new home).

On the other hand, if your child has a bottle only a few times a day, at specified times, and one of these happens to be in the middle of the night (or even late at night or early morning), you might try simply talking her out of it. Once your child is about two, she will probably understand something like "Tonight, neither Daddy nor I will bring you a bottle. We want to sleep all night. If you like, you may have one now before you go to bed"—not as she is falling asleep, though—"but then that's it until the morning." For many children whose bottle dependence is less developed, this tactic can work.

How to Retrain Your Nighttime Crier or Middle-of-the-Night Attention Seeker

Before you embark on any program to encourage your child's nighttime independence, you must carefully evaluate your own situation. If you are suffering from long-term exhaustion, feeling that your daytime activities are compromised by fatigue, and finding that your child's sleep problems are hurting your relationship with your spouse, it is definitely time to turn things around.

Also take a good look at your child. If, aside from recognizing your own needs, you also feel that your child still needs you at night, you have to overcome your ambivalence. Until you are convinced that sleeping through the night is to your child's advantage as well as your own, you won't succeed. Once you reach that point, read on!

If your child is still at the toddler stage (around eighteen months) and sleeping in a crib, the method for the trained night crier in Chapter Three will suit your needs. But if your child is well into her twos, the following method, which includes using the neutrality of a clock-radio to let her know when it is morning, takes into account the developmental advances that have occurred since the toddler stage.

By the time a child reaches two years of age, specific sleep problems tend to blend into a general pattern of sleep resistance. For instance, a child who is used to regular nighttime attention may also have been in her parents' bed off and on, may get an occasional bottle or other nourishment, may need a parent to fall off to sleep, and may have built up a lot of complex night fears. Wherever you need to, then, look to other sections so that you have a complete plan that is especially suited to your child. For example, sometimes moving a fearful child into her sister's or brother's room will reassure her enough to be able to sleep through the night.

Preliminaries

1. It is always a good idea to advise your neighbors of your intent. Then, if your child cries a lot in the middle of the night, they will know that she is not in any real distress. If you like, show them this book.

2. We have learned from parents who have succeeded with this method that it is important for them to choose a time (a week or so) when they are relaxed and committed and won't be distracted or deterred by other pressing demands in their lives. One mother told us that she had never been able to let her toddler cry until they went on vacation one summer. It was with a background of summer country sounds and farm animals that her son cried it out and learned to sleep through the night!

3. We recommend that the least involved parent (frequently this is the father, but not always) do the reassuring in this method. This parent can often be more effective in enforcing new limits. If this isn't practical, though, you can give it a try on your own. Just don't let yourself fall back into old nighttime patterns.

NIGHT 1

Step 1. Buy your child an inexpensive clock-radio and put it next to her bed. Set it for whatever time you would like her to get up in the morning. Then, before you put your two-year-old to bed, tell her something like "I can't get up at night with you anymore. I'm exhausted and I intend to sleep. We love you and will always make sure you are safe in bed; we always check on you. But you have to learn to not call for Mommy or Daddy at night. In order to help you know when it's okay to come to us, I have bought you something special, a clock-radio. When the music comes on in the morning, you can get out of bed and come see us. Remember, don't get out of bed or call for us until the music comes on." A simple, friendly bedtime discussion like this gives your child a clear idea that you are setting new limits and that you are firm about them.

Step 2. When your child wakes up in the middle of the night, go to her once and say, "It's still nighttime and time to go back to sleep. You'll know that it's morning when the music comes on. Don't call us or get up until then. Right now you are safe in your bed. We love you and will see you in the morning." Do not let her get out of bed and don't cuddle her (if she gets out of bed herself, see steps 4 and 5). Just stroke her quickly, reorient her to her love object, and leave the room.

Step 3. Continue to reassure your child at thirty-minute intervals by saying and doing the same thing. Don't stay with her, don't give her anything to eat or drink, and don't get involved in any lengthy interaction.

Step 4. If your child continues to cry (which she undoubtedly will the first night), she'll likely get out of bed and come to your room or doorway. Make the effort to get up again and lead her by the hand back to bed. Don't reinforce this behavior by getting angry and engaging her. Look her in the eyes and say, "You need to stay in your bed until morning. You're safe. Don't forget that your new radio will let you know when it is time to get up." Expect her to be angry and cry, but don't worry about her being afraid.

Step 5. If your child's getting-out-of-bed problem is particularly severe, as a last resort you can use a baby gate at her doorway. Tell her you are doing this because you want to sleep through the night and it will keep her safe in her room. If she gets out of bed and hangs on the gate or starts playing, try to ignore this behavior. If necessary, continue your short reassuring visits every thirty minutes or so *without* any other exchange. After this training process has started, don't bring your child to your room.

Step 6. The next morning, say something positive to your child like "I love the way you came to us this morning when the music came on." Don't mention anything negative that happened. At this point, you want to reconstruct only positive memories of your previous night's experience.

Step 7. As is always true, you will have to build your child's confidence during the day if you want this nighttime plan to work.

NIGHT 2

Follow the same procedure as Night 1. You may or not find that her crying is reduced.

NIGHT 3

Your two-year-old should call out or cry for you a lot less by the third night *if you have been consistent.* From now on, if you go to check her, *don't let her see you and don't interact with her in any way.* Remember, crying won't harm her in any way.

NIGHT 4

Repeat as in Night 3.

NIGHTS 5 TO 14

By the fifth night, some children will not call out at all or will only call out momentarily. Other children are more resistant and will take up to another ten days to sleep through the night (once your child is sleeping through the night you can stop using the clock-radio). Regardless of where your child stands on this two-week timetable, you will definitely sense that she is making the transition to independent nights. It works!

How to Defer Your Early Morning Riser

Early morning rising is only a problem if you, as parents, perceive it as such. If you don't mind getting your day started bright and early every morning when your child wakes up and calls for you, don't worry about it. Many children who wake before their parents are able to entertain themselves in bed, so again no one is disturbed. If, however, your child is waking and demanding breakfast or your attention at what you consider to be an unacceptable hour, there are some things you can do.

The most obvious thing for you to consider is whether your child's room gets too light early in the morning. Installing roller shades or other light-blocking window coverings may be all that you need to do to get her to sleep later.

Second, look at your child's overall sleep schedule. There is nothing you can do to change the total number of hours she needs to sleep a day, but you can do some manipulating of what specific hours these are. In other words, you can try putting your child to bed a little later in the evening or cutting down on her daytime napping. Both of these may allow her to sleep a little later in the morning.

If this doesn't work, the third thing you should look at is how you are responding to your child in the early morning. If you have built up a pattern of feeding her right away or inviting her into your bed as soon as she wakes up, she has probably become dependent on this interaction. Therefore, your goal is to change these expectations so that she can slowly become more independent in the early morning hours.

By the time a child is two years old and has fairly good language skills, we recommend a different retraining tactic than the one we recommended for a toddler. Therefore, if your child is still in a crib and at the toddler stage, refer to our method in Chapter Three. The following method, which involves using a clock-radio to signal your child when she can get up, is appropriate for a child who is two or older. In the following version of this method, we recommend that you start right away by setting the radio to go off at the time you would like your child to get out of bed. Another equally effective variation would be to gradually work up to your ultimate goal. In other words, if your child is now waking and getting up at five-thirty but you would like her to stay in bed until seven, you could set the clock-radio to five forty-five or six the first morning, six-fifteen the second morning, and so on until you finally reach seven. In either case, patience and consistency will be the keys to your success. And also remember that because one habit contributes to another, you will have to continue to pay attention to other aspects of her sleep habits.

DAY 1

Step 1. Buy your child an inexpensive clock-radio and place it next to her bed. Set it for seven o'clock, or whatever you feel is a reasonable time for her to get up. When you tuck your child in at night, tell her that she may not get out of bed until the music comes on. Tell her that she may play with her animals or other toys and books that are near her bed. If she is used to coming into your bed when she wakes up, tell her she is welcome only after the music has started.

Step 2. If she is used to a bottle or nursing, tell her the same thing: that she may come to you or call for you only after the music has started, and that only then can she have her milk. The neutrality of the clock-radio is important.

Step 3. The next morning, when she calls or comes to your room at the predictably too early time, make the extra effort to get out of bed. Firmly, gently, and without any great discussion, lead her back to her bed. Put her back in bed with her love object, and remind her of her new clock-radio. You can say something like "We love to see your happy smile in the morning, but you have to wait until the music comes on. That's when the whole family gets up. You may play quietly until then."

Step 4. If she starts to cry or call out, leave her room and ignore the crying as best you can.

Step 5. If your child continues to come after you or get out of her bed after only about ten minutes, take her promptly back to her bed without anger or a long discussion. You have to be prepared for this the first morning. At breakfast time, say something positive like "I love the way you spent a few minutes playing in your own bed waiting for the music to come on." She may have acted horribly except for those two minutes, but those two minutes are the part of the whole experience that you want to reinforce.

DAY 2

Step 1. The second evening, repeat everything from the night before and add a statement like, "I loved the way you played in your bed this morning," even if she didn't complete the time goal.

Step 2. If you anticipate that this won't be an easy process, you can add a physical barrier to your strategy. Your experience from the first morning will give you an idea if you need the extra help of a baby gate. If you do, go ahead and put it up that evening, telling your child something like "Mommy and Daddy like to sleep until the music comes on. We'll come get you at seven when the music

starts and the gate will keep you safe in your room until then."
Notice you haven't said anything negative like "You keep bothering us and that is why I put the gate up."

Step 3. When your child starts calling or crying the next morning, get up
once and go to the baby gate where she is probably standing.
Remind her of the new household rising time by pointing to her
clock-radio, shaking your head and saying, "It's not time to get up
until the music comes on. We'll come get you then. If you like,
you can play with your toys quietly." Leave her and go back to
bed without any more exchange. Let her cry if you have to, but
don't give in until seven, or whenever you said you were coming
for her. (If you can anticipate your child crying, notify your neighbors the day before of your plan. Explain to them that her crying
in this instance does not mean that she is in any real distress and
that she will settle down within just a few days.)

Step 4. Again at breakfast and at bedtime the next day, highlight some
positive aspect of your child's early morning behavior. Also try to
make her feel like a big kid during the day.

After several days to a week, you should see some progress. Consistency, patience, and building your child's self-esteem are your major keys
to success.

When you are finally sure that your child can stay in her bed until
seven, or whatever time you have set as your goal, you can gradually stop
using the clock-radio. You can do this by setting it only every second or
third night until she no longer needs it at all.

DEVELOPMENTAL FACTORS
THAT CAN DISRUPT SLEEP

Fears are a normal part of growing up. As we all know, the continuing
process of becoming independent and self-sufficient isn't always easy.
There are many surprises and conflicts along the way, and often there are
setbacks. As Ames and Ilg of the Gesell Institute have pointed out, children seem to alternate between stages of relative calm and contentment
and stages where they are easily upset.

The months between one and a half and three years of age are no
exception. Many children develop fears and anxieties, some of which can

keep them up at night. They may have trouble falling asleep or staying asleep, or their fears may come out during sleep, in the form of a nightmare. (We discuss night terrors, which are different from nightmares, in Chapter Five.) In any of these situations, you should realize that your child is going through a completely normal developmental stage. Even the most well-adjusted child who has always slept through the night without a hitch may now have a few unsettled nights. Once she has worked through whatever is bothering her, she will be able to return to her old sleep habits.

The approach for this type of developmental sleep disruption is to reassure your child so that she eventually feels comfortable again. This is quite different from the approach for correcting poor habits, in which you have to limit your nighttime attention so that your child can learn to become more independent. It is important, then, for you to sort out what is keeping your child up before you decide what to do.

The following discussion is designed for the child who normally sleeps well but is now having a few rough nights. If, on the other hand, your child doesn't usually sleep through the night on her own, you should review our sections on habits. Fears may well be intensifying her sleep problems, but once you get control of them, you will have to continue to work on improving her usual sleep patterns.

Bedtime and Middle-of-the-Night Fears

Young children, like anyone else, often become their most insecure and fearful at night, when they are tired. There are any number of things that can frighten a child at bedtime or in the middle of the night. Fear of the dark, of being alone, or of wetting the bed can make it difficult for her to either fall asleep or stay asleep. She may have a hard time relaxing because she has had a frightening experience during the day, or because her imagination is working overtime. In any of these cases, the following guidelines should help point you in the right direction.

GUIDELINES FOR HELPING YOUR CHILD OVERCOME FEARS

1. If you have more than one child, consider having your fearful child share a room with her brother or sister. Don't worry about one disturbing the other. They will probably work it out quickly on their own if you don't interfere. Although there are a lot of different age and temperament combinations that make each situation unique, here is one example of how easily children can help each other: The younger sister, Jenny, wakes up in

the middle of the night and starts to pester her five-year-old sister. "Alice, wake up. Hi, Alice!" Alice rolls over, sleepily opening her eyes, "Huh?" "Hi, Alice," says wide-eyed two-year-old Jenny. It's a lot if Alice gets out under her breath a muffled "I'm sleeping." The main point here is that the presence of the big sister is reassuring, and she is *naturally* doing just what is needed to help her sister sleep through the night. The little sister may keep trying to talk to her older sister, but after a few nights of being simultaneously ignored and reassured, she will finally be independent. She may still wake up, but she will get herself back to sleep. We urge you, then, to give this arrangement a try.

2. If you don't have another child, or if you prefer to keep your children in separate rooms, consider buying your fearful child a pet for nighttime company. Even a bedside fish tank may help.

3. Help your child become attached to a security object that she can keep in bed with her. This often helps a child feel more relaxed through the night.

4. No matter what your child seems to be afraid of, a night-light can help. The dark has a way of triggering almost any child's fears. You can also try leaving the door to her bedroom ajar, so she doesn't feel isolated from the rest of the family.

5. Don't make toilet-training an issue at night. If you keep your child in overnight diapers well past the time you think she needs them, she won't worry about wetting the bed.

6. If your child clings to you as you tuck her in for the night, or if she calls out or screams in fear, go back to her bed and ask her what is wrong. Even at eighteen months, she may be able to give you a clue. Then, you can say something like "Darling, you are safe; we are here to make sure you stay safe. We'll make sure nothing hurts you so you can be snug in your bed all night long." Continue in this reassuring vein, adapting what you say to the context of her fear. Be sure you communicate the idea of safety over and over again.

7. Similarly, if your child wakes up in the middle of the night and can't go back to sleep because she is frightened, go to her and reassure her. Repeat the message about being safe, that you are there for her, and that she will be fine.

8. Don't ever dismiss or make fun of your child's fears. Even something

as unlikely as a big truck or strange animal coming into her room are legitimate fears for her. Because of the stage of her development, she can't approach her fears rationally. Therefore, if you mock her fear, you undermine her confidence and the legitimacy of her feelings. Be sure to listen to what she is saying and reassure her.

9. It is equally important that you not build or embellish your child's fears. For example, if she is afraid of monsters on the floor, don't get out a broom and start sweeping them away! Nor should you go from drawers to closet to curtains to under the bed, saying, "No, I don't see a monster here!" If she sees you carrying on like this, it can only fuel her insecurities. (If you are interested in encouraging your child's imagination, you can invent and enact stories during the day. Your child will feel safer exploring her fantasies removed from the time of day and setting in which she is insecure.) There is also the possibility that this type of display can backfire on you in another way. If you have gotten yourself into a regular ritual of dramatically clearing the monsters out of your child's room, she might come to expect this nightly attention and entertainment. After a few nights, she might be telling you that she is afraid of monsters, when in reality she is enjoying your show!

10. Don't ask your child if she wants to get out of bed. Because you want her to learn to cope with and eventually overcome her fears, she should stay in bed and find out for herself that she really is safe. If you bring her into your room, or downstairs with you while you finish the dinner dishes, your message is that her bed isn't a safe place to be. It is much better for you to stay with her in *her* room than for her to join you.

11. If your child gets up in the middle of the night and comes into your room, take her right back and gently tuck her into bed. Again reassure her, but don't let her get up.

12. If your child is too frightened to stay in her room alone, it is okay to *occasionally* stay by her bed until she falls asleep. We don't recommend that you do this too frequently, or even two nights in a row, as she may come to depend on your presence.

13. Make a special effort to build your child's self-confidence during the day. If she feels secure during the day, this can help her feel more secure at night, too. Depending on how old she is and how well she can talk, you might try talking about what it was that bothered her the night before. This open discussion, perhaps combined with a demonstration, can help

her overcome her fear. If she is afraid of motorcycles, for example, you might ask her if she would like to see one close up and touch it. You can also explain that motorcycles *never* come into the house, so that she certainly is safe in her bed.

14. If your child's sleep disruption continues despite all your efforts, it may be simply that she has become dependent on your new attention. After a few nights, then, it is time to step up your efforts in being firm and consistent, at the same time as you reassure her that she is safe in her bed. Review our sections on habits.

15. In rare instances, a child's fears can accelerate and start to affect the rest of her life. If you find that your child is becoming increasingly fearful, it is time to consult your family doctor or pediatrician! It is always best to nip this sort of problem in the bud.

Nightmares

Childhood nightmares are a part of normal development. Like other dreams, nightmares, or "bad" dreams, occur during REM sleep. Their content, however, is frightening or unpleasant, especially for the young child who has a hard time differentiating her dreams from reality.

Most parents can easily tell when their young child is having a nightmare. She may cry out in her sleep and wake up frightened by some event that hasn't really happened. Depending on her age, she may or may not be able to describe the circumstances of her dream. She will, however, respond to you, and within minutes can be comforted enough to calm down. If, on the other hand, your child bolts upright while still asleep, obviously frightened but glassy-eyed and unresponsive to your presence, she may be having a night terror. Although rare, night terrors sometimes affect children of this age group. For a more complete discussion of what night terrors are and how they are different from nightmares, see Chapter Five.

There are lots of different theories about the causes and the significance of dreams and regular nightmares, but most experts agree that they are expressions of a person's innermost thoughts, feelings, concerns, and fears. It should come as no surprise, then, that the young child, who is working so hard to sort out her world, should have an occasional bad dream. At this age, for example, her dreams may reflect her conflict between her dependence on her parents and her drive for independence. The questions and fears that come up as she starts to make friends outside of her family circle and spend more time away from home may also come out in a dream.

As a parent, then, you should look on nightmares as normal expressions of your child's uncertainties and fears. They do not, by themselves, indicate that your child is seriously troubled, but simply that she is worried about something. Of course if your child seems exceptionally stressed during the day and is having regular nightmares, we suggest that you contact your pediatrician so that the two of you can assess what is going on. But if your child is normally happy and well adjusted during the day, don't worry about an occasional nightmare. On the positive side, once your child is able to talk to you about her dreams, you can look on them as a key to better understanding her concerns.

Of course, as parents, we all want to minimize any type of unpleasant experience for our children. With this in mind, there are a few things you can do:

GUIDELINES FOR DEALING WITH NIGHTMARES

1. To cut down on the incidence of nightmares, don't let your child watch frightening or violent TV shows. We don't think that young children should *ever* watch such shows, but especially not at bedtime. A soothing, relaxing bath, bedtime story, or chat with you is a much better way of preparing your child for bed.

2. If your child is simply moaning or complaining in her sleep, don't wake her up. She is probably dreaming, but the unpleasant sensation will probably pass more quickly if you let her stay asleep.

3. If your child suddenly wakes up and screams for you, go to her right away and comfort her. If she is able to tell you what happened in her dream, that may make her feel better. Many young children, however, respond best to physical comfort and distraction. If you calmly hold her on your lap and offer her a glass of water or her teddy bear, she should feel better soon. (Be careful, though, not to let your child get used to a glass of water or other attention in the middle of the night. The only time we recommend this is when she is sick or extremely frightened.) Let her know that she is safe.

4. If your child does tell you what frightened her, don't try to dismiss her fears by saying, "Oh, but that was just a silly dream." The dream was certainly *not* silly to her, and she needs to know that you understand how

she feels. At this age, she may not be able to understand the difference between dreams and reality, so any explanation to that effect may simply confuse her more.

5. On the other hand, don't confirm your child's fears. If you pretend to lock all the windows to keep the bears out or chase away the monsters from under her bed, for example, you are telling her that she has a real reason to be frightened.

6. If your child is too frightened to be left alone, stay with her. It is also fine to *occasionally* invite her into your bed when she is frightened, but don't let this become a habit.

7. If your child is afraid of the dark, put on a night-light or hall light and leave her bedroom door open.

8. If you can figure out what is frightening your child, try talking to her about it during the day, when she isn't so upset. If she has been dreaming about a ferocious dog, for example, you can explain that many dogs really are very nice, tell her stories about dogs, and perhaps take her to meet an especially friendly dog. Slowly, she should be able to overcome her fear.

9. If you find that your child's nightmares are making her afraid of getting into bed and falling asleep, read our suggestions for bedtime fears.

10. If your child seems to be having more and more nightmares or is becoming more fearful during the day, we recommend that you consult your pediatrician or family doctor for further advice.

SITUATIONS THAT CAN DISRUPT SLEEP

It is a rare child who goes through her early years without even occasional sleep disruption. Even if she isn't bothered by the usual habit- and developmentally based problems, there are bound to be situations that temporarily interfere with her usual sleep patterns. Some of the situations that most commonly affect a child's sleep in this age group are illness or hospitalization, the birth of a baby brother or sister, travel, and, occasionally, poor diet. For tips on handling other situations that may come up, refer to other chapters (for example, moving to a new home is discussed in Chapter Three and divorce and a death in the family are discussed in Chapter Five).

Once again, this gets us back to the importance of good sleep habits. If your child is used to sleeping through the night, she will be much less disturbed by the temporary situations that come up. She may have a few nights of poor sleep when she is sick, for example, but once she is better she will have her old good habits to fall back on.

On the other hand, if your child has a history of multiple, long-term sleep problems, illness, travel, or the birth of a new brother or sister can throw her off even more. As you undoubtedly know by now, you find yourself in the confusing situation of having to sort out what is wrong and figure out how to get her back on the right track. If this should happen, we recommend that you first help your child through whatever temporary situational or developmental problem she is having and then turn your attention to her habits. Within just a few weeks, you should see a real difference!

Illness

If you are like most other parents, you have discovered that it's not so easy to avoid the usual round of colds, sore throats, and ear infections. Young children with older siblings tend to get sick a lot because they are exposed to all of their brothers' and sisters' friends. Older toddlers and two-year-olds also thrive on playing with children their own age. Unfortunately, though, they also are at the stage where they rub their eyes and put their fingers in their mouths and noses as they go from one toy to the next, spreading infections. Because children are often at their most contagious when they are just coming down with a virus but before they have obvious symptoms, it is difficult to prevent this spread.

During the second eighteen-month period in your child's life, we feel that it is reasonable to approach illness-related sleep disruption in two ways. If your child is really ill, the most important thing you can do is to give her all your loving care. Do whatever you have to do to manage her illness, even if that means bringing her to your room or bed, or you spending the night in her room. In this case, you need not be concerned with upsetting her usual sleep routines. Your priority is keeping a close watch on her.

On the other hand, if your child has a garden-variety cold virus, try to keep to her usual routine. Don't get her out of her crib or bed and invite her into your bed. More than anything, she needs a good night's sleep, which is best accomplished in her own bed. You can help her breathe more easily by setting up a vaporizer. If she needs additional comforting in the middle of the night, go to her and resettle her quickly.

Normally, once a child is over her illness, she resumes her old sleeping habits. Life is not always this simple, though. Plenty of parents say that after an extended illness or a series of illnesses, they have to start all over getting their children to have good sleep habits. If you are in this position, a firm, no-nonsense approach will help your child get back on the right track. Say something like "I'm so happy you're well again. It's time for you to get back to going to bed and sleeping through the night. Mommy and Daddy want to sleep through the night, too. You need to stay in your bed all night tonight, and I will see you in the morning." Then, make sure you enforce the limits you have set. If she gets out of bed, take her right back, with as little discussion as possible. If she calls or cries, go once to quickly reassure her and tell her, "I'm happy to see that you are fine and it is time for you to get yourself back to sleep." Then leave. Don't give her water, food, juice, or anything else you might have offered when she was ill. You want to nip any of these new expectations in the bud. She must understand that now that she is well, she doesn't get special consideration at night.

Hospitalization

Hospitalization almost always causes some kind of sleep problems in young children, but they don't have to be long-term. Sometimes it is only the hospital routine or the discomfort associated with the illness, surgery, or medical procedure that interferes with sleep. For example, if a child is connected to an intravenous line, she is likely to wake up from the re-straint. Once the needle is taken out, she is able to sleep perfectly well.

Most often, though, a child can't sleep in the hospital because she is frightened. New surroundings, strange people, uncomfortable procedures, and the stress she can sense in you all combine to make hospitalization a traumatic experience for her. Because it is almost impossible to explain to a child of this age exactly what is going on, the best thing is for one of her parents to stay with her at all times, even through the night (many hospitals can provide you with a cot). Your continual presence is the best way to keep her feeling relatively happy and secure. Then, once she returns home, it shouldn't take her too long to get back to her normal schedule.

Don't be surprised, though, if your child does have some trouble settling down to either a nap or nighttime sleep when she returns home. It may take anywhere from a few days to a month for her to get over her hospital experience. In general, wait until she is *completely* well and healed before you try to change her habits. This will give both of you some time to rebuild your confidence and get used to being home again. Once you reach that point, though, she'll feel relieved that you are able to set limits for her, because she will interpret this as a message that she is fine and that any unpleasantness associated with her hospital stay is behind her. Your best tack is to be reassuring (in her room) while you help her enjoy and feel safe in her usual surroundings and bed. If she remains fearful, see our section on bedtime fears for other tips. And as always, if the problem doesn't seem to be getting better, talk to your pediatrician or family doctor.

Birth of a Baby Brother or Sister

Most young children can make an easy adjustment to a new baby brother or sister, provided they are doing well before she is born, and provided they have been properly prepared for his or her arrival. If you don't see to these things, however, you risk creating problems in all areas of your child's behavior, including her sleep.

When you think about it, the birth of a new baby can be one of the most sensitive times for a family. As parents, you are understandably pre-occupied with your infant. But if you communicate this to your older child, especially if she is used to having you all to herself (or only if she is used to being the baby in the family), the new baby can come to represent a competitive threat to her. Because this is the time that your older child's self-concept is evolving, it is particularly important to maintain her sense of security. In general, then, there are three important relationships you have to safeguard: (1) your (and your spouse's) relationship with your child, (2) your child's feelings about herself, and (3) your child's relationship with the new baby.

If you are trying to figure out how well your child is adjusting to having a new baby brother or sister, one thing you can do is look at how she is sleeping. Even if your child hasn't had a history of sleep problems, she may now have trouble falling asleep on her own or start waking up in the middle of the night if she is feeling insecure. Of course she may also be disturbed by the new noise and commotion in the house, so try to keep this in mind as you care for your baby at night.

In any event, common sense should guide you in maintaining special, quality time with your older child. You may not be able to put a lot of time aside to be alone together, but an effort in this direction will certainly help. Let her know that she is as special to you as ever. If it's possible, try to get your spouse or a baby-sitter to care for your baby once in a while so you can have an exclusive outing with her. Also, structure some opportunities for you and her to have happy, positive interaction. It's much easier to build on positive interactions than to have to cope with an escalation of whining and other attention-seeking behavior as the weeks go by.

Your child's feelings about herself are probably the most important of all and certainly will reflect on all her other relationships. If she feels good about herself, she's not likely to feel usurped by the newcomer. Her budding self-esteem can grow, too, as you help make her feel proud to be the big kid she so strongly aspires to be. The most successful way to build her positive self-concept is to compliment her when she handles any situation well. Let her know that she should be satisfied for a job well done! When she has difficulty, give her the tools that will help her cope better. As parents, we sometimes assume that young children should have all the social skills for handling little problems that come up. Most of the time, kids need to be clued in at their level of understanding.

If you work hard at safeguarding the first two relationships, you will find that you are naturally able to safeguard your child's positive feelings for her baby sister or brother, as they are all intertwined. While it is hard to imagine how a newborn can participate at so early an age, start to promote the idea that your children are part of a team. Let your older child know that since she is older, she has a special place on the team for now, and that the new baby will grow to admire her a great deal. Give her lots of positive reinforcement for all the wonderful ways she plays and entertains the baby, and also let her help with as many baby-related tasks as she wants to (for example, bringing a diaper, sitting down and holding the baby, giving the baby a bottle of water or milk). Keep in mind, though, to never leave the two children alone together, as a two-year-old isn't old enough to ensure the baby's safety. Also be sure to never single out your older child as the bad one and the baby as the good one. It's important to closely watch the development of this kind of pattern from the beginning, as children tend to live up to their reputations.

GUIDELINES FOR AVOIDING NIGHTTIME PROBLEMS WITH YOUR OLDER CHILD WHEN THE NEW BABY ARRIVES

1. Make sure your child has good sleep habits before the baby arrives. You are going to be too tired to cope with extra nighttime demands when you have a newborn to look after. Besides, you'll help your child feel more secure if she has a solid routine before the baby arrives.

2. If you are planning to have your baby in the hospital, let your older child know of your plans in advance. Even if you are only planning to be away one night, you must prepare her for your absence. Let her know who will be staying with her (or whom she will be staying with) so that there are no surprises at the last minute. If at all possible, arrange to have your older child visit you in the hospital. Many hospitals now have special visiting hours for older brothers and sisters.

3. Don't change your bedtime or nighttime expectations of your older child when the new baby arrives. Your firm, loving consistency will make her feel confident that nothing has changed. If you start to lower your expectations of her, you will not only wreak havoc with her habits, but you will also give her the message that she has good reason to feel insecure.

4. The arrival of a new baby is a good time to give your child something new and special to snuggle at night: a toy, stuffed animal, a doll, or new comforter. Or as you fix up the baby's crib or bassinette, you can let your older child choose some new sheets for her bed, as well. Other nice gifts include a cassette or record player, books, a new poster, or enticing wallpaper.

5. It is fine to have extra cuddling sessions in your bed after the baby is born, but not in the middle of the night. Also, don't let these cuddling sessions replace your child's regular bedtime ritual. If necessary, have your spouse or other helper take her through those steps on which she relies.

6. If your child wakes up in the middle of the night, give her your loving reassurance, but insist that she stay in her bed. If you start pitying her and take her to your room, you are actually building her feelings of displacement rather than reassuring her that she is safe and secure as always. If she awakens only because of the baby's crying, tell her that you are sorry that the baby has awakened her, but that for now she'll have to get herself back to sleep. Tell her that as the weeks go by, the baby will wake up less and less, until she is able to sleep the whole night the way big children do. Then make an effort to take your crying baby to the other end of the apartment or house.

7. If you plan to put your children together in the same room, inform your older child of your plans. Let her know that as soon as the baby is sleeping through the night, you'll move her into her room. This will give your older child the opportunity to look forward to sharing nighttime company with the baby. Say something to her like "As soon as the baby is

big enough to go without nursing at night, you lucky kids will get to sleep in the same room together."

8. If your children are not going to be sharing a room, make it clear to your older child that the baby will soon sleep in her own room, too. This way, you let her know that the baby is only in your room for a short time. Tell your older child that you know the baby will love her new bedroom just as much as she loves her room now.

Travel

As your child grows out of toddlerhood, she should make a reasonably good traveling companion. There is no reason why you can't have lots of good times in your travels as long as you pay attention to a few important points.

GUIDELINES FOR MINIMIZING SLEEP DISRUPTION WHEN YOU TRAVEL

1. Begin to prepare your child for your departure at least a few days before you actually leave. Tell her if you will be traveling in an airplane, or on a train, and perhaps even buy her a picture book that the two of you can look at together so that she can get used to the idea.

2. In general, children behave away from home as they do at home. If your child has poor sleep habits at home and you have not been consistent in managing her, you can expect her sleeping troubles to continue, or perhaps escalate, away from home. She will understand that you are concerned about disturbing others, so her demands for attention may increase accordingly. Therefore, if she has good sleep habits *before* you leave home, you will have a much better time traveling together. Don't set yourself up for a real disappointment!

3. Bring your child's love object, a familiar blanket, a familiar book or two, and several small toys with you. Besides her attachment to her love object, these other few things serve as pleasant reminders of home and reassuring routines.

4. If you are traveling by air through time zones, you should expect your child to be as affected as you are by the time change. Depending on how far you travel, the transition to a new time zone can take several days (as a rough rule, you can figure that it takes one day to adjust to each hour of difference). If you are only going to be away for a few days, you might not want to change your schedule at all. If you are planning an extended

vacation to a distant location, you might want to start making the adjustment to the new time zone *before* you leave home (perhaps half before you leave and half after you get there).

5. Most young children can't go a whole day without a nap. You may think that your child can, and she may be able to once in a while, but you are pushing her to her limits if you don't give her a chance to recharge during the day. Therefore, always try to put aside an hour or two for a nap (or at least some quiet time). Also keep in mind that kids this age are usually best in the morning, so plan your most energetic excursions for the morning.

6. Although you should be flexible, keep your child to her regular routines as much as possible. She'll feel safer with the same kind of routines and bedtime rituals that she has at home.

7. It isn't the best idea to use baby-sitters when you are traveling, but sometimes you just can't help it. Make sure your baby-sitter comes with references and that she has had ample awake time with your child before you leave.

8. If you are away from home for only a short time, and especially if you are moving around quite a bit, don't try to change a well-established sleep habit. When her surroundings are unfamiliar, your child may need all the security that old habits and attachments can offer. On the other hand, if you are in one place for several weeks or so and you don't have to worry about neighbors close by, this may be the opportune time to put an end to a bottle-in-bed habit or nighttime attention. Some families feel better equipped to face these situations when they are on vacation and removed from the regular pressures of their lives.

Poor Diet and Food Allergies

Although we feel that the most important factors in determining a child's sleep habits are the parent's attitudes and management of their child, there are occasional situations that warrant a closer evaluation. Poor diet and food allergies are increasingly mentioned as reasons for a child's out-of-bounds behavior, including bedtime behavior. Although we think that a poor diet or food allergies cannot be solely responsible for behavior problems, they may contribute to them.

Therefore, if you suspect that your child is sensitive to certain foods (such as milk, wheat, or citrus), try eliminating the suspect foods from her diet and see if it makes a difference. In addition, foods with lots of sugar or those that are heavily laced with preservatives and food dyes have been frequently cited as potential culprits.

Probably an even rarer diet-related cause of sleep problems is calcium deficiency. Therefore, at this age when many children give up nursing and taking a bottle, make sure that your child is continuing to get milk (or other dairy products such as cheese and yogurt) or some other source of calcium every day.

Also remember that a poor diet will be reflected as much in your child's daytime behavior as in her nighttime behavior. So keep a close watch on how she behaves and feels during the day as well as on what she is eating before you jump to any conclusions. If you suspect food allergies or poor diet, discuss this with your pediatrician or family doctor.

QUESTIONS/ANSWERS

1. My twenty-two-month-old goes to bed every night at seven-thirty. She almost always goes down without any fuss at all. The problem is that she sometimes talks to herself for an hour or an hour and a half before she falls asleep. If she hears me, she will call out. Otherwise, she entertains herself. I'm starting to feel guilty that maybe I'm putting her to bed before she is really tired. What do you think?

First, let us congratulate you. The fact that your child can stay in her bed independently means that you have encouraged good sleep habits. Let us reassure you, too. Because this is an age of rapid speech development, it only makes sense that a child would repeat and rehearse all the wonderful new sounds she has learned to string together during the day. A lot of children spend wakeful but peaceful time in their cribs consolidating their newly acquired language skills. The best approach is to let her be. In our experience, this evening wakefulness is temporary, and within a matter of weeks, her chattering will taper off and she'll start falling asleep earlier again.

If you are concerned that your child isn't tired when you are putting her to bed, you can make two minor alterations in her routine: put her down for an earlier afternoon nap and put her bedtime back to eight o'clock. If she continues her wakeful chattering, this will confirm that there is a developmental reason for her delayed sleep. Don't get her up and entertain her during this spurt of language development or she may not so easily resume her old falling-asleep pattern.

2. I just switched my twenty-seven-month-old daughter into a big bed and am having a horrible time getting her to stay there at bedtime. She seems to love the new freedom she has, and nothing I say seems to make a difference. My friends tell me that I'm not very consistent about bedtime and I guess it's true. Sometimes I let her get out of bed after I've tucked her in. Other times, I don't give her permission to get up and I lose my temper after the fifth or sixth time she gets up on her own, even threatening her with putting her back in her crib. What can I do to avoid this unpleasantness but still make her stay in bed?

First of all, it is important to understand that many young children like to test their parents by repeatedly getting out of bed. As in your daughter's case, this often happens at the time a child is switched from crib to bed. From your description, it sounds as if your problem results primarily from two mistakes that are easy to make: (1) not being clear enough in communicating with your child and (2) inadvertently rewarding your child with nightly entertainment when she continues to get out of bed.

Let's discuss the communication issue first. Since you haven't been consistent, you are giving your child what psychologists call a "mixed message." You may not realize that you are doing this, so let us explain how it works. For discussion, we have divided mixed messages into two types: those based on situations that crop up unexpectedly and those based on your own ambivalent feelings that you might communicate to your child.

As an example of a situational mixed message, you may say something to your child like "You may not get out of bed." But then, if your husband comes home unexpectedly, you might then allow her to get out of bed to spend some time with him. Another example of a situational mixed message could be that you say, "It's bedtime and you have to stay in your bed." She then proceeds to tell you that she is hungry so you let her out of bed for a snack. Or you could tuck her in for the night, begin another task or answer the phone, and then realize ten or fifteen minutes later that she is out of bed. The possibilities are endless, and in each case you gave your daughter a mixed message because your action didn't follow up your words. Another way of defining the mixed message is dividing it into the word message and the action message. When you do this, though, you must realize that a child will always take the part of the message that she likes the most, ignoring the rest.

The other type of mixed message comes about when parents feel torn or ambivalent about an issue themselves. This ambivalence may come from guilt or simply because they aren't sure themselves how they feel about an issue. For example, more and more we hear about working mothers who feel guilty about not spending as much time with their children as they would like. Children are amazingly adept at picking up this ambivalence, so even though a parent may say, "You have to stay in bed now," the child will understand it if she means, "I love your company and haven't seen enough of you today and I want to be with you."

The second reason, besides mixed messages, that your daughter might be continuing to get out of bed is the simple entertainment value of both your words and your actions. Many parents in your position go through a process of pleading, cajoling, lecturing, raising their voices, gesticulating, losing their temper, and maybe even passing the buck to the other parent. Although you may be hot under the collar, your child is finding your act the best in town! To make matters worse, you probably fall into the common pitfall of repeating your repertoire every night. If you give it a second thought, you will marvel at how, even though you're not getting successful results, *you keep managing the problem in the same way!*

So now let's look at some ways to change your situation and get on the right track! In a nutshell, you want to be as nonentertaining and clear in your message as possible. First, though, you have to be sure yourself of what you want and clear about your plans. Once you are committed, give yourself a week to get results. Tell your child when you tuck her in, "You must stay in bed tonight." (Linguistic specialists advise against saying, "Don't get out of bed." For some reason, young children don't process the "don't" message; they only hear the "get out of bed" part of the message!) Look your daughter right in the eyes to let her know that you mean what you say. Then leave her room, but stay alert and close by in order to be prepared to back up your words with actions. During this training period, don't let *any* situation be an exception. In this context, don't be concerned if your daughter cries, as this may be her way of resigning herself to her new limits. Or, if she gets out of bed and comes to you again, simply take her right back to bed and repeat, "You must stay in bed." Do this as many times as necessary, trying not to lose your temper. Keep in mind your goal of giving her one message only. We think you will be amazed at how fast your daughter catches on.

3. My two-and-a-half-year-old is in daycare every day from eight-fifty to four-thirty. Although his teachers tell me that he does very well once he gets going, I have a terrible time getting him settled there every morning. Maybe he's just not a morning person. I have to wake him up every morning at about eight-fifteen to give him breakfast and get him ready to leave the house. He seems to resent being awakened and resists getting dressed and having breakfast. What can I do to avoid our morning struggles and get us all off to a better start?

No doubt about it, running a household in the morning can be one of the biggest challenges of the day! With more and more mothers due at work along with fathers, getting everyone off bright and early can be extremely complicated. We all strive for the idyllic household that runs smoothly and in which everyone cooperates. Like just about anything else, though, this won't happen on its own. Once again, the key here is organization and planning. As unglamorous as this may sound, it can make a real difference in getting you off on the right foot.

First of all, your son should be getting up out of bed much earlier so he can begin his days in a more relaxed fashion. Quite possibly, he is going to bed too late. In order for a two-year-old to be rested by seven or seven-thirty in the morning, he probably should get to bed by seven or seven-thirty in the evening. Like many other working parents, you may be delaying bedtime so that you and your spouse can have more time with him. On balance, though, that extra evening time is probably not worth the problems it causes in the morning.

If you find that you have trouble getting your son to fall asleep at the earlier hour, find out if he is taking too late or too long an afternoon nap. Explain your situation to his daycare teachers. They should understand and be able to help you adjust his daytime schedule. Then, once he is going to bed early enough, he will be able to wake up on his own (or you can help him along with some normal morning household noises). This should help him feel less rushed and irritable.

Another good idea is to lay his clothes out every night before you put him to bed. This activity can become part of his bedtime ritual. It may also be helpful to establish a regular morning routine so that he can anticipate the steps without being nagged. For example, he could first get dressed, then have breakfast, and then be helped to brush his teeth and hair. Don't let him play or watch TV until all these things have been taken care of. He will quickly get used to this new pattern, and it is our bet that this, combined with the other suggestions, will make an enormous difference in easing his transition from home to daycare.

4. I adore my thirty-three-month-old son, but he is the type of kid who always seems to push limits. We don't have any significant bedtime problems, but we would if we relaxed our firm stand. He always comes up with a good reason to get us into his room after we have tucked him in for the night. His latest excuse is that he is cold and needs to be covered. It's not just once that he makes this request, either. Should we go in and cover him or should we just ignore him?

Congratulations on holding a firm stand. Although it may represent considerable work for you, in the long haul your efforts will pay off. While you are in the thick of the bedtime vigil, it is hard to appreciate the humor in the situation. But if you can step back momentarily, you will marvel at your son's cleverness and his ability to get your attention. His initiative should hold him in good stead for other pursuits in life!

Getting back to the present, though, the best way to manage your son's requests for covers is to tell him that you will come in to cover him only *after* he is asleep. Be sure to tell him this as you are tucking him in, so you don't need to interact with him once you have said good night. In order to make sure that he really isn't cold, dress him in warm blanket sleepers and make sure that the room temperature is comfortable. Given your description of your son, he may well begin requesting something else at bedtime, but your usual firm approach will eventually prevail. (For further discussion on bedtime delay tactics, see Chapter Five.)

5. My two-and-a-half-year-old is at the "why" stage! When I tell him he has to stay in bed, he asks, "Why, Mommy?" My friends tell me that I have foot-in-mouth disease! I always get sucked in and he ends up getting at least fifteen minutes of extra attention out of me. I love his curiosity, and it is something I would never want to stifle, but I don't know how to handle all his "why" and "what for" questions at bedtime.

Your child has cleverly found a way to prolong bedtime. He knows how much you adore him, and he is using it to his advantage! It's quite natural, of course, for you to appreciate your son's curiosity and talents. Many parents fall prey to this enchanting effort to stall bedtime. Like you, however, they also realize that it can get out of hand and lead to greater bedtime problems. The best way to approach this, then, is to encourage his curiosity during the day, but not when he is supposed to be getting ready for bed.

We suggest you say something to your son like "I love all your wonderful questions, and I'll be happy to answer them in the morning at breakfast! For now, it's time for bed. Good night. I love you." Then leave his room. Don't get involved in any more dialogue. If he gets out of bed, simply say, "You have to stay in bed," but don't offer any explanation. You're better off not repeating the message, even if you have to escort him back to bed another time. He'll get the message that it's bedtime if you are firm and friendly and don't offer any secondary gain.

6. I am a divorced, working mother with two young children. My younger child, who is two (the other is five), has had a lot of sleep problems since she was a baby. First, I have trouble getting her to bed in the evening. Then, once I get her down for the night, she doesn't stay down. She ends up in my bed every night. I feel bad for her that she has been in daycare and that she has been deprived of a life with her father. I also have ambivalent feelings about being too strict with her. My older daughter doesn't have any sleep problems. What can I do?

First of all, try not to be so hard on yourself and recognize that any child, not just a child of a divorced mother, can have sleep problems. And it isn't at all uncommon that one child in a family sleeps much better than another. It doesn't take something as major as a divorce to create sleep problems. It usually happens because parents either don't know how to manage a particular child or ,are too busy or unwilling to confront the problem until it is out of hand.

Ambivalent feelings often contribute to undesirable behavior. (For example: "I don't spend enough time with my child." "I just had another baby and she feels displaced." "I'm afraid she won't trust me if I let her cry." "I don't want to make her more insecure than she already is.") Unfortunately, this type of reasoning can act as a self-fulfilling prophecy. Your child will certainly pick up on your mixed feelings and respond in an equally confused way. Of course no situation is cut-and-dry, but at least try to give your child some real guidance. Otherwise, she will more likely than not live up to your fears.

Although we know of no magic solutions that will instantly rid you of your guilt and ambivalence, there are a few things you can do that will help alleviate some of these feelings. Since you have to work to support your family, you should try to organize your nonworking time so that you reserve some time for your children every day. Such time-saving tips as making several of your week's dinners over the weekend, freezing lunches, and doing household tasks after the children are in bed will give you an extra hour (or more) on workdays to play and relax with your children. Also, it is important to choose daycare carefully. If your child is having a wonderful experience in her daycare, you are less likely to feel bad about leaving her. Stay in close touch with her caretakers so that you can share her development with them and learn about her life away from you.

Once you have made a few concrete changes in managing your time together, you will start to feel more confident about what you have to offer your child. Pitying your daughter is not constructive for either of you. You'll help her a lot more in the long run if you work toward building her feelings of self-esteem and give her the ability to sleep independently at night. Provided you are friendly, firm, and consistent, your child will interpret your new enforcement of limits as a signal that she can relax and feel safe. You can also encourage her sense of community with her sister (this is particularly helpful to working mothers) by having the girls share a room. For specific suggestions for getting your two-year-old on the right track at night, see our section on habit-related sleep disruptions.

7. Every time I give my twenty-three-month-old some decongestant for a cold, she seems to be up all night long. Is there a connection between the medicine and her wakefulness, or is it just because she feels under the weather?

It is quite possible that your child is being kept awake by the medicine, and not just because she is not feeling well. Decongestants work in the body by causing vasoconstriction (shrinkage of blood vessels) and reducing edema (fluids) of the lining of the respiratory tract. But besides helping to dry up a cold, decongestants are also known to stimulate the brain, which can result in insomnia, restlessness, and hyperactivity. Some people seem to be more sensitive to this effect than others, just as some people are more sensitive to the stimulating effects of caffeine. Therefore, if you suspect that your child is being kept awake by the medicine you are using, we suggest that you first analyze exactly what you are giving her, and then see if she sleeps better without the medication. Because decongestants are intended only to make your child feel better (but not get rid of her illness), it isn't necessary that you use them. It is very different, for example, from when your doctor prescribes an antibiotic medicine that is necessary for combatting an infection. So if the decongestant is keeping your daughter up at night, it isn't really helping her to feel better at all, and she is best off without it.

Before you condemn all cold preparations, however, it is worth your while to analyze the different drugs that can be found in them. It is quite possible that one drug will have more of an effect on your child than another. Also, many cold preparations don't have just one ingredient, so you have to spend some time reading labels and figuring out exactly what you are giving your child.

To first get back to decongestants, then, the most common drugs are phenylpropanolamine hydrochloride and phenylephrine hydrochloride. The first drug, in particular, is known to have stimulant effects. Another common decongestant, pseudoephedrine hydrochloride, is sold under the trade name of Sudafed.

Frequently, though, decongestants are sold in combination with other drugs, mainly antihistamines, expectorants, and cough suppressants. Antihistamines, which work to combat allergic responses and dry up the nose and throat, also tend to make people sleepy. This way, the stimulant effects of decongestants are usually balanced by the sedative or drowsiness properties of antihistamines. The most common antihistamines are chlorpheniramine maleate and phenyltoxolamine citrate. Another common antihistamine, usually marketed not in combination but as a single preparation, is diphenhydramine (one brand name is Benadryl).

Expectorants are designed to loosen secretions in the respiratory tract (bronchial tubes), although their usefulness is questionable. They are not known to have any effect on behavior. Cough suppressants, on the other hand, inhibit a person's desire to cough. The most common cough suppressants are dextromethorphan, which may be a mild sedative, and codeine (by prescription only), which is a potent sedative.

And finally, other common ingredients in most liquid medicines designed for children are artificial coloring and flavoring. Although the evidence is not clear-cut, these substances have been linked to hyperactivity in sensitive children.

As you can see, then, deciding on using a decongestant or cold preparation is a complicated matter. Because we are deluged with so many advertisements for cold remedies and have such easy access to over-the-counter medications, we tend to get quite relaxed about giving our children these things. We must keep in mind, though, that they are drugs and carry with them the possibility for undesirable side effects, such as insomnia. Our advice, then, is to carefully evaluate exactly what you are giving your child and monitor the effect it has. If you have questions about the ingredients, ask your doctor or pharmacist for help.

8. My thirty-one-month-old goes to bed in his own bed but comes to our bed every night around midnight. He spends the rest of the night in our bed, nursing on and off. I have been waiting for him to wean himself, hoping that at the same time he will naturally give up sleeping with us. I haven't had a full, uninterrupted sleep in two and a half years. Besides feeling tired, I feel upset about a lot of things in my life. My husband and I have reached rock bottom in our relationship. My friends keep telling me that my child will not wean himself and that I'll have to force the issue. They give me a hard time about nursing him all the time, as he is pretty much on and off the breast all day, too. I feed him so much because he is underweight and doesn't seem to be growing very well; that is why I have been reluctant to wean him or cut down his feedings. What do you think I should do?

We think your first step should be to take your son to your pediatrician for a complete work-up. If he is not growing or gaining weight properly, you certainly want to get to the bottom of this situation. Also, you have to understand that if you haven't slept through the night for several years, you are operating at a real disadvantage. Your ability to analyze and respond to your situation in a reasonable and logical way is compromised by your fatigue. Therefore, before you can start to address your many feelings and problems, you must first teach your son to sleep through the night *in his own bed* so that you can get on top of your exhaustion. Then, because you have so many confused feelings, we think you should consider getting some professional help as well.

Although we are not physicians or psychologists, there are a few suggestions we would like to make. From your description, it sounds as if nursing is interfering with your son's normal growth and development. Although weaning is always a personal decision, we think it would be the best idea for your son. First of all, with him at your breast around the clock, nursing is most likely hindering, rather than helping, his nutrition. A two-and-a-half-year-old cannot thrive on milk alone, and a constant nursing habit definitely interferes with regular mealtimes. And besides interfering with his eating habits, nursing a child of this age and in this fashion interferes with his ability to comfort himself and with his growing need to become more independent. It is also quite possible that all this around-the-clock nursing has delayed the maturation of his sleep physiology.

Given this situation, we feel that the best way for you to wean your son is cold turkey. Because he nurses so frequently, he has grown to look to your breasts for emotional security, in much the same way that other children view their blankets or teddy bears. An attachment like this is very difficult to decrease gradually, because he will always think of your breasts first when he gets tired, cranky, or scared. Therefore, although you will have several difficult days, we think the easiest way for you to succeed is to provide him with a substitute security object and stop nursing him altogether.

When you get up tomorrow morning, then, tell your son firmly that you are not making any more milk. Make your breasts as inaccessible as possible by wearing clothes that are inconvenient for breast-feeding. When he comes to you and tries to nurse, pick him up in your arms, give him a big hug with a new security object, and then distract him by playing with him. Offer him three good meals a day, with only healthy snacks.

When you tuck him in at bedtime, tell him he has to stay in his bed all night. Make sure he has his cuddly love object with him. When he comes to your bed at midnight, take him right back to his bed and tell him that he needs to stay there until morning. If you need to, for the first few days, sit with him until he gets himself back to sleep. Don't nurse him and don't give him a bottle in bed. (For more suggestions, see our sections "How to Move Your Child out of Your Bed" and "How to Wean Your Child from Nighttime Feedings").

In the meantime, during this adjustment period, do everything you can to build your child's feelings of self-esteem and desire to be a big boy. At first he'll feel torn about what direction he wants to follow (some of his infantile desires will still tug at him), but as the first few weeks pass, you will notice that the scale will be tipped in favor of moving toward childhood.

Once the two of you have gotten over the initial shock of not nursing anymore, we feel confident that your sleep will improve, too. Although this may in itself straighten out your other problems, you may also find that you could still benefit from talking to a psychologist or other counselor. In any case, you have made the first crucial step!

Chapter Five

FROM THREE TO FIVE YEARS

The Preschool Years

The Preschooler's Self-esteem: On the Road to Independence

Developing the Art of Positive Communication

To Nap or Not to Nap

Sleep-Disturbing Habits

How to Enforce Bedtime

How to Help Your Child Be Independent at Night

Developmental Factors That Can Disrupt Sleep

Bedtime and Middle-of-the-Night Fears

Nightmares

The Parasomnias

Night terrors

Sleepwalking and sleep-talking

Bed-wetting

Situations That Can Disrupt Sleep

School-Related Stress

Illness

Hospitalization

Divorce

Death

Questions/Answers

My daughter didn't start sleeping through the night until she was four and a half. My seven-year-old nephew arrived at that time to start a six-month stay with us. For lack of space, I put him in the same room as my daughter. It was like magic! I guess his presence reassured her, because from then on, she began to sleep through the night. Let me tell you, going from four years of constant sleep disruptions to being able to count on a good night's sleep was like being visited from the heavens! By the time he left, my daughter had outgrown her night-waking problem.

—*Relieved Mother*

THE PRESCHOOL YEARS

The preschool years are a time of intense cognitive, social, and emotional development. Like children of all other ages, three-to-five-year-olds seem to alternate between periods of being calm, secure, and well adjusted and periods of being rebellious, insecure, and anxious. The overall trend, however, is toward becoming a more reasonable and accomplished person. The road toward maturity and away from complete dependence on one's parents is sometimes bumpy, but a lot of the time there's no alternate route.

According to Drs. Ames and Ilg of the Gesell Institute of Child Development, who have studied the development of thousands of children over the years, the typical three-year-old is a happy, secure, and friendly person. His emotions and behavior are usually under control, and he takes enormous pleasure in the company of other people. He especially likes being and doing things with his parents, but he also enjoys children his own age.

Sometime around the middle of the fourth year, however, children often become more rebellious and strong-willed. It's almost as if they are tired of always working to please someone else and are now testing ways to please themselves. As a result, your three-and-a-half-year-old may refuse to go along with even your simplest requests, stubbornly following his own inclination. Many three-and-a-half-year-olds have trouble with everyday routines; eating, getting dressed, and getting ready for bed can be trying experiences for everyone. And perhaps as an expression of this intense experimenting and testing, this is the age when many children become attached to imaginary friends, or perhaps take on the role of an imaginary character themselves. But although your three-and-a-half-year-old may be difficult to live with, remember that his behavior is perfectly normal.

Of course subject to the variations of individual temperaments and developmental timetables, the fourth birthday often marks the beginning of another stage. Enthusiastic, outgoing, and often boisterous, the typical four-year-old enjoys life and seems to revel in his own power and abilities. He is busy and active and loves new experiences. And not only does he feel comfortable with himself, he is becoming much more adept in social situations. Now in his second year of nursery school, he not only plays well in a one-on-one situation but also participates in group activities. He has slowly become less egocentric and more concerned with the welfare of others. His play is sometimes wild, and he is quite capable of spinning out of control, but all in all, this is a very happy and positive time.

Continuing along Ames and Ilg's model of six-month stages, children often begin a new period of disequilibrium at about four and a half. In between the relative security of four and five, the four-and-a-half-year-old can be unpredictable and therefore difficult to understand. One minute he can be his goofy old four-year-old self, and the next minute he is brooding about something that happened at school. He has learned to project into the future and may worry about what will happen tomorrow. Gradually, he is becoming more introspective and thoughtful and, as can be expected, is sometimes confused by the process.

For many children, five is a quiet, conservative, and conforming age. Gone are the wild, crazy days of a year ago. By and large, five-year-olds like being "good" and doing things "right." They enjoy following rules and take exception if someone doesn't follow suit. Many five-year-olds are homebodies, although most also enjoy their kindergarten class, once they have had time to get used to the new environment.

A lot of the five-year-old's calm is self-imposed. He doesn't fail because he doesn't take risks. This behavior often begins to loosen up after several months, though, as the five-and-a-half-year-old again begins to question and push limits. Of course this is healthy and necessary for his growth and increasing independence, but the process can be hard on everyone, especially his parents. So many times we have heard of children, described by their nursery school or kindergarten teachers as so well-behaved in school, who are terrors at home. Other children are unable to accept the rules at school, too, and act out there, as well. Sometimes it may seem as though you have a split-personality Dr. Jekyll–Mr. Hyde on your hands. One minute your son may be happily working on an art project, and the next minute he throws it and himself on the floor in frustration. Of course all of this makes you think back to the last time he acted this way—perhaps when he was two and a half. Don't worry, though; his behavior is completely normal, and like his previous stages, this, too, will pass.

Right about now you might be saying to yourself, "Thank goodness that doesn't sound like my son. He is much more reasonable than that." Or, perhaps, "You're right. That sounds like him. I feel better knowing that he is normal, but I never knew I was getting myself in for this!" True enough in both cases. As individuals, with different personalities and talents and varying home situations, children develop in their own ways, according to their own schedules. And of course, until you are a parent yourself, you can never fully appreciate what it feels like to go through the more difficult times with your child. So even though you shouldn't expect your child to rigidly adhere to the preceding overview, we hope that it has shed some light on his behavior, and in so doing, helped you to appreciate him for the person he is.

For most three-to-five-year-olds, sleep is not a major issue. By and large, the preschooler's life is so busy and active that sleep comes easily. The vast majority of children give up their daytime nap during this time, and most sleep about eleven hours at night. Although, as we point out in the introduction, many children continue to use delay tactics at bedtime, most do sleep through the night. Like the younger age groups that we have discussed earlier in this book, three-to-five-year-olds occasionally go through developmental stages or have stressful experiences that can temporarily disrupt their sleep. For example, this is the time when a group of sleep disorders known as the parasomnias, which includes night terrors, sleepwalking, and sleep-talking, can first show up. For other children, daily stresses may surface in the form of the more common nightmares or simple bad dreams. More than ever before, though, you should expect your child to have good regular sleeping habits. He has come a long way since he was the seemingly helpless baby of just a few years ago, and it is our hope that you can now look back on his many achievements with fondness and pride.

The Preschooler's Self-esteem:
On the Road to Independence

Sleep and bedtime behavior, like daytime behavior, can be considered reflections of a child's emotional well-being. This is not to say that all bedtime and sleep disturbances are symptoms of emotional instability, because many are based primarily on habit or circumstances, but a child who is insecure during the day is likely to be needy at night as well. Therefore, if your child is having trouble settling down to sleep in the evening or can't stay quietly in his bed throughout the night, one of the first things you should do is to evaluate how secure he feels during the day.

As we point out in the beginning of this chapter, the road to independence is not always easy, and almost all children go through unsettled but normal testing stages along the way. Look at life from your child's point of view: there are a lot of changes going on. Nursery school may well be the first time he has to test his resources outside of the security of home. All of a sudden, he doesn't just have the adoring eyes of mom or dad or the relative security of a daycare center; he is now more aware of other children's and the teachers' opinions as he tries to adapt to the nursery school routines. When he gets home after a demanding morning he may compensate by increasing his demands on you, or he may stubbornly refuse to go along with your simplest requests.

As trying as these times may be, it is important to recognize that part of your child's behavior is aimed at testing his relationship with you. He experiments with his feelings for you and needs to know how you feel about him, now that he is becoming more independent. He may act out just to see your response. This is where your confident parenting skills come in. Don't hesitate to discipline him as you see fit, but be sure he understands that you still love him, no matter how he behaves. Also be sure to compliment him when he behaves well and help him feel proud of all of his achievements. All of this will help him build a foundation of self-esteem that will benefit him for the rest of his life. With your unconditional love backing him all the way, he will feel secure enough to move forward on his own, during the night as well as the day.

Developing the Art of
Positive Communication

In the preceding sections we talk about the importance of feeling comfortable enough to set appropriate limits on your child's behavior. But once you decide on the limits you will set, there are many ways of going about enforcing them, some more successful and positive than others.

Our first piece of advice is to choose your issues carefully. It just doesn't make sense to come down too strongly on something that really isn't that important. If your child wants to pick out his own school clothes, for example, why not let him do it? It may not be what you would have chosen, but does that really matter? If you find yourself at odds with your child about too many things, you will both be too worn out to deal with the issues that really matter, and perhaps unable to enjoy each other's company at all.

Then, once you have decided on the issues that matter most to you, set realistic goals for yourself. If you expect your four-year-old who has never slept through the night on his own to suddenly stop needing you at night, you're setting yourself up for disappointment and frustration. Once a child has developed a strong habit, it will take lots of patience and consistency to change his ways. Just make sure you're moving in the right direction.

When it comes to the actual methods you use for enforcing limits for your preschooler, one of the most important goals is to avoid constant power struggles. If you find yourself frequently reprimanding your child, losing your temper, or shouting at him or spanking him, you are paving the way for future hostilities.

Behaviorists believe that you should always express your thoughts about your child's behavior in a positive way, no matter how critical you are feeling. Their studies have shown that you are much more likely to get results if you emphasize the good and ignore the bad. This approach should be your goal most of the time, although sometime a direct approach is best. Occasionally a strong "No, you can't do that" is the most effective. There are other times when it seems more appropriate to distract, cajole, ignore, reason with, or even bargain with your child. With time you learn what works when, but it isn't so much the actual technique that matters as much as your ability to keep your relationship friendly and positive.

Also, by the time your child is three or four years old, he is old enough for the two of you to have honest chats about his behavior. If you sit down together when you are both calm and unhurried during the day (don't reinforce your child's waking behavior by having a long discussion in the middle of the night), you can explain your expectations to him in a way that he will understand. If he has been getting up every night and coming into your room at 3 A.M., you can explain to him that this behavior is *not* acceptable and that his nightly visits are making you too tired. Try not to get emotional or angry, and finish your talk with lots of hugs and kisses. That way, he'll understand that you still love him, even though you would like to change one aspect of his behavior. You are also laying the groundwork for a future relationship that is based on openness and respect.

To Nap or Not to Nap

Probably about half of three-year-olds take a daytime nap, with most giving it up by the time they are five. Whether your child takes a nap depends on your personal preference and the way you organize his schedule as well as his physiological needs. Whether he naps or not, however, he will probably wind up sleeping the same number of hours a day. For example, a three-year-old who doesn't nap may sleep from 7:30 P.M. until 7 A.M. Another three-year-old may sleep only from 8:30 P.M. to 6:30 A.M. but also nap for an hour and a half during the day.

As we discuss in Chapter Four, the complete transition to not needing a nap can take several months. Your clue that your child is entering this transitional period is obvious: on some afternoons, he simply won't fall asleep. When this first begins to happen, you can do one of two things, depending on your preference: either encourage him to have at least a "quiet time" every afternoon or help him to give up his nap altogether. Although you certainly can't insist that your child sleep when he isn't tired, many children benefit from having a regular time every afternoon to relax and perhaps listen to music or look at picture books. Some afternoons, he may even fall asleep. On the other hand, if your child has been staying up late at night, and you would like him to go to bed earlier, this may be your golden opportunity for change. If you offer him a snack, take him for a short outing, or offer him some other diversion at his normal nap time, he will probably be good and tired and ready for bed earlier in the evening.

In either case, try to be consistent. As we keep stressing, children thrive on regularity in their lives, so it is best to figure out one routine that works for you and try to stick to it. On the other hand, your child may be in an awkward transitional stage for several months, and it won't harm him to have several naps a week during this time.

SLEEP-DISTURBING HABITS

By the time your child is three years old, his sleep patterns are probably quite predictable: either he falls asleep happily and sleeps through the night on a regular basis or he continues to resist bedtime and wake up for one reason or another almost every night. What you have to realize, though, is that sleep patterns, good or bad, don't just happen. Rather, like other aspects of his behavior, they have developed over time. His personality, development, and special situations certainly have all played a part in this picture, but it is also the way you have responded to him, night by night since he was born, that has made the difference.

Regardless of your child's current sleep habits, however, it is our firm belief that *all* healthy children can learn to sleep through the night. One of your most important clues, then, is your child's daytime behavior. If he is happy and well-adjusted during the day, you are safe interpreting his long-term nighttime problems as little more than poor habits. And sometimes troublesome daytime behavior comes from fatigue. Parents often see a marked improvement in their child's daytime behavior once his sleep habits improve.

On the other hand, if your child is extremely anxious, fearful, shy, or having difficulty with his peers, his poor sleep may reflect how unsettled he feels on the whole. His sleep problems could be just another one of his many signals that he is having trouble. If your child fits into this pattern, we urge you to focus on building his feelings of self-esteem, independence, and social competence. If necessary, get some extra guidance from your pediatrician, nurse practitioner, psychologist, or family counselor. The preschool years are a critical time for children, and a lot of the feelings they form about themselves and the world around them stick with them for a lifetime! This is definitely the time to get a handle on your child's problems and turn them around before they compromise his development any further.

Most bedtime and nighttime problems are not emotionally founded, however, and a fresh approach can go a long way in turning things around. If you are like most parents, your heart is in the right place, you love your child more than anything in this world, and your goal is to have him go to bed reasonably happy, without waking up fearful and needy in the night. What may have eluded you is the skills to be effective with your child. So even if your child has always been a problem sleeper, don't be discouraged.

It is just as possible to improve his behavior at bedtime and when he wakes in the middle of the night as it is to improve any other aspect of his behavior. In the following sections, we will show you how. Then, once you get him on the right track, he will quickly get over the occasional situational or developmental disruptions that come up. He will have a firm foundation of good sleep habits to fall back on.

How to Enforce Bedtime

Bedtime resistance seems to be the most common sleep problem among preschoolers. For example, data from the New York Longitudinal Study analyzed by Drs. Beltramini and Hertzig reveal that two thirds of the preschoolers studied required more than thirty minutes to fall asleep every night. Similarly, about half of the preschoolers regularly used delay tactics, calling their parents back for a glass of water, a second good-night kiss, and so on, after being tucked in for the night.

So if your preschooler resists settling down to sleep for the night, he is not unusual. There are, however, several things you can do to avoid nightly struggles and make bedtime pleasant for everyone:

GUIDELINES FOR BEDTIME

1. Before you do anything else, you have to be convinced that your child should have and will benefit from a regular bedtime. If you have been inconsistent for three years or so, this will require a real commitment on your part; without it, you won't succeed.

2. Be sure that you and your spouse are in agreement before you attempt to change your child's bedtime pattern. Talk over a strategy together, and decide *in advance* how you will cope if your child cries for two hours the first evening! Also, if necessary, you might want to tell your neighbors that you are setting new bedtime limits for your child so they won't be alarmed if he cries.

3. Since life-styles, napping patterns, and overall sleep needs vary considerably from one individual to the next, there is no one ideal bedtime for preschoolers. The only way to arrive at a suitable bedtime for your child is to first figure out how many hours of sleep he needs a day and then make sure that these hours fit in with the family schedule. So for two weeks, jot down the number of hours he sleeps each day. Add up the total and divide by fourteen; this will give you a good idea of his daily sleep needs. Given

this figure, you can then try to organize his sleep times to fit the family schedule. For example, if he seems to need eleven and a half hours of sleep a day, is enrolled in a morning nursery school or daycare program, and doesn't nap, you can put him to bed at 7:30 P.M. and expect him to be well rested by 7 A.M. Or you can put him to bed at 8:30 P.M. and let him nap for an hour during the day. Or, if he doesn't have to go anywhere in the mornings, you might choose a later bedtime. But you always get back to the premise that he needs a base line of eleven and a half hours a night (although he may need more if he is sick or under stress).

4. Be sure that your child is actually tired when you are putting him to bed. This may seem obvious, but sometimes parents do try to enforce bedtime for their own convenience. It's easy to understand that children can build up negative feelings about bedtime because they are not in the least bit tired when their parents put them to bed.

5. Make sure your child's bed and bedroom are inviting and comfortable.

6. Once you have decided on your child's bedtime, be *consistent* about it. It will make it easier for him to accept a bedtime if it falls at the same time every day. Establishing a regular bedtime is much like setting an internal clock. It is all right to make occasional exceptions, but too much inconsistency can throw him off.

7. Be sure to incorporate a regular bedtime ritual as part of your child's wind-down transition before bed. An evening bath and bedtime story are valuable ways to help calm your child down after a busy day. Some children have more difficulty than others making transitions and, in particular, falling asleep. If your child is like this, his bedtime ritual may need to be more soothing or longer than that of another child who happens to fall asleep easily.

8. If your child doesn't already have a love object, you can encourage him to bond to one now. Although his attachment may be less intense than that of a two-year-old, it can still be a source of comfort and help him make the transition to sleep. A stuffed animal, a doll, or a blanket is a good choice for a favored love object.

9. Evaluate your bedtime interaction with your child. If you have a struggle every evening, first recognize that whatever you are doing now is *not* working. Step back and think about what is wrong; it could be that you are giving him a mixed message. A mixed message can be made up of

conflicting verbal messages, a verbal message that conflicts with your action, or a verbal message that conflicts with your intent. For example, do you tell your child that he has to stay in bed and then allow him to get out of bed for a snack or some other reason? Or when you tell him that it is bedtime, do you feel guilty or ambivalent at the same time and wish that he might stay up? If you fall into one of these common traps, remember that a child will always take the part of the message he likes the most. When it comes to setting limits for your child, you have to be clear.

10. Although it is natural to feel angry when your child misbehaves, don't let yourself fall into the pattern of regularly losing your temper. Your objective is to have your child feel as secure and positive about bedtime as he does about himself! Being punitive *doesn't* help a child build positive feelings about himself or the task in question.

11. Another reason bedtime can fail is that you may be providing the best show in town. If you are one of those parents who lecture, cajole, plead, and lose their temper, your child may be finding you entertaining. If you were to do a videotape of yourself (and perhaps your spouse) you would see lots of humor in the way you act each night. And if you can see the humor, imagine how much more entertaining you are to your child! Therefore, when you are ready to tuck your child in at night, *be boring and repetitive.*

12. Before you start your new nighttime program, sit down with your child during the day and explain your new expectations. Tell him calmly, but firmly, that you can no longer put up with all his bedtime shenanigans and that, starting tonight, he will have to go to bed on time. Don't make your conversation too long or involved; just make sure that he gets the idea.

13. If your child is toilet-trained, make sure he uses the toilet right before you tuck him into bed. This way, he'll have one less reason to get out of bed.

14. When you are ready to say good night to your child, tell him in a friendly voice that he may not get out of bed and that if he has anything to ask you or tell you, now is the time—before you leave his room. Then, if he gets out of bed, take him by the hand and lead him right back. Be friendly but firm and brief. Repeat this as many times as necessary to make your point. If your child calls out, remind him *once only* that you won't answer him. If he cries or has a temper tantrum, ignore him as best

you can. Don't be alarmed if he complains and cries for as long as two or
three hours the first night. If you are consistent, he will complain less each
succeeding night, and probably not at all within three days to a week. By
the time a month has passed, his bedtime will be a secure landmark in his
daily life.

15. During the day, be sure to reinforce all positive aspects of your child's
bedtime behavior. Say something each morning like "I love the way you
looked at your book quietly in bed last night" or "You are such a big kid
for being able to stay in your bed!" Don't dwell on the problems you
might have had the evening before. In general, the more upbeat and
positive you are with your child, the more he will reward you with his
pleasant self. Remember, you are an important role model for him.

16. If your child has bedtime fears, reassure him *in his own bed* (see our
section on bedtime fears). Keep in mind that you can reinforce your
child's bedtime fears by making a bigger deal out of them than they
actually are. And frequently children insist that they are scared beyond the
time they really are. Perhaps this is because they have grown dependent
on the attention they get, or perhaps the idea of being scared becomes a
habit. In any case, you want to give him the confidence to cope with his
bedtime fears until he completely grows out of them. So use your own best
judgment. As a general rule, be an active listener, tell your child he is *safe*
and snug in his own bed, and that you are there to protect him.

How to Help Your Child Be Independent at Night

By the time your child is three years old, you should feel absolutely
confident that he doesn't need you during the night. Except for the occasional times that he is sick or perhaps frightened, you shouldn't hear from
him at all! Remember, though, that many children who "sleep through
the night" actually wake up periodically; they have learned, however, to
get themselves back to sleep without disturbing the rest of the household.

No one knows for sure what comes first: poor habits or the temperament and sleep physiology that is more prone to night waking. It doesn't
really matter though, since sleep specialists confirm that training plays a
critical role in a child's ability to sleep through the night. This allows us to
be optimistic and assume that all children can learn good, solid sleep
habits as long as we allow for individual differences. Our suggestions, then,
are designed to help your child be independent at night, but not to make

him sleep the same number of hours or at exactly the same time as another child his age.

In the following guidelines, we discuss the most common nighttime problems you might be having with your preschooler. There is no set timetable as to how long it should take your child to learn to sleep through the night, as the degree of his sleep problems, the length of time he has had them, and how consistently you set about changing his ways all make a difference. We warn you, though, to be patient; it takes time to replace old habits with new ones. Although instant solutions sometimes come about, it is more realistic to expect it to take weeks, not days.

One of the most important things you can do while you are helping your child to form new nighttime sleep habits is build his general feelings of confidence and self-esteem during the day. Devise activities at which he can succeed, provide him with playmates to reinforce his developing feelings of social competence, and make a special effort to interact with him in a positive way. These extra steps will make it so much easier for you to enforce the new nighttime limits. Also, the better your child feels about himself, the more confident you will feel about your parenting and your ability to retrain him at night. Feelings of guilt or ambivalence won't help you achieve your goal!

GUIDELINES FOR NIGHTTIME INDEPENDENCE

1. If your child is afraid of the dark, has expressed a lot of bedtime and nighttime fear, or has had frequent nightmares or night terrors, first read our section on developmental factors that can disrupt sleep. It is important for you to sort out as best you can whether your child is currently afraid or whether what was once a fear has become little more than an act of habit. Unless your child is fearful or otherwise disturbed during the day, we think it is unlikely that he is experiencing sustained fear over a period of months or years. So take a close look and decide for yourself. If you believe that your child really isn't so scared after all, you will be able to reassure him with new confidence and firmness. Try to adopt the attitude that he can cope with and eventually master any leftover fears that do exist; having them is not incompatible with learning to sleep through the night.

2. If you have more than one child, consider having your child with the nighttime problems share a room with his sister or brother. Even if you don't want this to be a long-term arrangement, it is one of the best ways to

first get your child sleeping independently at night. After several months go by and he feels confident, you can then put him back in his own room, if you want. In the meantime, don't worry about one child disturbing the other; if you don't intervene, this rarely becomes a problem.

3. Make sure your child's bed and bedroom are inviting. If you haven't already done so, set up a bedside table with a lamp, a special place for your child's favorite toys and books, and perhaps a clock-radio or cassette player. Decorative sheets and attractive posters are another way of making his room more attractive. If your child needs or wants one, also set up a night-light. This can be a closet light, a hall light, or a traditional child's night-light, but it shouldn't be a regular glaring overhead light.

4. If your child doesn't already have a love object, it may not be too late for him to bond to one. Although his attachment may not be as intense as it would have been when he was younger, he can still find a love object comforting at sleep times.

5. Before you try to retrain your child to sleep through the night, you and your spouse should agree as to how you are going to proceed. Don't wait until the night to discuss your strategy. If you talk out your plan ahead of time, you minimize the possibility of misunderstandings. As a team, you have a much greater chance at success.

6. Pick a time in your life when you are feeling relaxed. If you have a lot of outside pressure on you, you are much less likely to be consistent. Chances are that not only will you be ineffective but you may also end up feeling more ambivalent and angry toward your child. It's better to not even try to change your child's sleep behavior until you are prepared to give it at least a few weeks of your undivided attention.

7. Similarly, pick a time when your child isn't under stress. If he is just starting nursery school or you have recently moved to a new home, for example, wait until he feels settled in before you try to change his sleep habits.

8. As you start to build new nighttime habits, the "least involved" parent (this may or may not be the father) may be more effective in enforcing new limits and in fostering independence. If this isn't possible, give it a try on your own. Just be extra vigilant about not going back to your old nighttime interactions with your child.

9. With three-to-five-year-olds, you have language on your side, so before you begin any program, talk to your child about your expectations. That doesn't mean that he will always share your logic or interpret things the way you do, but he is perfectly capable of understanding your position if you keep your conversation simple and friendly. It is important that you have this conversation during the daytime, as you should minimize your interaction at night when he is supposed to be sleeping. You can tell him something like "I'm a very tired and cranky mommy [or daddy] almost all the time because I don't get enough sleep at night. I love your company during the day and in order to have lots of good times together, I need to start sleeping through the night. From now on, then, you're going to have to learn to get through the night without waking me. If you wake up and have trouble getting back to sleep, you can look at a book, talk to your stuffed animals, or watch your fish [or whatever you think is a suitable way to be quiet at night] until you are ready to fall back to sleep. It's not okay, though, for you to come into my room or call for me. If you have to get up to go to the bathroom, that is fine, but then you must get right back into bed." Remember, the idea is not to bully your child into sleeping all night long (it won't work anyway) but to help him feel good about himself and his ability to be independent through the night.

10. If your child has gotten into the habit of calling or crying for you in the middle of the night, your only solution is to let him cry it out. You have to teach him that his crying no longer gets the results he wants: your attention. Your first step is to explain to him during the day or as you tuck him into bed that you expect him to stay quietly in his bed all night long and that you won't be taking care of him in the middle of the night. That night, when he wakes up and begins to cry, go see him *once only*, reassure him that you are there and that he is safe, and tell him that he has to stay quietly in his bed until morning. As hard as it may be, stick to your guns and don't go in to see him again (if you want to check on him, wait until he is asleep). Otherwise, all you will be teaching him is that he eventually gets your attention if he cries long enough. Be prepared for the fact that your child may cry for as long as two or three hours the first few nights. But if you are consistent, his crying will be greatly reduced, and eventually eliminated, within a few nights to a week. If you have neighbors close by, you may also want to prepare them for his nighttime crying.

11. If your child has become used to sleeping in your bed, you must be especially committed and consistent. Many parents have changed their

minds so many times about this sleeping arrangement that it is small wonder that the child feels confused. So if you just feel lukewarm about getting your child out of your bed, don't try for the moment.

Once you are ready to follow through, have a daytime chat with your child. Explain calmly and clearly that he can no longer sleep in your bed. Then, when that first night arrives, you must be prepared to back up your words with action. Take him right back to his own bed as soon as he makes an appearance in your room or bed *regardless of the hour.* As you lead him back to his bed, you can say something like "Remember, darling, from now on you will be sleeping in your own bed." If he starts to fuss or cry, don't negotiate. Just kiss him good night, tell him that he is safe and snug in his own bed, and leave. If he comes after you, repeat this process of bringing him immediately back to his room without comment or anger. If he starts to carry on, don't allow yourself to pity him. Unless you are firm, you won't get results.

During the first few days, be sure to praise your child in the morning: "You did so well staying in your bed last night. Pretty soon, you'll be sleeping like big kids do, all night long in your own bed." This, combined with generally positive interactions throughout the day, should help him feel better about himself and his newly found independence.

12. If you are having trouble setting new nighttime limits, you can back yourself up with the neutrality of a clock-radio (if you don't already have one that he can use for a while, you can buy an inexpensive clock-radio at a drug store). When you tuck him in at night, tell him that he must stay in bed until morning and that the music will come on to let him know when it is time to get up. If he gets out of bed in the middle of the night, take him back immediately. Remind him that it is still night, and time for sleep, and that the music will let him know when it is morning. Some preschoolers find this neutral limit-setting device much easier to follow than the directions of their parents.

13. If your child is accustomed to eating a snack, having a bottle, or nursing in the middle of the night, it's time to cut out all of these eating habits entirely. First, tell your child in advance that he's not going to be eating at night. Even if he hasn't had a good dinner and tells you that he is hungry, you can gently but firmly say something like "The kitchen is closed for the night. I'm so glad you will be hungry for breakfast!" If he carries on, ignore it as best you can and don't get involved in any discussions. Don't even worry for a second that your child is *really* hungry or

that he will starve. There is no way that a healthy child will suffer from not eating at night! He has used the line "I'm hungry" as a means of getting attention from you, but hunger is not the reason he is getting out of bed. He just knows what works with you. So don't even weaken to the point where you leave a snack out for him so that he can help himself; this can escalate into an even bigger problem. You have to be able to defer him to teach him to sleep through the night.

14. If your child refuses to stay in his bed and predictably does other than you ask him to, it's time for you to reevaluate your entire interaction with him. If you feel your child never listens to you, we would guess that you are either giving him mixed messages (you say one thing and then contradict yourself a few minutes later or you don't follow through) or you frequently use punitive measures that result in power struggles. In either case, it may be time for you to talk to a family counselor to learn more effective ways to manage your child. If you feel that your problem is not yet out of hand but you need some extra help, look into community workshops and courses on child care and parenting. Talking to other parents will help, too; ask them how they would manage the problem you are having with your child. Be prepared to really listen!

15. If your child is getting up too early in the morning, there are two things you can do. First, you can try changing the hours he sleeps. Either putting him to bed a little later at night or having him give up his nap (if he is still having one) may make him sleep later in the morning. If this doesn't work, though, you can also try the clock-radio approach that we recommend for middle-of-the-night problems. Set the clock-radio for the time you would like your child to get up and tell him that he is supposed to stay in his bed until the music comes on. Tell him that if he wakes up before the music, he can play, but only quietly, and in his own room. Then make sure that he has a few favorite toys nearby. If he disturbs you before the music comes on, gently lead him back to his room, and remind him to wait for the music. If you are consistent and careful not to entertain him when he gets up, we think you will see a real difference in just a few mornings.

DEVELOPMENTAL FACTORS
THAT CAN DISRUPT SLEEP

Even children with good sleep habits have occasional problems sleeping through the night. These problems can result from a specific situation or, as we discuss in this section, they can be associated with a developmental stage.

As described in the introduction, the preschool years are full of change. Continuing steps toward independence, new social pressures, and the changes in sleep organization that are associated with giving up daytime napping often seem to cause nighttime sleep disruption. Some children may become fearful at bedtime and have a hard time relaxing enough to fall asleep. Other children may become frightened in the middle of the night and either be unable to fall back to sleep or have nightmares. The preschool years are also the time that some children first show the signs of a relatively common group of sleep disorders known as the parasomnias, which include night terrors (these are different from nightmares), sleepwalking, and sleep-talking. And sometime around the age of five, continuing bed-wetting becomes a situation worth evaluating.

Bedtime and Middle-of-the-Night Fears

As parents, we would all like to have the power to erase away our children's fears. Of course this usually isn't possible. Often we feel helpless and frustrated as our little ones toss and turn or cry out in their beds, too frightened to sleep. Fortunately, though, bedtime and middle-of-the-night fears are usually not severe, and the following suggestions should help you work through the rough times.

GUIDELINES FOR DEALING WITH BEDTIME AND MIDDLE-OF-THE-NIGHT FEARS

1. If your child is too frightened to fall asleep or wakes up afraid of something and cries for you in the middle of the night, go to him right away. There is nothing to be gained by making him wait.

2. Encourage your child to talk about whatever is bothering him. Most preschoolers have the language skills to at least give you an idea of their fears. It isn't a good idea to get into a long drawn-out discussion at night,

so try to keep it short and simple. Many times, children respond best to some hugs and a few reassuring words.

3. Other times, you may find that your child's fears are triggered by something that is relatively easy to correct. For example, if he is afraid of the dark, get him a night-light. Or if he is afraid of being alone, you can either keep his bedroom door open or let him share a room with a brother or sister. Other children seem to get enough comfort by having a pet dog, cat, or even fish in their rooms.

Sometimes, sharing a room with a sister or brother is all the reassurance a fearful child needs to sleep through the night. Every family situation is unique because of the different combinations of temperament, age, sex, and history of sleep problems among siblings. But these different factors seem to matter less than the constant reassurance the other sibling's presence provides. Here is an example of how one child can help another: The younger brother Mark wakes up in the middle of the night and starts to call to his older brother, "Justin, wake up. I want to tell you something." "What?" says Justin, sleepily. "I'm sleeping, tell me in the morning." The most important part of this exchange is that Justin is *naturally* providing reassurance by his presence, but he is not providing Mark with any entertainment or secondary gain. Even if Mark is able to engage Justin in conversation or mischief the first few nights of this new arrangement, the novelty quickly wears off. Justin will start to sleep through or ignore Mark's nightly chatter. Mark may continue to wake up, but if Justin keeps ignoring him, he'll quickly learn to be independent. Therefore, if one child complains about being bothered by the other, it's important for you to stay neutral. Say something like "I'm sure you kids will be able to work out your differences. If you don't like your brother to talk to you when you are trying to sleep, the best thing you can do is ignore him." You can then continue to monitor your children's interaction from behind the scenes.

The only reason we make such a big pitch for this arrangement is that it works. Many children who have never slept through the night without disturbing their parents magically do so when they are put in the same room with another child. You may not even need to read on!

4. Don't worry about toilet training at night. Although most preschoolers are dry at night, some normal, healthy children continue to need diapers until they are five years old. And in any event, your pressure won't help. It can, however, make your child too worried to sleep at night.

5. No matter how ridiculous your child's fears may seem to you, don't dismiss or belittle them. Your child will feel much more comforted if he knows that you are taking him and his fears seriously.

6. On the other hand, don't embellish your child's fears. It's enough that he's afraid of a monster in his closet, but if he sees you trying to scare it away, he might become even more frightened!

7. If you can, try to have your child stay in his bed. The best way for him to learn that his bed is a safe place to be is to stay there, and get over whatever is bothering him. If he seems to need you, it is much better for you to stay with him in his room than for him to get up and come to you.

8. If your child is willing, try to have a longer conversation about whatever was bothering him the next morning or afternoon. The daytime is the time for you to go into more detail about his fears. If you have found, for example, that he is afraid of bears, you can talk about bears together, look at pictures of bears, and perhaps even visit one at the zoo. If you stay down-to-earth and reassuring, this should help him come to grips with his fear.

9. If you find that your child isn't feeling any better after a few nights, try to figure out if he has just become attached to your nightly attention. Some children seem to form habits more easily than others, so this may be the time for you to start reducing the time you spend with him. Continue to be reassuring but brief. On the other hand, if you feel that his fears are continuing or even getting worse, it is probably time for you to talk to your family doctor or pediatrician.

Nightmares

Nightmares, or "bad" dreams, seem to affect between one quarter and one half of preschool children. Like other dreams, nightmares occur during REM sleep. Unlike that of other dreams, however, their content is frightening to the young child, who may either cry out in his sleep or wake up with a terrified scream.

No one knows for sure what triggers nightmares, but often they seem to result from daytime stress. For the preschooler, this could be stress from starting a new school, having a new baby brother or sister, moving to a new home, or a hospital stay. Sometimes a frightening experience or a violent television show can trigger a nightmare. At other times there may not be such an easily identifiable cause.

No matter what the cause of preschoolers' nightmares, however, they often have common themes. The characters are usually animals or monsters, not people, and the child is being either chased or threatened or can't find his way home. The most frightening part of this experience for the young child is that he may have a hard time differentiating his dream from reality. He may have trouble falling back to sleep, convinced that the lion will chase him again.

Yet as disturbing as these experiences are for you and your child, try to keep in mind that nightmares are common and usually not serious. We hope that the following suggestions will help you handle them in a constructive way.

GUIDELINES FOR DEALING WITH NIGHTMARES

1. If your child begins to cry or lets out a terrified scream in his sleep, go to him right away. This is the time when he needs your attention, regardless of the hour.

2. If you find that your child is still asleep when you get to his room, it isn't necessary to wake him up. Unless he is extremely agitated, he may get over the nightmare more quickly by simply continuing his normal sleep cycling. Even if he is asleep, you may be able to comfort him by gently stroking his head or giving him a light kiss. Stay with him until he seems to be sleeping peacefully again.

3. If your child wakes up, your primary thought should be to comfort him. Remember, though, that to calm him down, you will have to be calm yourself. So put your arms around him and talk to him quietly as you give him some gentle hugs. You might want to distract him by offering him a glass of water or asking him if he would like to hold his favorite stuffed animal. Some children feel better if they can talk about what it was that scared them, but don't force the issue in the middle of the night.

4. If your child does tell you what the nightmare was about, don't dismiss it by saying, "Don't worry; that was just a silly dream." Rather, you can try explaining the concept of a dream as being somewhat like "a story that you tell to yourself." Although a three-year-old may be too young to understand this, many four- and five-year-olds will be comforted by this explanation. It also then gives you the chance to help your child conclude his story on a positive note: you can suggest, for example, that the bear decided to stop chasing him, or that the monster took off his frightening

mask and was just a normal person underneath. As you continue in this vein, however, be careful *not* to embellish your child's fears. If you start locking all the windows to protect him from the bears, for example, you are only fueling his feelings of insecurity, and probably confusing him at the same time.

5. Stay with your child until he is feeling better. If you are calm and reassuring, this shouldn't take too long. Most likely, he is tired and ready to fall back to sleep. You might want to bring him into your bed for extra comforting, but don't let this become a habit. This may not be an option if your child has a history of sleep problems.

6. The next day, you can try having a more in-depth discussion with your child about his fears; on occasion you might find that you get a clue about something that has been bothering him in the day, too. A lot of the time, though, a nightmare is an isolated event without clear significance.

7. To help avoid future nightmares, don't let your child watch frightening or violent TV shows, especially at bedtime. Reading bedtime books, telling stories, and listening to soothing music are more appropriate bedtime activities. Many children are also comforted by a night-light and by having their bedroom door left open.

8. If, despite all your efforts, your child seems to be having more frequent and severe nightmares, and particularly if he seems fearful during the day, we recommend that you talk to your pediatrician or family doctor for further advice. The two of you can work together to assess whatever stresses he may be experiencing.

The Parasomnias

The parasomnias are a group of sleep disorders that include night terrors, sleepwalking, and sleep-talking. Although each is a distinct entity, they have certain characteristics in common: they all occur during a prolonged period of the deepest type of sleep, stage 3–4 NREM, usually between 70 and 120 minutes after a child falls asleep and right before a transition to REM sleep; they affect boys about four times as frequently as girls; and they seem to run in families, sometimes all in the same person.

Unlike dreams, which occur during REM sleep, the parasomnias are not associated with specific mental images. The victims are not acting out a role or an event. In fact, when awakened from a bout of sleepwalking or sleep-talking, or from a night terror, the child has no recollection of anything at all.

Although they are classified by sleep researchers as disorders, we should emphasize that in preschoolers, the parasomnias are not associated with physical or emotional problems. Dr. Anders has mentioned the stress associated with starting school and making friends and the fatigue associated with giving up naps as possible triggers of the parasomnias. Most likely they also have a physiologic basis such as immaturity of the nervous system. In the vast majority of cases, psychological counseling or medication is not indicated, and the parasomnias disappear on their own.

Night Terrors

Night terrors are generally more frightening for the parent than for the child. Although from the outside it may seem that the child is experiencing a terrifying dream, he is not. A typical attack, which can last anywhere from thirty seconds to five minutes or so, goes something like this:

> The child screams and sits bolt upright in his bed. Glassy-eyed and unresponsive to anyone or anything in the room, he may moan and groan. His heart is pounding, he breathes heavily, and he may be sweating. He is obviously agitated but inconsolable, and within a few minutes he relaxes and resumes peaceful sleep.

As a parent, the most difficult aspect of such an episode is that there really is very little you can do. When a child is having a night terror, he is extremely difficult to arouse, as he doesn't respond to anyone or anything around him. You can try turning on the light, talking loudly, holding him, stroking his head, and perhaps wiping his forehead with a cool washcloth. It is important that you stay calm, though, because if he does wake up, your anxiety can frighten him. It is also important that you stay nearby until he resumes peaceful sleep, as children who get up and walk around during a night terror can easily get hurt.

The typical night terror is over as quickly and mysteriously as it began. The child either passes into peaceful sleep or, if he wakes up, has no memory of the event, although he may have a vague uneasy feeling. Although most children never have a night terror (researchers estimate that night terrors affect about 3 percent of children, primarily preschoolers), don't be alarmed if your child does. In most cases, the tendency runs in a family, so chances are that either you or your spouse or some other relative had similar episodes as a young child. If the night terrors become more frequent, though, or begin to frighten you at all, don't hesitate to discuss the matter with your pediatrician or family doctor.

Sleepwalking and Sleep-talking

Like children who are experiencing a night terror, children who sleepwalk or sleep-talk are not acting out the elements of a dream. Rather, they walk or talk while in the deepest stages of NREM sleep, and without intent or meaning.

In one study, Dr. John F. Simonds of the University of Missouri and Dr. Humberto Parraga of Southern Illinois University found that almost half of their subjects had talked in their sleep at one time or another. Dr. Anders estimates that about 15 percent of children sleepwalk one time between the ages of five and twelve, and that between 1 and 6 percent of children sleepwalk on a continuing basis. And even though sleep-talking is much more common than sleepwalking, the two frequently occur in combination. A typical episode may go something like this:

> The child sits up abruptly in bed. He is not distressed but unresponsive. His eyes may be open, but he doesn't see. His movements are awkward and purposeless; he may move his hands and fingers in a repetitive fashion. He may either stay in bed and perhaps mumble incoherently or get up and stumble about. If he remains in bed, he may well resume peaceful sleep on his own. If he wakes up, perhaps in a strange location, he will only be confused and not remember the event at all.

The primary message in all of this is the importance of protecting your sleeping child. Because sleepwalkers lack normal judgment, they can easily hurt themselves as they wander about. The popular representation in films and books of sleepwalkers accomplishing tremendous feats of unusual coordination and daring while in a trance is a myth! We all tend to dismiss stories we hear about young children who wander outside in the middle of the night, but the potential dangers of such a situation are very real. And the problem is that sleepwalkers, unlike children who scream while having a night terror, do not necessarily attract attention. Their parents may not hear them at all as they quietly stumble around, perhaps putting themselves in great danger.

If your child walks in his sleep, then, do what you must to ensure his safety. It's probably not a good idea for him to sleep on the top bunk bed, for example. You might want to install a safety gate at his bedroom door and make sure that all of his bedroom windows are locked. Some parents find it necessary to install an alarm system on their child's bed.

If all this sounds worrisome, keep in mind that despite the obvious physical danger the child faces, sleepwalking is not a serious problem. It is not linked to emotional or physical abnormalities and almost always stops on its own by the time a child is fifteen. In the meantime, if you take reasonable precautions and make a special effort to respond to your child without anxiety or fear, you will both do fine.

Bed-wetting

Bed-wetting (medically known as enuresis) is divided into two distinct conditions: primary enuresis, when a child has never achieved regular bladder control at night; and secondary enuresis, when a child who has had at least six months of nighttime dryness again begins to wet his bed.

It is necessary to make this distinction because only primary enuresis is a sleep disorder. Secondary enuresis, on the other hand, is associated with physical problems (a urinary tract disorder, pinworms, or diabetes, for example) or emotional stress (commonly the birth of a baby brother or sister, moving to a new home, beginning a new school, and so on). Therefore, if your child begins to wet his bed after six or more months of dryness, he needs a medical evaluation. Many times there is nothing serious going on, but you must rule out this possibility.

Primary enuresis, previously linked to the parasomnias, is now recognized as occurring in any stage of sleep, REM as well as NREM. Like the parasomnias, however, bed-wetting is much more common in boys than in girls, and tends to run in families. In any case, bed-wetting should not even be an issue until a child reaches five or six years of age. Until that time, lack of nighttime bladder control is not unusual and does not require immediate evaluation. Just keep your preschooler in diapers for at least a month or so beyond the time he seems to need them. Don't pressure him or make him feel embarrassed for needing them. When his body is ready, he will stay dry; in the meantime there isn't anything for you to do.

Once your child reaches five or six, however, he should be evaluated by your pediatrician or family doctor if he is still wetting his bed on a regular basis. At this point, you must rule out a physical or emotional cause. Once this has been done, there are a variety of treatment options available. Because this is stretching the upper age range of this book, we only list them briefly to give you an idea of what may be in store.

At this time, there isn't any one treatment that is overwhelmingly effective. The best approach seems to be trial and error, with some treatments more effective for one child than another. Alarm systems that awaken a child when he first begins to urinate are sometimes helpful, especially for older children. Behavioral techniques, such as star charts, work for other children. Some children respond to daytime bladder-capacity training exercises, and older children are encouraged to take responsibility for the situation by changing their own sheets. And finally, as a last resort, some doctors prescribe medication (for example, imipramine) that, while effective when taken, doesn't seem to have any long-lasting results. In any event, it is most important that you continue to support and reassure your child. Help him not to feel ashamed, as the psychological scars can last for years, far beyond the time that he wets his bed.

SITUATIONS THAT CAN DISRUPT SLEEP

There are many situations that affect a young child's nighttime as well as daytime behavior. As examples, starting nursery school, illness and hospitalization, divorce, and a death in the family will not only influence the way a preschooler acts and feels during the day, but they may also disrupt his sleep (for a discussion of moving to a new home, travel, and the birth of a baby brother or sister, see Chapters Three and Four). Sometimes these situations are self-limited and the sleep disruption is resolved as soon as things get back to normal. Other times the situation may trigger developmental fears that can wax and wane for months or even years (for suggestions on how to deal with these fears, review our section on developmental factors that can disrupt sleep).

Regardless of the situation, however, a child's habits are going to determine his nighttime behavior more than anything else. Any of the circumstances that we discuss in this chapter are less likely to have as strong an effect on the child with solid sleep habits; the child who is most prone to situational sleep disruptions often has a long history of poor sleep habits. Therefore, if your child's bedtime and nighttime behavior has challenged you all the way along, it's important not only that you deal with the particular situation that is currently causing his night problems but also that you work on helping him form good habits. It still isn't too late to get him on the right track before he starts his school years.

School-Related Stress

For most three-to-five-year-olds, nursery school is a happy, enriching experience. But that doesn't mean there aren't the usual ups and downs for the young child who is learning to test the waters outside of home. Initially, a three-year-old may resist going to school in the morning and go through a daily struggle separating from his parent at the school's front door. More frequently than not, however, this child will then settle down and enjoy himself immensely once his parent has left. In most cases, this natural ambivalence normally gives way to feelings of enthusiasm and confidence by the middle of the first year or certainly by the second year of nursery school. Provided the school is good and suited to your child's temperament and to your philosophy, there is no reason to suspect that these separation struggles will trigger sleep problems.

But occasionally, even in the best schools, a child may not click with the other children or with the teachers. This social awkwardness and inability to fit into the group reinforces the child's fears about his new school life and his wish to be at home in a safe environment. It is this type of school-related stress that can lead to sleep problems and nightmares.

Therefore, if your child seems intensely distraught about school, the first thing to do is to talk to his teachers. Find out what they're thinking; most of the time, experienced nursery school teachers are right on target! Many nursery schools also have one-way mirrors so that you can observe him without him knowing that you are there. You first want to rule out that his behavior isn't for your benefit alone! You also want to be confident that this is the right environment for your child.

Frequently, night waking and nightmares resulting from anxieties about school are short-lived. Provided that you are satisfied with what you saw at your child's school, the best thing you can do is to reassure your child. Help him cope with his new independence; the more easygoing and confident you are about sending him to nursery school, the faster he'll adjust. If he is having a hard time making friends, you can invite children from school to play at your home. Often the friendships cultivated at home will continue at school.

Also, it's a good idea to read the other sections in this chapter that might help you cope with various aspects of your child's night problems. If your child is showing signs of stress that are either prolonged or more intense than expected, check with your pediatrician.

Illness

Unless your child is really ill, you should make every effort to help him maintain his regular sleep habits. Preschoolers get a lot of colds, and a good night's sleep is probably the best thing to help him feel better. If anything, he might require extra sleep when he is feeling under the weather.

On the other hand, if your child is ill enough for you to be concerned, don't hesitate to attend to him during the night. The most important thing is that he recover as soon as possible. A preschooler who has had good sleep habits before becoming ill will quickly resume his old habits when he feels better. Often, though, a child who has shared his parent's bed during a lengthy illness will resist being moved back into his own bed. If you are in this position, read our section on helping your child to become independent at night, but first make sure that he is completely over his illness. You may have to start all over training your child to have good independent sleep habits, or he may have developed only a single new nighttime expectation such as a glass of juice at bedtime. Whatever the case, if you are firm, consistent, reassuring, and friendly, you should achieve quick results.

Hospitalization

A hospital experience is bound to be traumatic for any child. In the first place, because he is either extremely ill, in pain, or in need of some procedure (surgery, tests, etc.) when he is admitted to the hospital, he will be less able than usual to cope with the new and frightening surroundings. The combination of his anxiety and his discomfort will take its toll.

Because a hospital is such a potentially frightening place for a child, with all the intimidating equipment, unfamiliar people, and uncomfortable procedures, it is most important that you stay with your child at all times, if possible. Most hospitals will provide you with a cot so that you can even spend the night by your child's side. If your child is scheduled for surgery, advanced preparation can be very helpful. Some hospitals have special programs that deal with explaining hospital routines and various surgical procedures to children. Even young children can benefit from a simple explanation of what will happen to them.

Don't be surprised if your child is having trouble sleeping when he gets home from the hospital. He may have trouble falling asleep, wake up frightened in the middle of the night, have nightmares, or have any number of other sleep problems. For tips on how to cope during this adjustment period, see our section on developmental factors that can disrupt sleep.

Once your child is completely recovered, it is time for you to help him resume his old sleep habits. When you feel relaxed and confident that he is his old self again, you will be able to reassure him and set bedtime and middle-of-the-night limits for him. For specifics, see our section on helping your child to be independent at night.

Divorce

Divorce is an unsettling experience for children, no matter what their age. Even as young as three to five years old, a child can feel that his world is being turned upside down when his parents split up. Sleep problems, as well as daytime behavior problems, are a common result. Therefore, no matter how preoccupied you may feel by your separation and divorce, you must also consider the effect it has on your child and take whatever precautions you can to soften the blow for him.

One of the biggest fears for children of divorced parents is a fear of the unknown. He may well be wondering if you still love him, now that you no longer love his other parent, and he may also be frightened by the thought of what might come next, now that this terrible thing has happened. Therefore, one of the most important things for you to do is to *talk to your child*. Even though his speaking vocabulary may be quite limited, he will understand you if you keep things simple. Tell him that you still love him, and that nothing could ever change that. As much as you can, prepare him for how your divorce will affect his life. Even a preschooler should be told well ahead of time if, for example, you and he will be moving to a new house, or if Daddy will be moving to a new house, or if there is another major change in store. If you just spring something like this on him, how can he help but feel frightened?

You must also explain to your child that he is in no way responsible for the breakup of your marriage. With their limited experience, young children tend to be quite egocentric and often feel that they are to blame for their parents' problems. Along with all the rest of their pain and confusion, they feel guilty! As much as you can, then, talk to your child, and reassure him that this isn't so.

Another way you can maintain your child's sense of security and well-being is to keep to his regular routines (including bedtime and sleep habits) as much as possible. By doing this, you tell him that things haven't changed that much after all. If you want to give your child extra attention because he is having a rough time, arrange your life so you can spend extra time with him during the day or in the early evening. Of course, if he occasionally feels especially frightened or rejected at bedtime or in the middle of the night and can't sleep, it's important to comfort and reassure him (for suggestions, see our sections on developmental fears). Just don't let your guilt or your insecurities contribute to his sleep problems. If you all of a sudden let him sleep in your bed or let him stay up as late as he wants, you may actually make him feel more insecure and unloved. He may be confused by your new leniency and thrown even further off balance. Remember, you can be extra reassuring and loving while you continue to set normal limits.

If your child is spending a fair amount of time with both you and your ex-spouse, also try to make your household routines as consistent as possible. His adjustment will be much more difficult if the two of you have very different expectations for his behavior, sleep and otherwise. For example, if you try to get your child to bed at seven-thirty but your ex-spouse allows him to stay up until he finally falls asleep on the living room floor, he is bound to get confused.

As much as you try, though, don't be surprised if you can't handle all of this on your own. Divorce can be one of life's biggest traumas for a family, and you may all benefit from professional help. Sometimes just a few sessions with a family counselor will go a long way toward helping you and your child through these rough times.

Death

As much as we wish to protect our children from the concept of death, it is still as much a fact of life as birth. Don't be surprised, then, when your preschooler begins to question what it means to be dead. Not all children experience the trauma of the death of a family member or a close friend, but all children observe death in some way, either through the loss of a pet or by observing the death of an insect or some outdoor animal.

Children who do lose family members express their loss differently because of the inherent uniqueness of each family circumstance. If a child has been close and emotionally dependent on the family member (a parent, a sibling, a caretaking grandparent, or someone closely involved in the child's everyday life), he is likely to have feelings of loss, and perhaps anger and fear, when this person dies. He may feel extra trauma if the death is sudden, accidental, or violent. A preschooler lives in the present, however, and is not likely to be affected too much by the death of someone who has only occasionally been present in his life, even if that person is a grandparent. He may feel some degree of empathy with his parent's sorrow, but it is usually short-lived.

Whatever the circumstances of death are in your child's life, the most important thing you can do is talk to him about what has happened. If someone close to him has died, help him to express (mourn) his sorrow, fear, and anger. It isn't a good idea to dwell on death, but you should reassure him and answer his questions as honestly and simply as you can. Being egocentric creatures, many young children may feel that they were in some way responsible for the death. Other children may worry about dying themselves or, more commonly, that their parents will die.

Although it doesn't always happen, the loss of a loved one or even just general fears and concerns about death can interfere with a child's sleep. Preschoolers are by and large so resilient, though, that this rarely becomes serious or continues for more than a night or two. For guidelines for dealing with such temporary insecurities, see our section on developmental fears. If you don't seem to be making progress, we suggest that you seek outside counseling.

QUESTIONS/ANSWERS

1. Our children have always had good sleep habits, and we have had relatively few problems at bedtime. Lately, however, our four-year-old son has been complaining every night that he can't fall asleep and that he's not tired. I know that he is tired because he doesn't nap anymore, and he has a very active day. I don't know why he is having trouble settling down. Do you have any suggestions?

First of all, you should realize that it is quite common for a four-year-old to have trouble settling down to sleep. Four-year-old boys, in particular, tend to get revved up and act silly as a part of their normal behavior. Sometimes it seems it's hard for them to turn their motor down so that they can make the transition to sleep. Also, it is not unusual for children this age to get overtired, which only adds to the problem. Luckily, there are a few easy things you can do to help your child settle down more easily. You may already be following many of these steps, but it's worth reviewing them.

First figure out the total number of hours your child needs to sleep every night in order to feel rested, and set his bedtime accordingly. It sounds like he would benefit from a slightly longer than usual pre-bed wind-down time (at least until he gets over this restless stage), so start getting him ready for bed at least forty-five minutes to an hour before you think he should be asleep. If his bedtime is seven-thirty, for instance, start getting him ready at about six-thirty. A bath is usually a good way of calming an active four-year-old. Then, once he is in his pajamas and ready for bed, try not to let him roughhouse or run around. Restrict his television viewing to age-appropriate nonviolent shows. You can continue your bedtime ritual with a relaxing book or story, or perhaps a few songs. If he seems to need it, you can then give him another five or ten minutes on his own, but only in his bed. Tell him he can look at a book or listen to a cassette or record and that you will be in to turn off the light in a few minutes.

If your son complains about not being able to fall asleep when you come in to turn off the light, tell him it's fine for him to just lie there with the light off and create his own stories. Reassure him that he doesn't have to be in a rush to fall asleep but that he is on his own. You might also consider whether he is telling you he can't fall asleep because he likes the extra attention he is getting. If this is the case, you'll have to be firm and tell him that it's okay to stay awake in his bed but that he can't call or get out of bed anymore. If you want, you can let him turn his light on again and play quietly in his bed, but we see this only as a last resort.

One last thing to consider: make sure your son isn't eating chocolate or drinking caffeinated beverages, such as cola, at bedtime; stimulants such as these may intensify his restlessness.

2. My four-year-old daughter is the original bedtime staller! I'm pretty wise to most of her techniques, but the one that always gets me is the "I'm hungry" routine. I know that this is my daughter's way of delaying bedtime, but it goes against my nature to send a hungry child to bed. Do you think I can solve the problem by putting a little snack next to her bed at bedtime?

No, we don't think that is a good idea. By putting a regular bedtime snack next to her bed, you're playing right into her delaying tactics, because, after all, that is what her hunger plea is all about. She doesn't really need to eat at this time; she has just learned what works with you.

We suggest you do the following: Tell her at dinnertime that she will no longer be able to have a snack at bedtime, so that if she is hungry she should be sure to eat enough dinner. According to your own preference, you can give her dessert immediately following dinner or later, before you start to get her ready for bed. Also offer her a glass of milk or a yogurt at this time so that you can be sure she won't be hungry. Then, if your child tells you that she is still hungry as you tuck her in to bed for the night, you can say something like "Darling, I'm glad you're hungry. I'll look forward to making you an extra special breakfast in the morning! Remember, we talked about no more food at bedtime." Be friendly but brief; say good night right away, and leave. She may complain, but she'll adjust to this new fact of life in a few days.

Of course there are times you should make an exception. When your child is sick, it's perfectly reasonable to wait on her and bring her something to eat or drink in bed. Also, there is something quite special about an occasional treat or surprise. But keep in mind that neither situation should grow into a regular expectation or habit.

3. We have a very busy household, and getting our kids down for the night hasn't ever been a big priority. Our seven-year-old seems to do fine going to bed late every night and gets by fine on nine hours of sleep. Our three-year-old is another story, though. He stays up until ten or later, at which time he usually falls asleep on his own. During the day he's often cranky and out of control. He also doesn't want to get up and go to nursery school in the morning. In the late afternoon he starts to fall apart; if I'm driving around, he'll fall asleep. Otherwise he doesn't nap, and I guess he isn't sleeping enough at night either. We always thought of him as a great kid until recently, when he started becoming difficult. What should we do?

It sounds like you're correct in attributing a lot of your three-year-old's behavior problems to fatigue, and no wonder! He really can't be expected to maintain the same schedule as your seven-year-old. He simply needs more sleep.

Since your son has to be ready for a morning school program, your only solution to this problem is to get him to bed earlier in the evening. He sounds as if he's past the stage where he'll voluntarily nap, so you might as well not force that issue. Because he is not accustomed to having a regular bedtime, though, you have to be prepared to make this new routine a priority in *your* life for the first month or so. Keep in mind that overtired three- and four-year-olds often have a hard time making the transition to sleep, so you will have to help him along.

Every evening, then, put everything else on hold until you've gotten him to bed. For starters, begin getting him ready for bed (bath and bedtime ritual) at about 7 P.M. every night so that you can make sure he's settled in by about seven-thirty or eight. Your goal is to have him fall asleep early enough so that he'll awaken on his own in the morning, without your having to wake him. His transition from home to school should become much more pleasant once he has enough time to have a relaxed breakfast and perhaps even play a bit before setting off.

If you follow this program, we're willing to bet that your child's behavior will improve enormously in a matter of weeks, or even days. The better rested he is, the more he can get on with the business of being a kid: playing and making friends. You will probably find that your interaction with him improves too, once he isn't tired all the time.

4. I'm the father of a four-year-old daughter who has been sleeping off and on in our bed since she was born. My wife seems to tolerate her sleeping in our bed; in fact, I think she even encourages her to share our bed with us. I don't feel comfortable with this arrangement; it's really beginning to bother me more and more. My daughter is also going through a stage at which she seems to be enamored of me. Is there something wrong with her sleeping in our bed? If so, how can I convince my wife to go along with a plan to have her sleep in her own bed?

There is nothing "wrong" with having your child share your bed with you in an absolute sense, but we don't think that it is a good idea. Although we encourage the closeness that can come from sharing a family bed, we think that this closeness can be achieved in other ways. We also worry about several other things that happen in the process of sharing a family bed.

We are concerned primarily about a young child's developing sense of independence when she sleeps with her parents at this age. Of course your daughter needs lots of nurturing and love, but she also needs the opportunity to cope on her own with such a primary experience as sleeping in her own bed. Therefore, we think it is better for you to offer her your love and close physical contact during the day, instead of throughout the night. In this way, you also show her *your* confidence in her ability to build her independence away from you. Although she may initially be unhappy about sleeping apart from you, those feelings won't last.

This is also a good time for you to start having your daughter sleep in her own bed because, as you point out, she is at the age where she is especially infatuated with you. Many children, both girls and boys, go through similar stages of having intense feelings for their parent of the opposite sex. This is the natural time, then, for you to start drawing the appropriate boundaries for your family relationships. This doesn't mean that you sit down and talk to your daughter about things that are beyond her experience or comprehension, but a simple act like having her sleep in her own bed, while you sleep with your wife, gets the message across.

A final reason for not sharing your bed with your four-year-old concerns your relationship with your wife. Although every couple must make up their own minds about this issue, we see sharing a bed every night with a child as inhibiting intimacy and communication between husband and wife. From your description, it sounds as if your wife feels ambivalent about this issue. Granted it is a difficult issue to face, but it is one you can't ignore.

Your first step, then, should be to have a frank talk with your wife. It is most important that the two of you agree, no matter what you decide. If you do decide to reclaim your bed for yourselves, recognize that your job may not be easy, and that you will need a definite plan. For specific suggestions, see our section on helping your child become independent at night. And good luck! We feel that you will also be helping your relationship and your family life by not allowing your daughter to become a wedge in your marriage.

5. My four-year-old daughter has had sleep problems all her life. We finally got fed up and refused to let her come into our bed, so now she comes and falls asleep on the floor next to us. She also talks to us and tells us about what she did during the day! She is wide awake, and acts as if it were perfectly normal to be chatting away in the middle of the night. How can I get her to stay in her own bed, or at least in her own room?

The most obvious place for you to begin is by having an open and friendly chat with your daughter during the day, when you're not tired or angry. Explain to her that her nightly visits are making you a very cranky mother (or father) and that she must learn to stay in her own bed. You can ask her if there is anything that she would like to keep her company in her room, such as a new stuffed animal or fish, and you might also let her help you pick out new sheets or a blanket to make her bed more desirable. Reassure her that you understand that she gets lonely in the middle of the night and that you are there for her if she *really* needs you, but that she is old enough to sleep on her own.

Then, the first night when you tuck her in, remind her in a loving way that she may no longer come to your room. When she does, lead her right back to her bed and tell her once only that she has to stay there. After that, don't get involved in a discussion. Just lead her back to her bed as many times as necessary. You may be in for several rough nights, but if you are firm and consistent, you will get results.

Also, if you have another child, consider moving your daughter into your other child's room, at least for a few weeks or so. In most cases, the presence of a sleeping brother or sister is reassuring enough to initiate good sleeping habits. Even if you don't want this to be a long-term solution, it can help her develop the initial confidence to get through the night on her own. For a longer discussion and other tips (such as using a clock-radio as a neutral limit-setting device), see our section on training your child to be independent at night.

No matter what tack you take, however, remember that almost all children wake up in the middle of the night in the normal process of sleep cycling. Your child, however, has learned to wake up and expect attention at these times. If you stop providing her with a secondary gain, she'll learn to be independent. Her pattern of waking up may or may not change, but you can expect her need to interact with others to disappear.

6. My four-year-old daughter, Margot, and my two-year-old son, John, share a room. I guess they both have their fair share of sleep problems now, although Margot didn't start waking up at night until our son was born and he moved into her room. Lately, they're both up at least three times a week in the middle of the night. Once Margot's awake, John wakes up too, and then they start talking and carrying on. Margot sometimes gets out of bed, taunting John, who is stuck in his crib. Other times it seems (according to Margot, anyway) that John wakes her up. Some-

where along the line my husband or I get up and try to settle them down; sometimes we get so frustrated that we lose our tempers, at them as well as at each other. We consider ourselves fairly good parents and we try to be consistent with our children, but this pattern has been going on for months. Margot and John have a regular bedtime and go to bed without any problem, but how can we get them to sleep through the night?

Your situation may seem more complicated than average because you are dealing with two children instead of one, but the underlying principles are the same: somehow, in some way, your children's sleep pattern has been reinforced. This isn't to say that you and your husband aren't great parents, or that you aren't consistent most of the time, but simply that you have allowed this pattern to become a habit.

Your first step, then, should be to examine the ways you treat your children when they wake up in the middle of the night. From your description, it sounds as if you are giving them a fair amount of attention, even if it is negative attention. Also keep in mind that some children are more physiologically and psychologically susceptible to sleep problems than others. This doesn't mean that you should give up but that you may need more than the average amount of patience and consistency to get the results you want. You should be encouraged, however, that your children don't seem to need you most nights; this is your best clue that they are capable of getting through the night on their own.

In order to get on top of your problem, you are going to need a carefully planned tactic. Basically, there are two approaches you can take: either keeping your children in the same room or separating them. In either case, you will have to stop giving your children any type of nighttime attention (unless, of course, they are sick or frightened).

Because keeping them in the same room is less drastic, we suggest that you try it first. You might, however, want to move their beds (or bed and crib) a little farther apart. This way, the children are less likely to disturb each other, but they can still be reassured by the other's presence.

Start your program by talking to your children about your new expectations. Tell them (you can scale down your language for your two-year-old) that they are no longer allowed to talk to each other or get up in the nighttime. Explain that all of this nighttime activity has made you too tired, and that you can no longer get up in the middle of the night. Tell them they will be on their own from now on, but that you are always there to make sure they are safe and fine. In order to reinforce this new limit-setting and make it more neutral, you can put a clock-radio in their room. Tell them they are not allowed to get out of bed or talk until the music comes on in the morning. Demonstrate to them how *it will tell them* when it is time to get up.

The first night, if either one of them starts to disturb the other, go to them right away to remind them of the new nighttime policy. In order to be effective, be clear, boring, and brief (don't get angry until you're at least in the privacy of your own room!) and then leave their room. For the rest of the night, don't get involved. This is the hardest part, but it is necessary. If you are able to stay away, we think that you will get results.

If this doesn't work after a few nights, though, you can consider separating them, but don't do this in a punitive way. In a friendly voice, tell them that they will be able to share a room again when they learn to sleep through the night without disrupting the family. We think that Margot, in particular, will respond to this type of logic. If you are consistent about *not* giving them *any* attention in the middle of the night, you should get fast results.

7. Our four-year-old daughter has always slept through the night, but recently she has started having nightmares once or twice a week. It's probably not a coincidence that the beginning of these nightmares coincided with our moving to a new town. Laura seems to be a well-adjusted child, but she has been having a hard time getting used to her new school. I think some of the problem may be with another child who she says is mean to her. Is there anything we can do? Are nightmares a normal response to this type of situation or do you think that they signal a deeper emotional problem?

Nightmares are a perfectly normal response to the type of stressful situation that you describe. Moving and starting a new school are difficult adjustments for any child, and it is quite common for this type of stress to interfere with sleep, in one way or another. We cannot tell you for sure whether Laura has an emotional problem, but none of the information you give us would make us think so. If she continues to be happy and well adjusted most of the time, chances are that she is simply going through a tough adjustment period.

Our guess, then, is that Laura will outgrow her nightmares as she settles into her new life. And in the meantime, there are a few things you can do to help her along. Speak to her teachers and find out exactly what is going on at school. If the problem seems to revolve around one particular child, or anything else at school, perhaps they can help. You can also talk to Laura and suggest ways to manage problems as they arise. She may also enjoy having children from school play at your house. This can help her bond to this new group of children and build her confidence in her new home.

When Laura does have nightmares, it's important to go reassure her and let her know that she is safe. Be sure to give her the opportunity to tell you what's scaring her in her dream. If it is a repetitive theme, it may help her to talk about it during the day. For other suggestions, see our section on nightmares.

In summary, we encourage you to be patient and supportive during Laura's adjustment period. This doesn't mean that you should become overly indulgent, because that won't help her in the long run, but try to help her along as best you can. If her nightmares continue well beyond the time that she seems to have adjusted to school and her new home, don't hesitate to contact your pediatrician or family doctor for more advice.

8. My three-and-a-half-year-old appears to masturbate with her stuffed animal. When she is falling asleep at night she takes her prized teddy bear and puts him between her legs and rocks back and forth. It doesn't bother my husband much, but it bothers me. I'm embarrassed that she does this in order to fall asleep and I don't want anyone else to put her to bed. I don't let her have her teddy during the day because I don't want her to start doing this in other situations. Is there anything I can do to get her to stop?

Chances are that your child's rocking with her teddy or masturbating is perfectly normal. Since she is only doing this at night, to help herself fall asleep, there is no obvious cause for concern. The best way for you to look on it is as just one of the various self-comforting acts (for example, thumb-sucking, sucking a pacifier, or stroking a love object) so common to the preschool years.

On the other hand, if your child masturbates constantly, then you have cause for concern. Whenever a child is engaged in a self-comforting act that interferes with her social interaction, it is a sign of greater anxiety and distress. If you have any doubts about your child's overall well-being, speak to your pediatrician or a psychologist.

In the meantime, do your best to ignore your daughter's self-comforting behavior. If you instead focus on building her self-esteem and social competence and security, you'll probably find that she needs to do this less and less. For example, provide her with lots of opportunities to play with other children her age, and help her find activities that she enjoys. From our experience, nagging a child to stop doing a habitual, annoying behavior almost never works. Parents find they are much more successful in reinforcing positive behavior that slowly replaces the bothersome habit.

9. My four-and-a-half-year-old son is having a tough time. I am a single (separated for six months) working mother. Although my son seems to be okay at school and at daycare, he becomes belligerent and testy a lot of the time in the evening. He frequently defies me at bedtime and then I have a big struggle getting him to bed. Sometimes he is up a couple of times in the middle of the night, either going to the kitchen and helping himself to something to eat or just wandering around. One night I found him playing with the fish in the fish tank! Another night I found him pouring milk and spilling it all over the floor! He's a good kid, but I'm beginning to feel desperate about his sleep problems. Since I don't see him all day long, I want so much to have nice evenings with him. I'm also tired and need to sleep. What can I do to get him to go to bed easily and stay in bed through the night?

First, let's try to shed some light on your child's evening and night-time behavior. Since you've been separated from your husband for only six months, chances are he is still feeling upset and rejected. As his mother, you're probably the only person in the world with whom he feels entirely safe and at whom he can lash out. Since he has to stay "glued together" all day long in the care of others, it's only natural that he would let all his feelings spill out with you. In addition to his feelings of anger and hurt, he may also just be exhausted. A full day in daycare is bound to leave him tired and he may need a much earlier bedtime. Also think about your feelings of pity or guilt and consider whether they have interfered with your management of his bedtime.

In order for you to help your child feel loved and reassured, it is important to rebuild his feelings of security. This can happen only when you are prepared to be consistent and set firm (but always friendly) limits to his behavior. First start with bedtime (at the same time every night) and see what you can do to turn things around.

One way of handling your son's bedtime belligerence is to let him know that if he doesn't cooperate, you will leave the room. Say something like "I'm sorry you're having trouble, but you may not talk that way to me. Let me know when you're ready to try again. I'd love to read you your bedtime story when you're ready." Don't lose your temper and don't just stand there and let him abuse you. If he still resists when you return in a few minutes, say something like "We'll try again tomorrow with your bath and story; good night, darling," and leave the room. If he gets up and comes after you, you can either lead him right back to bed without comment, anger, or fuss as many times as is necessary or you can *pretend* to ignore him. Either way, you are no longer giving him attention and reinforcing his behavior. He'll protest vehemently for a few nights, but he'll catch on fast.

During the night, you can take a similar approach. Tell him that he must stay in his bed but that he may look at a book if he likes. Tell him you're happy to serve him an extra big dinner and dessert but that then the kitchen will be closed for the night. Do not let him get up and help himself to food in the middle of the night. If he does get up, lead him right back to bed without comment.

Finally, on weekends, mornings, and evenings, do everything you can to build your son's feelings of security and reinforce his willingness to cooperate. In addition to providing the two of you with lots of opportunities for positive interaction, also do everything you can to build a normal home life for him, such as inviting his friends to play on the weekend. Although it may be difficult for you, try to make his well-being a priority during this adjustment period.

BIBLIOGRAPHY

Ames, Louise Bates, et al. *Your One Year Old.* New York: Delacorte, 1982.

———, and Ilg, Frances L. *Your Two Year Old.* New York: Dell, 1976.

———, and Ilg, Frances L. *Your Three Year Old.* New York: Dell, 1976.

———, and Ilg, Frances L. *Your Four Year Old.* New York: Dell, 1976.

———, and Ilg, Frances L. *Your Five Year Old.* New York: Dell, 1981.

Anders, Thomas F. "Biological Rhythms in Development." *Psychosomatic Medicine* 44 (No. 1): 61–72, 1982.

———. "State and Rhythmic Processes." American Academy of Child Psychiatry, 1978.

———, et al. "A Longitudinal Study of Nighttime Sleep-Wake Patterns in Infants from Birth to One Year." In *Frontiers of Infant Psychiatry*, edited by Justin Call et al. New York: Basic Books, 1983.

———, and Guilleminault, Christian. "The Pathophysiology of Sleep Disorders in Pediatrics. Part I: Sleep in Infancy; Part II: Sleep Disorders in Children." *Advances in Pediatrics* 22: 137–74, 1976.

———, and Keener, Marcia A. "Sleep-Wake State Development and Disorders of Sleep in Infants, Children, and Adolescents." In *Developmental and Behavioral Pediatrics*, edited by M. Levine et al. Philadelphia: Saunders, 1983.

———, and Weinstein, Pearl. "Sleep and Its Disorders in Infants and Children: A Review." *Pediatrics* 50 (No. 2): 312–24, 1972.

Beebe, Brooke M. *Tips for Toddlers.* New York: Dell, 1983.

Behrstock, Barry and Trubo, Richard. *The Parent's When-Not-to-Worry Book.* New York: Harper & Row, 1983.

Beltramini, A. U., and Hertzig, M. E. "Sleep and Bedtime Behavior." *Pediatrics* 71 (No. 2): 153–58, 1983.

Brazelton, T. Berry. *Toddlers and Parents.* New York: Dell, 1974.

———. "Why Your Baby Won't Sleep." *Redbook Magazine,* October 1978.

Brenner, Barbara. *Love and Discipline*. New York: Random House, 1983.

Briggs, Dorothy C. *Your Child's Self-Esteem*. Garden City, N.Y.: Doubleday, 1975.

Brody, Jane E. "Sleepwalking and Other Nocturnal Oddities." San Francisco *Chronicle*, August 17, 1983.

Brooks, Jane B. *The Process of Parenting*. Palo Alto, Calif.: Mayfield, 1981.

Brown, Saul L., and Reid, Helen. *Infant and Toddler Sleep Disruptions*. Los Angeles: Preschool and Infant Parenting Service, 1983 (cassette tape).

Caplan, Frank, ed. *The First Twelve Months of Life*. New York: Grosset & Dunlap, 1973.

———. *The Parenting Advisor*. Princeton, N.J.: Princeton Center for Infancy, 1976, 1977.

———, and Caplan, Theresa. *The Second Twelve Months of Life*. New York: Grosset & Dunlap, 1977.

Carey, William B. "Breast Feeding and Night Waking." Editorial correspondence in *Journal of Pediatrics* 87 (No. 2): 327, 1975.

———. "Night Waking and Temperament in Infancy." *Behavioral Pediatrics* 84 (No. 5): 756–58, 1974.

Christophersen, Edward R., ed. "Incorporating Behavioral Pediatrics into Primary Care." In *The Pediatric Clinics of North America* 29 (No. 2): 281–86. Philadelphia: Saunders, 1982.

Church, Joseph. *Understanding Your Child From Birth to Three*. New York: Simon and Schuster, 1973.

Committee on Psychosocial Aspects of Child and Family Health. "The Pediatrician's Role in Discipline." *Pediatrics* 72 (No. 3): 373–74, 1983.

Coons, Susan, and Guilleminault, Christian. "Development of Sleep-Wake Patterns and Non-Rapid Eye Movement Sleep Stages During the First Six Months of Life in Normal Infants." *Pediatrics* 69 (No. 6): 793–98, 1982.

DeLorenzo, Lorisa, and DeLorenzo, Robert. *Total Child Care: From Birth to Age Five*. Garden City, N.Y.: Doubleday, 1982.

Dement, William C. *Some Must Watch While Some Must Sleep*. Stanford, Calif.: The Stanford Alumni Association, 1972.

Dinkmeyer, Don, and McKay, Gary D. *The Parent's Handbook*. Circle Pines, Minn.: American Guidance Service, 1982.

Dodson, Fitzhugh. *How to Parent*. New York: Signet, 1970.

Douglas, Jo, and Levere, Ruth. "Behavioral Management of Sleep Disturbance in Young Children." Unpublished paper from the Department of Psychological Medicine, the Hospital for Sick Children, London.

Dreikurs, Rudolf, and Cassel, Pearl. *Discipline Without Tears*. New York: Hawthorn, 1974.

Dreikurs, Rudolf, and Grey, Loren. *A Parents' Guide to Child Discipline*. New York: Dutton, 1970.

Dreikurs, Rudolf, and Soltz, Vicki. *Children: The Challenge*. New York: Dutton, 1964.

Dunn, Judith. "Feeding and Sleeping." In *Developmental Psychiatry, Scientific Foundations*, edited by M. Rutter. London: Heinemann Medical Books, 1980.

Emde, Robert N., and Walker, Stephan. "Longitudinal Study of Infant Sleep: Results of 14 Subjects Studied at Monthly Intervals." *Psychophysiology* 13 (No. 5): 456–61, 1976.

Gerber Library. *500 Questions New Parents Ask*. New York: Dell, 1982.

Glazer, Robin K. *Letting Go*. Secaucus, N.J.: Citadel, 1983.

Hales, Dianne. *The Complete Book of Sleep*. Reading, Mass.: Addison-Wesley, 1980.

Ilg, Frances L., and Ames, Louise Bates. *Child Behavior*. New York: Harper & Row, 1955. Rev. ed., New York: Barnes & Noble, 1982.

Jacklin, Carol Nagy, et al. "Sleep Pattern Development from 6 Through 33 Months." *Journal of Pediatric Psychology* 5 (No. 3): 295–303, 1980.

Jones, Sandy. *Crying Baby, Sleepless Nights*. New York: Warner, 1983.

Kaban, Barbara. *Choosing Toys for Children*. New York: Schocken, 1979.

Keith, Parl R. "Night Terrors: A Review of the Psychology, Neurophysiology, and Therapy." *Journal of the American Academy of Child Psychiatry* 14: 477–89, 1975.

Kelly, Jeffrey. *Solving Your Child's Behavior Problems*. Boston: Little, Brown, 1983.

Klaus, Marshall H., and Kennell, John H. *Maternal-Infant Bonding*. St. Louis: Mosby, 1976.

Lawrence, Ruth A. *Breastfeeding*. St. Louis: Mosby, 1980.

Leach, Penelope. *Babyhood*. New York: Alfred A. Knopf, 1983.

———. *Your Baby and Child: From Birth to Age Five*. New York: Alfred A. Knopf, 1983.

Levine, Milton I., and Seligmann, Jean H. *The Parents' Encyclopedia of Infancy, Childhood, and Adolescence.* New York: Harper & Row, 1973.

Michaels, Evelyne. "How to Handle Your Child's Nightmares." *Chatelaine Magazine,* July 1983.

Moore, T., and Ucko, L. "Night Waking in Early Infancy." *Archives of Disease in Childhood* 32: 333–42, 1957.

Moore-Ede, Martin, et al. "Circadian Timekeeping in Health and Disease, Parts I and II." *The New England Journal of Medicine* 309 (Nos. 8 and 9): 469–76, 530–36, 1983.

Nelson, Waldo E., ed. *Textbook of Pediatrics,* 11th ed. Philadelphia: Saunders, 1979.

O'Donovan, J. Crossan, et al. "The Failure of Conventional Drug Therapy in the Management of Infantile Colic." *The American Journal of Diseases of Children* 133: 999–1001, 1979.

Paret, Isabel. "Night Waking and Its Relation to Mother-Infant Interaction in Nine-Month-Old Infants." In *Frontiers of Infant Psychiatry,* edited by J. Call et al. New York: Basic Books, 1983.

Parmelee, Arthur H. "Remarks on Receiving the C. Anderson Aldrich Award." *Pediatrics* 59: 389–95, 1977.

Richards, Martin. *Infancy.* New York: Harper & Row, 1980.

Richman, Naomi. "A Double Blind Drug Trial of Treatment in Young Children with Waking Problems." Unpublished paper from the Institute of Child Health, London.

————, et al. "Behavioral Methods in the Treatment of Sleep Disorders—A Pilot Study." Unpublished paper from the Institute of Child Health, London.

Roffwarg, Howard P., et al. "Ontogenetic Development of the Human Sleep-Dream Cycle." *Science* 152: 604–19, 1966.

Rubin, Richard R., et al. *Your Toddler.* New York: Macmillan, 1980.

Samuels, Mike, and Samuels, Nancy. *The Well Baby Book.* New York: Summit, 1979.

Schaefer, Charles E., and Millman, Howard L. *How to Help Your Children With Common Problems.* New York: New American Library, 1981.

Schaffer, R. *Mothering.* Cambridge, Mass.: Harvard University Press, 1977.

Schmitt, Barton D. "Infants Who Do Not Sleep Through the Night." *Developmental and Behavioral Pediatrics* 2 (No. 1): 20–23, 1981.

Simonds, John F., and Parraga, Humberto. "Prevalence of Sleep Disorders and Sleep Behaviors in Children and Adolescents." *Journal of the American Academy of Child Psychiatry* 21 (No. 4): 383–88, 1982.

Smith, Lendon H. *The Encyclopedia of Baby and Child Care.* New York: Warner, 1972.

Spock, Benjamin. *Baby and Child Care.* New York: Dutton, 1976.

Stoutt, Glenn R. *The First Month of Life.* New York: New American Library, 1977.

Tackett, J. J. M., and Hunsberger, M. *Family-Centered Care of Children and Adolescents.* Philadelphia: Saunders, 1981.

Thevenin, Tine. *The Family Bed.* Minneapolis: Tine Thevenin, 1976.

Weissbluth, Marc. "Sleep Duration and Infant Temperament." *The Journal of Pediatrics* 99 (No. 5): 817–19, 1981.

White, Burton L. *The First Three Years of Life.* Englewood Cliffs, N.J.: Prentice-Hall, 1975.

White, Paul J. "Management of Infantile Colic." *American Journal of Diseases of Children* 133: 995–96, 1979.

Yogman, Michael W., and Zeisel, Steven H. "Diet and Sleep Patterns in Newborn Infants." *The New England Journal of Medicine* 309 (No. 19): 1147–49, 1983.

Zimbardo, Philip, and Radl, Shirley. *The Shy Child.* Garden City, N.Y.: Doubleday, 1982.

SUGGESTED BEDTIME/SLEEP BOOKS

The following is a sampling of good bedtime books, many of which we have read to our own children. Because the possibilities are limitless, we have restricted our list to books that have something to do with sleep, nighttime fantasies, nighttime fears, and transitional objects. Of course, this doesn't mean that these are the only books that you should read to your children at bedtime. The age recommendations are only guidelines. We have included many books that are suitable for a wide range of ages in the youngest possible group; often these books will be interesting for many years beyond the indicated age.

From Ten to Eighteen Months Old

Boynton, Sandra. *The Going to Bed Book*. New York: Simon & Schuster, 1982.

Brimax Books. *Bedtime*. "Show Baby" series.

Cosgrove, Stephen, and Reasoner, Charles. *Sleepy Time Bunny*. Los Angeles: Price/Stern/Sloan, 1984.

Fernandes, Eugenie. *The Good Night Book*. New York: Golden, 1983.

Fujikawa, Gyo. *Sleepy Time*. New York: Grosset & Dunlap, 1975.

Golden Touch and Feel Book. *The Good Night Book*. New York: Golden, 1983.

Hill, Eric. *Baby Bear's Bedtime*. New York: Random House, 1984.

Kunhardt, Dorothy. *Pat the Bunny*. New York: Western, 1962.

Oxenbury, Helen. *Good Night, Good Morning*. New York: Dial, 1982.

Peek, Merle. *Roll Over! A Counting Song*. New York: Clarion, 1981.

Rice, Eve. *Goodnight, Goodnight*. New York: Greenwillow, 1980.

From One and a Half to Three Years Old

Allison, Alida. *The Sweet Dreams Book.* Illustrated by Laurie Gray. Los Angeles: Price/Stern/Sloan, 1984.

Brown, Margaret Wise. *A Child's Goodnight Book.* Illustrated by Jean Charlot. Reading, Mass.: Addison-Wesley, 1943.

―――. *Goodnight Moon.* Illustrated by Clement Hurd. New York: Harper & Row, 1947.

Burningham, John. *The Blanket.* New York: Harper & Row, 1962.

Coatsworth, Elizabeth C. *Good Night.* Illustrated by Jose Aruego. New York: Macmillan, 1972.

Eastman, Philip D. *Big Dog, Little Dog: A Bedtime Story.* New York: Random House, 1973.

Gerstein, Mordicai. *Roll Over.* New York: Crown, 1984.

Harris, Dorothy. *Goodnight Jeffrey.* Illustrated by Nancy Hannans. New York: Warne, Frederick, 1983.

Hutchins, Pat. *Good-night Owl.* New York: Macmillan, 1972.

Ipcar, Dahlov. *The Song of the Day Birds and the Night Birds.* Garden City, N.Y.: Doubleday, 1967.

Koide, Tan. *May We Sleep Here Tonight?* Illustrated by Yasuko Koide. New York: Atheneum, 1983.

McPhail, David. *The Bear's Toothache.* Boston: Little, Brown, 1972.

Morris, Terry N. *Goodnight, Dear Monster!* New York: Alfred A. Knopf, 1980.

Murphy, Jill. *Peace at Last.* New York: Dial, 1980.

Ormerod, Jan. *Moonlight.* New York: Lothrop, Lee & Shepard, 1982.

Walsh, Ellen Stoll. *Brunus and the New Bear.* Garden City, N.Y.: Doubleday, 1979.

Watson, Jane Werner. *Good Night.* Illustrated by Eloise Wilkin. New York: Golden, 1949.

Wells, Rosemary. *Noisy Nora.* New York: Dial, 1973.

Wilkin, Eloise. *My Goodnight Book.* New York: Golden, 1981.

Zemach, Margot. *Hush, Little Baby.* New York: Dutton, 1976.

Zolotow, Charlotte. *Wake Up and Goodnight.* Illustrated by Leonard Weisgard. New York: Harper & Row, 1971.

From Three to Five Years Old

Brown, Margaret Wise. *Wait Till the Moon Is Full.* Illustrated by Garth Williams. New York: Harper & Row, 1948.

De Paola, Tomie. *When Everyone Was Fast Asleep.* New York: Holiday, 1976.

Fair, Sylvia. *The Bedspread.* New York: William Morrow, 1982.

Feder, Jane. *The Night Light.* Illustrated by Lady McCrady. New York: Dial, 1980.

Flora, James. *Grandpa's Ghost Stories.* New York: Atheneum, 1978.

Freeman, Don. *Corduroy.* New York: Viking, 1968.

Goudey, Alice E. *The Day We Saw the Sun Come Up.* Illustrated by Adrienne Adams. New York: Scribner's, 1961.

Hoban, Russell. *Bedtime for Frances.* Illustrated by Garth Williams. New York: Harper & Row, 1960.

Hofmann, Ginnie. *Who Wants an Old Teddy Bear?* New York: Random House, 1978.

Jarrell, Randall. *Fly by Night.* Illustrated by Maurice Sendak. New York: Farrar, Straus & Giroux, 1969.

Jewell, Nancy. *Goodnight Calf.* Illustrated by Leonard Weisgard. New York: Harper & Row, 1973.

Johnston, Tony. *Night Noises and Other Mole and Troll Stories.* Illustrated by Cyndy Szekeres. New York: Putnam, 1977.

Katz, Bobbi. *Bedtime Bear's Book of Bedtime Poems.* Illustrated by Dora Leder. New York: Random House, 1983.

Levine, Joan Goldman. *A Bedtime Story.* New York: Dutton, 1975.

Marzollo, Jean. *Close Your Eyes.* Illustrated by Susan Jeffers. New York: Dial, 1978.

Mathews, Geda Bradley. *What Was That!* Illustrated by Normand Chartier. New York: Golden, 1975.

Mayer, Mercer. *Just Go to Bed.* New York: Golden, 1983.

———. *Little Monster's Bedtime Book.* New York: Golden, 1978.

———. *There's a Nightmare in My Closet.* New York: Dial, 1968.

———. *You're the Scaredy-Cat.* New York: Four Winds, 1974.

Plath, Sylvia. *The Bed Book.* Illustrated by Emily Arnold McCully. New York: Harper & Row, 1976.

Preston, Edna Mitchell. *One Dark Night.* Illustrated by Kurt Werth. New York: Viking, 1969.

Robison, Deborah. *Bye-Bye Old Buddy.* Boston: Clarion, 1983.

———. *No Elephants Allowed.* Boston: Clarion, 1981.

Ryan, Duran. *Hildilid's Night.* Illustrated by Arnold Lobel. New York: Macmillan, 1971.

Schubert, Ingrid and Dieter. *There's a Crocodile Under My Bed.* New York: McGraw-Hill, 1980.

Sendak, Maurice. *In the Night Kitchen.* New York: Harper & Row, 1970.

———. *Where the Wild Things Are.* New York: Harper & Row, 1963.

Seuss, Dr. *Sleep Book.* New York: Random House, 1962.

Showers, Paul. *The Moon Walker.* Illustrated by Susan Perl. Garden City, N.Y.: Doubleday, 1975.

Stevenson, James. *What's Under My Bed?* New York: Viking Penguin, 1984.

Ungerer, Tomi. *Moon Man.* New York: Harper & Row, 1967.

Van Allsburg, Chris. *Ben's Dream.* Boston: Houghton Mifflin, 1982.

Viorst, Judith. *My Mama Says There Aren't Any Zombies, Ghosts, Vampires, Creatures, Demons, Monsters, Fiends, Goblins, or Things.* Illustrated by Kay Chorao. New York: Atheneum, 1979.

———. *Sunday Morning.* Illustrated by Hilary Knight. New York: Atheneum, 1968.

Waber, Bernard. *Ira Sleeps Over.* Boston: Houghton Mifflin, 1972.

Ward, Andrew. *Baby Bear and the Long Sleep.* Illustrated by John Walsh. Boston: Little, Brown, 1980.

Weiba, Barbara. *Amanda Dreaming.* Illustrated by Mercer Mayer. New York: Atheneum, 1973.

Wells, Rosemary. *Good Night, Fred.* New York: Dial, 1981.

Zolotow, Charlotte. *The Summer Night.* Illustrated by Ben Schecter. New York: Harper & Row, 1958.

INDEX